LEFT-HANDED PEOPLE

Originally published as THE OTHER HAND

*An Investigation into the
History
of Left-Handedness*

MICHAEL BARSLEY

Published by
Melvin Powers
WILSHIRE BOOK COMPANY
12015 Sherman Road
No. Hollywood, California 91605
Telephone: (213) 875-1711

To
MY MOTHER
Who let me be Left-Handed

Originally published as THE OTHER HAND

First American Edition: 1967

ISBN 0-87980-087-9

Printed by
HAL LEIGHTON PRINTING COMPANY
P.O. Box 3952
North Hollywood, California 91605
Telephone: (213) 983-1105

ACKNOWLEDGMENTS

My researches for this book go back for more than ten years, and the people who have, through those years, given advice and experience are too numerous to mention individually. I am, however, very grateful to those whose interest encouraged me in my sinistral task.

Particular thanks are due to Mr R. D. Burrows, librarian, now at Ealing Technical College, London, who has been consistently helpful since the idea first arose; Miss Sandra Noble, of Wimbledon, whose educational advice has been valuable; Mr Barry Bingham, of the *Louisville Courier*; Mr John Kipps, of the Automobile Association; Mr. Alan Hodge, of *History Today*; Mr Tony van den Bergh; Miss Scott Eliot, Keeper of Prints and Drawings, the Royal Library, Windor Castle; Mr Bancroft, Superintendent of the British Museum Reading Room, under whose wedgwood-blue cupola most of this book was researched; Messrs Waterman's, with whose left-handed pen this book was written.

The Author would also like to thank the following for permission to quote copyright material:

The Macmillan Company, New York (*Lefthandedness*, by Beaufort Sims Parson); Lothrop, Lee and Shepherd Co., Boston (*Handedness, Right and Left*, by Ira S. Wile); Robert Hale Ltd (*The Dark World of Witches*, by Eric Maple); Oxford University Press (*The Witch-cult in Western Europe*, by Dr Margaret Murray); Sampson, Low Ltd (*The God of the Witches*, by Dr Margaret Murray); Quality Press (*Adventures with Phantoms*, by R. Thurston Hopkins); Messrs Collins (*The Desert King*, by David Howarth); Macmillan & Co. (*Ritual and Belief in Morocco*, by Edward Westermarck); Angus and Robertson Ltd (*Duet for Three Hands*, by Cyril Smith); The Bodley Head (*My Autobiography* by Charles Chaplin); University of London Press (*The Backward Child* by Sir Cyril Burt); McGraw-Hill, New York (*The Ape and the Child* by W. N.

Kellogg); University of Edinburgh Press (*Lefthandedness* by Dr Margaret Clark); Routledge, Kegan Paul (*Aion*, by Jung); Cohen & West Ltd (*Death and the Right Hand* by Robert Hertz); International Universities Press, New York (*Annual Survey of Psychoanalysis*—E. Gostynski); Macmillan & Co. (*King George VI* by Sir John Wheeler-Bennett); Chapman & Hall Ltd (*Reading, Writing and Speech Problems in Children* by Dr S. S. Orton); Farrar and Rinehart, New York (*Psychology of the Elementary School Subjects* by Miss Cole); Messrs Kegan Paul (*Mirror Writing* by Dr Macdonald Critchley); Methuen Ltd (*The First Five Years of Life*, ed. Arnold Gesell); Cassell & Co. Ltd (*The Romance of Leonardo da Vinci* by Merejowski); American Orthopsychiatric Association (*The Master Hand* by Abram Blau).

The Author hopes that all sources have been covered, but apologises if there have been any inadvertent omissions.

M.B.

ILLUSTRATIONS

CONTENTS

INTRODUCTION

"To either action, there is an equal and opposing action; for the mutual action of two bodies are always equal and oppositely directed."

ISAAC NEWTON

Duality is the essence of all life, human, animal, and organic. An electric connection has the plus and minus sign. The earth, when surveyed looking towards the magnetic pole, revolves from left to right. In Britain, a motorist can be prosecuted for driving on the right side of the road; in most other countries, for driving on the left side. Man was born with a brain capable of controlling the activities of his two hands. The verdict of history has given the right hand overwhelming preference, and the minority preference has been either ignored or forbidden. Yet, it has been estimated that in this world, there must be between one and two hundred million people who are originally left-handed.

It is remarkable that so little has been written about this minority, and the prejudice against it. Left-handed Man lives in a Right-Handed World, a world in which the dextral is exalted in religion, and catered for in everyday life. Perhaps, therefore, the neglect is not surprising, but to the left-hander, who has to grow up in this world and become accustomed to it, the prejudice is always present. The curious eyes which follow a left-hander as he writes in school, or in a post office, or at a hotel desk, or when signing autographs, are unconsciously resenting the odd boy or the odd man out.

For centuries, and in many countries today, left-handedness has been like the negative sign in electricity—an essential compensation, but the weaker side, the second best, indeed morally the evil side. The prejudice pervades every sphere of life, and the more primitive and superstitious the environment, the greater the prejudice. There are some countries, even in this supposedly enlightened age, where the subject is almost literally *tabu*: the reason is given in the chapter on The Unclean Hand. But a simple matter of personal hygiene is, in my opinion, responsible for a large amount of the prejudice. It is not merely a matter of the majority casting out the minority on a numeral basis.

Right-handedness, in the opinion of Thomas Carlyle, who became a sinistral in the later years of his life through the loss of use in his dextral hand, is "the very oldest institution that exists". Upon it, much human activity has been based, and nearly all religious practises have been founded. The Biblical quotations in praise of the right hand are echoed by the Koran and the Torah. But to be left-handed is not the deliberate choice of the individual. Whether hereditary or acquired, it becomes manifest in early childhood. There are some who think that a child who insists on using his left hand in defiance of parental or tutorial disapproval is being wilful and cussed. But this is to deny something which, to the left-hander, is the obvious and easiest way of doing things—going against nature.

In a later chapter, the American psychiatrist Abram Blau gives his estimate of the left-hander's characteristics, and it is by no means a flattering description.* I prefer this summing up by W. S. Inman:

"Independence is the characteristic of the left-hander, and seems to be related to the development of the abnormality. Whether a left-hander was born with a capacity for complete ambidexterity, and tenaciously clings to such left-handed activities as have survived parental pressure, resenting strongly meanwhile the interference with his personal desire to do as he likes with his own hands, or whether he has actually adopted left-handedness as a sign of his desire to be different from the authoritative parent, the fact remains that the left-handed child is almost invariably more critical and self-sufficient than his squinting and stammering relatives. . . . In opposing authority,

* *The Master Hand:* American Orthopsychiatric Association: New York, 1946.

the left-hander as a rule maintains a mental poise which generally, though not always, saves him from suffering too much in his own person."

It is perhaps natural to expect that a sinistral is likely to be something of a rebel, as well as an individualist. The very novelty and peculiarity of his manual activities set him apart as an object of curiosity, if not actual derision. How far such characteristics are manifest in left-handers was one of the enquiries I tried to undertake.

My own experience in handedness is, I suppose, typical of many left-handers brought up in an allegedly enlightened democracy. There was an early attempt, at a kindergarten school, to change me from left to right hand, and this appears to have made me unwell. My father took me to a specialist, who diagnosed the trouble, and said I was to be allowed to write left-handed. I have remained sinistral ever since, for writing and drawing and about half the normal activities of life, but as in many other cases, an amount of ambidextrality has taken place, for instance in golf and right-handed batting in cricket and cutting with scissors. I have not been consciously aware of the duality, and no pressure, social or parental, has been brought to bear on me. At one stage I remember telling myself that I must improve the legibility of my handwriting, and deliberately set out to form certain letters which were troubling me. This was a natural course, since both my father and brother were artistic, and my father particularly specialised in lettering. Both were right-handed, as is my mother, my two children, and my grandchild. Incidence of sinistrality can be traced only to my maternal grandfather.

I must have accepted being left-handed in a right-handed world, and was probably much more concerned about having to wear spectacles from an early age. Certainly the epithets "goggles" and "four-eyes" and "gig-lamps" were much more common at school than "cack-handed"—a north-country expression in Liverpool, where I grew up.

The idea of being an apologist for the left-hander, and studying his history came only late in life. Two separate circumstances prompted it. The first concerned the late King, George the Sixth. It was one of my jobs as a radio producer to edit the King's speeches—the first time this had been done. A fuller account of this is contained later in the book, when we consider stammering, but investigation of his condition revealed the information that he had been originally left-handed.

The second circumstance concerned the Coronation of Queen Elizabeth II. Months before the actual ceremony, the Coronation route from Buckingham Palace to Westminster Abbey was marked out, pace by pace. *The Daily Telegraph* printed a photograph of a Scots Guards officer making notes, as men walked backwards, step by step, through Piccadilly Circus. The officer was writing with his left hand. This immediately aroused my curiosity, since I had always imagined that left-handedness was discouraged, even *tabu*, in such exalted military circles. A left-handed Guards officer—surely that was sacrilege!

Later correspondence in the same paper disclosed that such sinistrality was permitted; but the letters also brought out several interesting facts and theories about handedness, and from that moment on I was committed to the present investigation.

Some well-known left-handers have clear memories of painful experiences arising from their sinistrality in early life. The Bishop of Southwark, the Rt Rev. Mervyn Stockwood, admitted:

"I am left-handed. It isn't my fault. I was born that way. But as a small boy I was punished for it because my schoolmasters thought it was a deliberate perversity. I tried and cried. Scrawls and smudges on the paper: and, when the master wasn't looking, back went the pen into my left hand because *that was natural for me.* . . ."

Many humorists and satirists appear on my list of left-handers. This may be a variation on the "odd-man-out" theory: that, being pin-pointed or isolated, they tend to hit back at society and the Establishment. An obvious example was Harpo Marx. His creation of a downtrodden figure, bereft of speech and responding only to the most primitive of instincts, had nothing outwardly to do with his being left-handed, but this condition became apparent when he played the instrument after which he was named. (It is said that when Harpo was auditioned for playing with the Boston Symphony Orchestra, the conductor could not think what was different about Mr Marx. Only after several performances did he realise that the harp was on the wrong shoulder.)

Left-handedness even creeps into the Marx Brothers' scripts, even though Harpo, the only sinistral among them, cannot speak the lines. In the vintage *Animal Crackers* (1931) they are arguing about the Beaugard, the famous painting which has been stolen. The argument begins: "This portrait was painted by a left-handed painter", but since it has disappeared, Groucho's explanation is: "This picture was eaten by a left-handed moth."

The satirical line of artist Ronald Searle is a sinistral one: those diabolical *jeunes femmes fatales*, the schoolgirls of St Trinian's, are the product of the right-hand side of Mr Searle's brain. But so, equally, are his many fine artistic works, from the lively sketches of New York and Paris, to the portraits of the Japanese who kept him prisoner in Singapore during the Second World War. Mr Searle confesses that, very occasionally, sinistrality gets the better of him. In the early part of the war, he was asked to draw the figure of a British Home Guardsman standing resolutely with rifle at the slope. Unfortunately but quite naturally, he put the rifle on the wrong shoulder, an error which was not spotted until the drawing appeared.

Other sardonic left-handers in this field include William Rushton of *Private Eye* and a number of illustrators for *Punch*. The *New Yorker*, which one might expect to include several sinistrals, can apparently produce none of note. No Thurber, no Steinberg, no Peter Arno. All are determinedly dextral.

Mention of Charles Chaplin, Sinistral Extraordinary, is made in the chapter on music. Like Harpo Marx, he showed his left-handedness by playing an instrument, in his case the violin. Rex Harrison is another sharply satirical character, who in *My Fair Lady*, demonstrated that his Professor Higgins made all his notes on Eliza Doolittle with the left hand.

The Left-Handed Ladies of stage and screen provide a

mélange in which there seems to be no distinguishing feature, except that, as with the Gentlemen, they are mostly light-hearted and amusing creatures. Kim Novak, as Moll Flanders, even duels left-handedly. Jessie Matthews, once the darling of the British cinema screen, and later the perennial Mrs Dale, the doctor's wife in the B.B.C. radio serial, has admitted that left-handedness has its drawbacks, particularly in certain household jobs. Elizabeth Allan and Brenda Bruce agree, and use left-handed ironing boards. Perhaps in the United States the ironing is done for you, otherwise Judy Garland, Betty Grable and Olivia de Havilland, all left-handers, would suffer the same difficulty. The surprising inclusion among the sinistrals is Mandy Rice-Davies, a witness in the Profumo Case in London in 1963, who was photographed writing her memoirs with the left hand.

There have been other books on left-handedness, more detailed and technical than this one, but I cannot recall any previous volume which has included every aspect of the subject. My "Gallery of Experts" pays tribute to pioneers such as Sir Thomas Browne and Sir Daniel Wilson, as well as to outstanding researchers of our own day. But the present survey, for those who have a wide and catholic taste, stretches from the Bible to the Beatles, and attempts to answer very popular and obvious questions, such as the direction taken by bath-water and the reasons for driving on the left or right side of the road. Such simple questions may have a long history, and their implications keep recurring. Direction of bath-water, as so many other things, depends on the rotation of the earth. This we cannot consciously feel, but it is there. When the Soviet scientists examined two dogs which had been weightless in outer space for three weeks, they found they could not stand upright, being subject to the renewed "pull" of a directional world.

Handedness cannot therefore be confined to the classroom, the clinic, or the church. It affects almost everything we do, and the numbers of left-handers are increasing, owing to greater tolerance. In sport, there has always been freedom of choice, from the days of the Roman gladiators to the more sedate pleasures of the lawn-tennis court, the baseball field and the fencing gymnasium. The often-held theory that sinistrality is in some way connected with the criminal, the delinquent or the mentally afflicted is becoming a thing of the past.

I

THE UNCLEAN HAND

By way of preface, it is important to consider one aspect of handedness about which writers have been very guarded and polite, referring in general terms to "hygiene" and "uncleanness". The epithet "cack-handed" is often used (not only in the North of England) but its meaning is rarely understood. The time has come for us to realise that one hygienic action of humanity is done by nine-tenths, or more, with the left hand, because they are right-handed. In civilised countries today this distinction no longer matters: but through the centuries it has mattered very much, and it is in many ways responsible, not only for the *tabu* and the physical prejudice against the left-hander, whose allegedly "unclean" hand is his preferred hand, but in reinforcing the social prejudice against the physical minority.

If this seems hard to believe, consider these words of Ira S. Wile:* "Just as pariahs and untouchables should use only the left hand for contact with impurities, many others would reserve it for use exclusively in the excretory areas. The left hand is the unclean hand; and this incidentally would favour the social usage of the clean and virtuous hand. The hand accursed—unclean—inferior—should have a prominent part in the mysterious, magic drama of life . . ."

The sense of shame associated with the genital organs goes back to the Garden of Eden and the fig-leaf, and survives to this day. Phallic worship may have been, from time to time, one of the most popular rituals, but the excretory functions of the body, though very frequent in swear-words and imprecation, have otherwise been delicately overlooked. The close physical

* *Handedness: Right and Left:* Lothrop, Lee, Boston, 1934.

association of the sexual and excretory parts—indeed, their partial duplication—has led to a dichotomy in man which he has never resolved, and has often shunned. The parts are called "privy" or "secret". The vagina, even in dictionaries, has been given the Latin name *pudendum muliebre*, and it was not until the law-case over *Lady Chatterley's Lover* that two of the main Anglo-Saxon words were allowed to be publicly printed without prosecution. (Eric Partridge revealed, in his *Dictionary of Slang*, how Sir John Murray lost his nerve when compiling his *Oxford Dictionary*, although one word occurs in Chaucer's *Miller's Tale*, with a different spelling.)

As far as the other functions are concerned, dextrals and sinistrals usually perform them with their opposite or "unclean" hand; i.e. wiping, making love. It is our purpose to discover how far this physical distinction has affected the social and religious attitude. From it, fanciful though it may seem, one could deduce that Solomon was left-handed, when the unknown poet makes the Shulamite say: "Stay me with flagons, comfort me with apples: for I am sick of love. His left hand is under my head, and his right hand doth embrace me." Twice she says this—and it is the action of a left-handed lover.

Left-handers like to have a woman on their left, for caressing with the right hand, and vice versa. (It is an ironic thought for right-handed Englishmen that, in cars, with right-hand steering, it is the left-hander who has the advantage in making the advances: on the Continent, and the U.S., the reversed position favours the right-hander.)

Among the Jews, ablution was not only part of their religious life, but was obviously connected with hygiene. In the Zohar, it says: "Whosoever sleepeth in his bed at night tasteth of death, for his soul leaveth him for the nonce. Being thus bereft of its soul, an unclean spirit possesseth his body, and defileth it. Wherefore I say, let no man pass his unwashed hand over his eyes in the morning, by reason of the unclean spirit which resteth on it." The Cabalists, going further, maintained that a man incurs the penalty of death if he walks a distance of four yards from his bed without ablution.

From the 12th-century writer Asaph in his *Book of Medicine*: "Shivta is a bad spirit: at the time the woman comes from the river or the privy, or when she discharges her faeces and does not wash her hands and gives bread to her son or milk, there is a bad ghost, Saturn by name, which seizes youths, and bends and breaks the neck. . . . There is no cure but to burn with fire. . . ."

From the *Talmud*: "The unwashen hand leads to blindness, the hand leads to deafness, the hand causes a polypus."

It has been the same ritual in Middle-Eastern and North African countries where the food is traditionally eaten by hand. E. W. Lane describes feeding habits in "Modern" Egypt (which is the Egypt of more than a century ago).*

"The persons who are about to partake of the repast sit upon the floor round a tray; or, if the tray be placed near the edge of a low divan, some may sit on the divan and others on the floor. They sit round it with the left knee on the floor and the right knee raised. Each person bares his right arm to the elbow. Before he begins to eat he says *bismillah!*. Neither knives nor forks are used; the thumb and two fingers of the right hand serve instead of those instruments. . . .

"When a fowl is placed whole upon the tray, two persons, using the right hand alone, perform the operation together. Many of the Arabs will not allow the left hand to touch food excepting when the right is maimed. . . .

"It is a rule with the Muslims to honour the right hand above the left: to use the right hand for all honourable purposes, and the left for actions which, though necessary, are unclean. . . .

"At the ceremonial washing of hands, the Muslim faces the Koran. First the right hand is washed, then the left. The speaker says: 'Place the book of my actions in my right hand. Place not, as at the resurrection, the book of my actions in my left hand.'"

One could match this style of eating with a present-day example from Morocco, where the traditional *cous-cous* (lamb or chicken, on a base of root vegetables and semolina rather like

* *Manners and Customs of the Modern Egyptians*: Charles Knight, London, 1846.

an Irish stew with porridge) is still eaten, on ceremonial occasions, in homes, or in the more expensive tourist restaurants, with the guests on cushions or on low divans, and without any cutlery. The author has had to explain to a provincial Governor, in Fez, that he is left-handed by nature, and remains so by the indulgence of the British way of life, and that for him to eat his *cous-cous* with the right hand would be difficult, because unnatural, but that no disrespect would be intended towards His Excellency if the left, or traditionally unclean hand, was used. Permission was of course given readily by an enlightened Moroccan with a French wife: but there were uplifted eyebrows from the white-robed servants who came in with silver kettles, to pour rose-water over the favoured right hand before the arrival of the main dish.

Jesus himself obviously expressed impatience at the orthodox Jewish insistence on ablutions, and this led him to ignore the Pharisaic rule, as described in St Luke.

"A certain Priest besought him to dine with him: and he went in, and sat down to meat. And when the Priest saw it, he marvelled that he had not first washed before dinner."

But the retort from Jesus came quickly and characteristically:

"Now do ye Pharisees make clean the outside of the cup and the platter, but your inward part is full of ravening and wickedness."

There is another account involving his disciples in the same practice, contained both in St Matthew's (XXV) and St Mark's Gospels (VII). Mark's version is the more detailed:

"Then came unto Him the Pharisees, and certain of the scribes, which came from Jerusalem. And when they saw some of his disciples eat bread with defiled, that is to say, with unwashed hands, they found fault. For the Pharisees, and all the Jews, except they wash their hands oft (literally "with the fist") eat not, holding the tradition of the elders. And when they come from the market, except they wash, they eat not. And many other things there be, which they have received to hold, as the washing of cups, and pots, brasen vessels, and of tables.

"Then the scribes and the Pharisees asked Him, why walk

not thy disciples according to the tradition of the elders, but eat bread with unwashen hands? He answered and said unto them, 'Well hath Esaias prophesied to you hypocrites, as it is written. This people honoureth me with their lips, but their heart is far from me.'" Jesus's point is that the Pharisees hold the tradition of men, "as the washing of pots and cups", and lay aside the Commandment of God. The Mosaic Law has been made an ass.

"There is nothing from without a man that entering into him defileth him: but the things which come out of him, those are they that defile the man."

He goes on: "Because it entereth not into his heart, but into the belly, and goeth out into the draught, purging all meats." (Revised version "making all meats clean".)

Jesus adds this phrase: "To eat with unwashen hands defileth not a man."

Now this is capable of two interpretations. There is, in this Biblical story, no distinction of hands. It is known that Jewish tradition imposed ablution particularly whenever there was any possibility of defilement: that meats were divided into the clean and the unclean: that the ablution was religious as well as hygienic. The literal word for wash is here to "baptise".

The attitude of Jesus is that these ceremonies didn't matter, compared with man's attitude towards God, his father and mother, and the sins which could befall him—a list of sins longer than the seven deadly ones. He regarded purgation into the "draught" (which has been variously translated as "intestines", according to the Ancient Eastern translation, "closet", or "sewer", in the Ronald Knox modern version) as the answer to the previous segregation of food.

This was the first interpretation. But it is obvious that the washing of hands before eating has always been closely bound up with the clean and the unclean hand. To what extent were the Pharisees referring to this? In their view, it was the hands which were defiled, not the food. To wash both was desirable, especially after a visit to a middle-eastern market: to use the left hand at all when "dipping into the dish", as Judas may have done during that fateful moment in the Last Supper, was a further sacrilege.

The book, or set of books, most heavily loaded against the left is the Holy Bible, as we shall see in a later chapter. The word 'hand' is mentioned so often that there are, in one modern Concordance, more than one thousand six hundred separate references to it, some merely directional, but the majority emotional or superstitious.* From the early chapters of Genesis, it is obvious that the right hand is preferred, and later it is exalted. There have been, as we shall also see, many reasons for the emergence of dextrality as the majority tribal cult, from the Bronze Age onwards. Later came its exaltation, partly as a result of the turning to the right, to the dawn, to the Light which was to be worshipped in the symbol of the Sun; to the favoured position of Apollo on the right side of Jove, and Jesus on the right side of the Father.

But to what extent, one may ask, was the converse disapproval of the left hand dependent, not simply on the unpopularity of any minority, but upon the physical dislike of mingling and eating with those who used the unclean member openly?

We could choose examples from many religions of the world, but the evidence seems strong enough in the case of Christianity for us to look no further.

Visitors to the Holy Land, if the author's own experience be typical, get a new view of their hitherto "European" religion. Sir Thomas Browne, however, declared that he was glad he had never seen the Holy Places.

"Some believe the better for seeing Christ's Sepulchre; and when they have seen the Red Sea, doubt not the Miracle. Now, contrarily, I bless myself and am thankful that I lived not in the age of Miracles, that I never saw Christ nor his Disciples. . . . 'Tis an easie and necessary belief, to credit what our eye and sense hath examined."

To others, brought up on the paintings of the great masters, on the western music of Bach and Palestrina, on the glories of

* *Complete Concordance*: Nelson, London, New York, 1957.

Gothic cathedrals and the majestic flow of the Bible prose, Jesus himself had been appropriated for the West. It is forgotten that Nazareth is still today a seething, entirely Arab town with Jews living only in the suburbs, and a life scarcely changed in two thousand years. The chief guide to the Holy Places is himself a Muslim. One realises with a shock that, racially and in some of their habits, the Jews were as much Arab as Semite. They had been brought up in captivity in Egypt. Their religion teemed with *tabus* and superstitions, many of them connected with the Hand. It was the Children of Israel, far more than any other race, who were most swayed by, and eloquent about, handedness. Later the Arabs were equally eloquent on the subject as followers of the Prophet.

Detailed Bible references are given in a later chapter, but there is one New Testament example so important and so relevant to our theme that it must be quoted now. This is the uncompromising, definitive Vision of Judgment in St Matthew, Ch. XXV.

"When the Son of Man shall come in his glory, and all the holy angels with him, then shall he sit upon the throne of his glory:

"And before him shall be gathered all nations, and he shall separate them one from another, as a shepherd divideth his sheep from the goats:

"And he shall set his sheep on his right hand, and the goats on the left:

"Then shall the King say unto them on his right hand, Come ye blessed of my Fathers, inherit the Kingdom prepared for you from the foundation of the world."

There follows the catalogue of kindnesses offered to Him by the sheep, and then the King deals with the goats.

"Then shall he say also unto them on the left hand, Depart from me, ye cursed, into everlasting fire, prepared for the devil and his angels. . . . And these shall go away into everlasting punishment: but the righteous into life eternal."

No one could object to the division between good and evil people, or to the reason for the division: that the sheep helped "even the least of my brethren" and the goats ignored him. It was, presumably, in the Arab way of story-telling (and story and parable tellers still exist in Arab markets) essential to conjure up a mental picture of the Judgment Seat, and the relative position of the sheep, a favoured animal, and the goat—one of the most unpopular of creatures since the scapegoat in Leviticus, chiefly due to its predatory habit of eating everything (presumably the pig, another allegedly unclean animal, could have been chosen as an alternative).

It is true also that sidedness, not handedness, is technically involved. But there is no doubt whatever, in our opinion, that this Vision of Judgment has been more responsible for 'fixing" the prejudice against left-handers than any other pronouncement, and this prejudice has come down through the ages, adopted by Inquisitors, judges, soldiers, artists, teachers, nurses and parents as the supreme example of the association of sinistral people with wickedness and the Devil, whose popular disguise is in the shape of a goat, with cloven hoof.

Charles Lamb wrote in his Elian Essay, *Witches and Other Night-Fears*: "When the wicked are expressly symbolised by a goat, it was not to be wondered at so much, that *he* (the Devil) should come sometimes in that body, and assert his metaphor."

The word Satan, most commonly applied to His Satanic Majesty, has no connection with the left. The Hebrew word means merely "adversary". The Talmud agrees, however, that there is a Chief of Satans and Prince of Demons, Samael. His name is clearly associated with the Hebrew *se'mol*, meaning left, as far as sides are concerned. In the angelic hierarchy, it is Michael who is on the right, Samael on the left (he is later replaced by Gabriel, against whom no stigma seems to have been attached).

The whole Vision, which is about the last parable uttered by Jesus before events began to hurry to their destined climax, may of course have as its key the phrase "before him shall be gathered all *nations*". In the opinion of Conrad Noel, the remarkable "Red" vicar from Essex:* "Many people have been

* *The Life of Jesus*: J. M. Dent, London, 1937.

so impregnated with the individualistic virus that they are quite incapable of seeing that this parable deals with corporate bodies and not with separate souls. But history is strewn with the carcasses of unrighteous nations and both the Old and New Testaments make no question of the fact that God visits with his judgments nations as well as individuals. . . . The communal interpretation of the parable can hardly be avoided, and this interpretation is good for all time. It comes as a searching challenge to modern nations and empires as regards their internal economy and their foreign policy."

The conclusion allegedly reached by Jesus (and every left-hander surely hopes that it is merely in the imagination of Matthew, the former tax collector) is inescapable. It can be used, and has been used, in many spheres of life. To take but one example: most early paintings of the Crucifixion show the sun shining on Jesus and the penitent thief, and sometimes on a church. On the left side, the moon shines on the impenitent thief, and a synagogue. The wounds of the crucified Saviour are always on the right side. The soldier pierced that side with his spear, from whence flowed blood mingled with water. If the Christians could have associated the Jews with left-handedness, they would gladly have done so (their method of writing has often been called left-handed, because of the movement from right to left). But Jews and Arabs alike were just as anti-sinistral. This was the Parable of the Unclean Hand.

II

THE ORIGINS OF HANDEDNESS

"The left hand, as we are born: the right hand, as we make it."

OSBERT SITWELL: *Left Hand, Right Hand*

The word "handedness" is a comparatively recent addition to the English language. "Laterality", or sidedness, has a longer tradition. "Southpaw" is 20th-century sporting slang. But whatever the words used, the subject dates back to the dawn of man's history. Why are most people right-handed? When did the asymmetry, or preference for one hand begin? What caused this preference? What can, or should, left-handers do about being a minority in a right-handed world? What is the average size of that minority?

These primary questions have no simple answer. To delve into the evidence is to discover a lot about the brain as well as the body, and about the fears and superstitions of man as well as his physical structure. Ignorance and prejudice have played their part through the centuries, and only within the last century has a rational medical and educational approach been made to this important subject.

In succeeding chapters, we shall discuss the origins of handedness, the problem of heredity, the habit of primitive man, and the proportion of sinistrals in the population, before going on to the wider implications in religion, superstition, the educational world, the arts and sciences, and finally the problems of everyday life for the left-hander.

Theories about handedness go back to Aristotle and Plato. Then there is a remarkable lapse of time until the Norwich doctor, mystic and author, Sir Thomas Browne noted, in 1648, that "many are sinistrously disposed, and go through their lives left-handed" and proceeded to an informed and remarkably thorough investigation into the origins and superstitions. Another lapse of time followed, until, supplementing the works of Darwin and Huxley on man generally, various authorities began to reconsider this human phenomenon in physical terms. Sir Daniel Wilson of Toronto was one of the first (1872) and about the same time Thomas Carlyle (whose early misfortune had been that of the maidservant mistakenly burning the manuscript of his *French Revolution*) suffered another misfortune, losing the use of his right arm in his 75th year. The following observations appear in his Journal of June 15th, 1871:

> "It is curious to consider the institution of the Right hand among universal mankind; probably the very oldest human institution that exists, indispensable to all human cooperation whatsoever. He that has seen three mowers, one of whom is left-handed, trying to work together, and how impossible it is, has witnessed the simplest form of an impossibility, which but for the distinction of a 'right hand' would have pervaded all human beings. Have often thought of all that—never saw it so clearly as this morning while out walking, unslept and dreary enough in the winter sunshine. How old? Old! I wonder if there is any people barbarous enough not to have this distinction of hands. . . . Why that particular hand was chosen is a question not to be settled, not worth asking except as a kind of riddle; probably arose in fighting; most important to protect your heart and its adjacencies, and to carry the shield in that hand."

Presumably Carlyle had not read Sir Thomas Browne, whose *Vulgar Errors* described as a fallacy the belief that the heart was, in fact, on the left side. Yet there were several experts who supported Carlyle's reasoning.

Those who have written at length about handedness and its cause have usually set out a list of alternative reasons. This is the list compiled by the American writer, Beaufort Sims Parson.* Handedness, he says, could be determined by:

* *Lefthandedness: a New Interpretation*: Macmillan, New York, 1924.

1. Habit and upbringing.
2. Hereditary transmission.
3. Nursing and early education.
4. Visceral distribution and displacement of centre of gravity (in the human body).
5. Primitive warfare.
6. Inequality of blood supply to the brain.
7. Origin of subclavian arteries. (They are under the clavicle, or collar-bone.)
8. Superior development of one cerebral hemisphere.
9. Ocular Dominance.

Parson, whose work is often quoted, concentrated mainly on the ninth interpretation, and based his findings on a visual correlation between the dominant eye and the favoured hand. He was in favour of sight-tests with a black spot on a white card, to determine which eye is the dominant one.

Now compare, since the evidence from this point on will accumulate rapidly, a list made by John Jackson in 1905, in an impassioned plea on behalf of Ambidexterity (with a Foreword by Major-General R. R. S. Baden-Powell, who comes into this book later as Lord Baden-Powell, of the Left-Handshake among the Boy Scouts).

Jackson's classification on the origin of handedness:

1. Nursing (includes Plato).
2. Practice in writing.
3. An acquired habit.
4. Warfare, Education, Heredity.
5. Hereditary impulse.
6. Mechanical Law.
7. Internal organic reasons.
8. Instinct or endowment.
9. Visceral distribution.
10. Blood-vessel arrangement.
11. Brain one-sidedness.
12. Natural selection.

This is a tall order, since not more than two of the above can presumably have any real importance in determining handedness. There is one item of agreement on the two lists which we shall next consider: the visceral distribution.

This mechanical theory, as it has been called, had already been referred to by Sir Thomas Browne. But it was given greater credence and impact in the 19th century by the Professor of Physiology in the University of Glasgow, Alexander Buchanan. He claimed that a child usually realises the mechanical advantage of the right side, because of the displacement of the centre of gravity in the body itself. With the greater weight of the liver and lungs on the right, man tends to be able to balance better on the left foot, leaving the right-hand free and ready for action, and in time the muscles on the right side develop more strongly, just as Aristotle observed that the right claws of most lobsters were larger. This still did not explain why apes were ambidextral.

Buchanan was supported by a fellow Scot, Sir John Struthers, who put the greater gravity to the right as much as three-tenths of an inch. Livers and other viscera were weighed, and another apparently irrefutable reason for right-handedness was deduced. The only omission was to explain what caused left-handedness, unless it was a displacement of the various viscera. But the theory would explain dextrality in primitive fighting. Palaeolithic man lived in days before the shield with which a man could protect his heart. His first weapon might have been a stone or any piece of wood which came to hand: and by "came to hand" might mean that, in leaning down, the whole emphasis was to the right, and the right hand was therefore the instinctive weapon hand.

The idea of cerebral dominance—the superior attributes of one side of the brain, controlling the opposite side of the body—had already been put forward in the 17th century by Browne, and later appeared in the lists of Parson and Jackson and others. But in 1861 Robert Boyd, an English medical man used to post-mortems, stated definitely that in most cases the left lobe of the brain was the heavier.* Sir Daniel Wilson confirmed this at the dissection of a dead friend, and he was supported by the Italian Cesare Lombroso and France's Joseph le Conte, in 1883, who also noted that most people who were left-eyed or left-footed were also left-handed. The anatomical difference was described as arising from "a foetal asymmetry of the cerebral blood supply, producing an unequal development of the hemispheres".

In 1890, Dr. Giuseppe of Pisa explained it in more detail:

"In left-handed persons the centres of the neuro-psychic factors of language are situate in the right hemisphere, as has been shown by well-studied cases. These persons, however, learn to write with the right hand and not with the left. And yet in their right hemisphere there is a potentiality which is very favourable for their education in the co-ordination and the memory of the movements for writing. Left-handed persons perceive that they could learn to write with greater facility with the left hand than with the right; but education succeeds in awaking and conveniently bringing into action in the left-hand sphere a latent cortical centre, which did not present so favourable a potentiality as that of the right hemisphere."

In a notable Huxley Memorial Lecture given in 1902, Dr D. J. Cunningham asserted: "Right-handedness is due to a transmitted functional pre-eminence of the left brain," and added: "Left-brainedness is not the result, but, through evolution, it has become the cause of right-handedness." He was a believer in the hereditary principle, and attempted to disprove the visceral explanation of the human organs as a factor in handedness.

These were years of intense interest in the whole problem, an interest probably as great as at the present time, when many of the theories are taken for granted, and the question of handedness has mainly become one of treatment for a familiar, accepted phenomenon.

* "Tables of the weights of the Human Body and Internal Organs in the Sane and Insane of both Sexes of various Ages, Arranged from 2614 Post-mortem Examinations". Royal Society of London, 1861.

III

HOW MANY SOUTHPAWS?

There are two main questions which are always asked about handedness. The first is, what causes left-handedness in a proportion of the people? The second, what proportion of the population is either openly or originally sinistral? The first has been discussed, and there is a wide divergence of views. The second has engaged the attention of many types of expert, and many authorities, including military commands, which have to account for a proportion of left-handedness among each intake of recruits.

Obviously the proportion will vary according to the degree of tolerance exercised in the country concerned. While, in the United States, Canada, Britain, Western Europe and Israel, among others, left-handed writing is permitted in schools (sinistral preference in games is hardly ever forbidden, as we shall see when we come to consider sport) this handwriting is *verboten* in both Western and Eastern Germany, in the Soviet Union, and in all countries beyond the Iron Curtain. There would seem to be no political significance in this: it is merely the desire for conformity. A typical Soviet school writing book has illustrated instructions on the cover, showing how to hold the pen, in the right hand.

The rule is even more strict in Arab countries, probably the strictest of all. Africa, India, Asia also adhere to the rule, but since this often applies only to actual handwriting and not to other activities, it is very difficult for the expert to get his information except by sample. Nino Lo Bello, in the American *Science Digest** put the world sinistral population at anything up

* April, 1960.

to 200 million, a very high proportion. Dr Wile, in his work on handedness, judges the range between 2 and 30 per cent of the population. Dr Bryng Bryngelson, of the University of Minnesota, who has spent thirty years studying the problem, declared:

"If there were no interference on the part of parents and teachers, 34 out of every 100 children born today would be left-handed, and about 3 per cent would be using hands with equal dexterity."

Sir Cyril Burt, who has had long experience in the educational world, estimates that about 5 per cent of the ordinary school population in Britain might be left-handed. There is a marked sex difference, the proportion of boys being 6 per cent and girls only 4 per cent.

It is noteworthy that, in his examination of mental defective schools, Burt found a very different statistic. Here are the two compared.

	Elementary Schools	Special Schools
Boys	6·2%	13·5%
Girls	3·9%	10·3%
Average	5·1%	11·9%

Another examiner, Hugh Gordon, taking 3,000 London school-children as his sample, arrived at an average of 7·3%. His survey of mental defective schools brought the figure of 18·2% (from 4,000 pupils) but the surprising variation in this case was that the proportion of girls outnumbered that of the boys, one of the only examples of this to be found. The general consensus of opinion seems to give the greater share of sinistrality to the male sex—perhaps because girls do sewing and household work at an early age, and are less independent.

With typical German throughness, the High Command of the Kaiser's army before the first world war employed the psychiatrist Stier to make a report on handedness among the troops. Stier had already studied the subject. His theory was that it was hereditary, and very prevalent among primitive tribes. His findings, published at Jena in 1911, form one of the longest book titles on record.* The proportion of sinistral soldiers he judged to be about 4 per cent: but the examination took IQ into consideration, and when it came to the number of "unintelligent" left-handers, the proportion jumped to 13 per cent.

Let us take a much later example, from a more enlightened age and a more tolerant country, the United States.

In 1952, the Surgeon General of the U.S. Army ordered an enquiry into left-handedness, in the expectation, among other things, that this might become an index for sinistral statistics in the whole U.S. population. The results were listed in a magazine by Karpinos and Grossman.† They are certainly detailed, and are divided into the various armies and the regions where they operate, so that one can see at once that there were appreciably more left-handed rejects in the New York and Washington area than in, say, the Middle West. Many of the other details are obscure, but the overall figures are illuminating.

Each recruit is normally asked to answer, among other questions, are you (a) right handed? (b) left handed? on the entry forms he receives. Of 6,040 men who qualified in 1952, left-handers numbered 471. Of 6,119 who failed to qualify, left-handers numbered 593. The total U.S. Army rate is reckoned at 7·9% left-handers (qualified) and 10·1% left-handers (disqualified). Total of both, 8·6% left-handed, which, if taken as a sample of the entire population, adds up to quite a number of southpaws.

Other miscellaneous calculations of various dates include:

Ohio school subjects (18,000) examined in 1930, revealed 4 per cent left-handed. In Stuttgart, 10,000 children (1932) revealed nearly 8 per cent, which is a high figure for Germany, and no doubt Hitler, with his right-handed swastika, changed all this. W. H. Pyle and Alice Drouin found, in American elementary schools, 862 left-handed pupils out of 13,438—

* *Untersuchungen über Linkshädigkeit und die funktionellen Differenzen den hirhalften nebst einem Anhang über Linkshandigkeit in der Deutschen Armee.*

† *Left-handedness in the U.S. Army*: Human Biology, Vol. 25, The Johns Hopkins Press, Baltimore, 1953.

about 6·4 per cent. Basing his case on left-eyedness, the American, Beaufort Parson, came to the astonishing proportion of 30 per cent, the sample being about 800 cases. A similarly extravagant claim was made by Stanley Jackson, the protagonist of Ambidextrality at the beginning of the century. He stated: "Out of every 100 children born, 17 were naturally right-handed, 3 were naturally left-handed, and 80 might have been either, or both." Since he was actively engaged in promoting the Ambidextral Culture Society this sounds like a piece of special pleading.

An examination of Palestinian children (2,000 of them) undertaken in 1933 by the German E. Arnstein, revealed a left-handed proportion of more than 10 per cent. The present author's visits to what is now Israel, in recent years, has revealed comparative freedom for left-handers in schools, even though the Old Testament books were so determinedly dextral. One school authority in Galilee estimated the proportion as "at least 10 per cent".

So, between the 1 per cent and the 30 per cent, there must obviously be an approximately accurate figure, but no one's statistics have been universally accepted. We might estimate that 4 or 5 per cent is likely in a civilised democracy with an enlightened educational outlook, but that in a more prejudiced and traditional Muslim country, with all the emphasis on the Unclean Hand and the Evil Eye, 1 per cent is probably an exaggeration.

There is no limit to the endurance, ingenuity and dedication of the investigators into sinistrality. It isn't a peculiarity which most people feel worth investigating or confessing: there has been, in the last few centuries, no Inquisition and no Senator McCarthy to conduct a witch-hunt against the sinistrals.

Investigation has been the hard way. Thousands of school-children seem to have been interviewed and since most of the schools are American, there has been no reluctance by the pupils to admitting left-handedness. Yet the investigations often contradict each other, or cancel out any hope of a final conclusion about sinistrality's cause and effect.

The lengths to which the patient investigator will go is illustrated in an example from the indefatigable Dr Wile of Boston. At one stage of his enquiry, he stationed himself at a street-corner, presumably in Boston, and observed, first, the habits of passers-by in carrying single packages held in the hand or under the arm, just as Sir Daniel Wilson watched the steamboat porters on the Mississippi. 76 per cent were carried on the left side, 24 per cent on the right side. But as far as women's handbags were concerned (the female sex, as investigators agree, being less prone to left-handedness than the male) 27 per cent held them on the left side, and 73 per cent on the right. Wile's investigation coverd 5,000 people.

More remarkable still is his testimony to the use of the umbrella, an article which one might think more common in Birmingham, England, than in Boston.

It is not merely the incidence of umbrellas, or even the handedness thereof, which impressed Wile, but the percentage of left-handers *who carried a closed, or rolled umbrella*. The figures are as follows:

Closed umbrellas carried   in right hand 30%
                                in left hand 70%
Opened umbrellas carried   in right hand 80%
                                in left hand 20%

"Here then," concludes Wile, "was a transfer of handedness according to need and purpose but fairly consistent in pointing out the latest functional preferences. Possibly the number with the freed right hand (umbrella closed) is greater than the freed left (umbrella open) owing to the pressure of social traffic habits. . . ."

But surely, the weather at the time of Wile's great Watch must have had something to do with the state of the umbrella, open or closed. It is no easy thing to roll an umbrella properly (some folklore experts might regard it as the privilege of the British Foreign Office) and a sudden shower in Boston might well have upset Dr Wile's calculations.

In addition to this, it is difficult, frankly, to understand what he proves by it. In his survey into sinistrality, Wile seems to have become obsessed by his enquiry, and saw left-handedness in everything, even in rolled umbrellas. And if he dreamed left-handed dreams, then Professor Jung would be only too happy to interpret them.

There is a legend that, during his conquests, Alexander the Great discovered a country of predominantly sinistral people, whose greeting was a handshake with the left hand. But even legends like this are rare.

"No purely left-handed race has ever been discovered," wrote a correspondent of the *Medical Record* in 1886, "although there seems to be a difference in different tribes. Seventy per cent of the inhabitants of the Punjab use the left hand by preference; and the greater number of the Hottentots and Bushmen of South Africa also use the left hand in preference to the right," and the London *Times* of 1876, in an article on Fiji, reported that left-handed men were more common among them than among white people. But these were mainly random notes and individual observations by travellers. In those years no attempt could be made which would provide statistical proof.

Four to 6 per cent of the people of Britain, the United States, France and Greece show preference for the left hand, according to Dr Margaret Clark in 1951.

Jane Clem, in 1954, writing in the *Business Education World* on "Helping your Left-Handed Typing Students", estimates that 5 to 8 per cent in the U.S. are totally left-handed, while 30 per cent are inclined to be left-handed in certain principles.

D. C. Rife in 1951 (*Science Monthly*, New York) asserted that the U.S. had a left-handed population of between 10 and 15 million.

An extensive study of 225,000 students in Michigan in 1947—this is an extremely large and therefore valuable sample—revealed that 10·1 per cent of students in Grade I were left-handed, compared with 6·6 per cent in Grade XII.

In Detroit in 1941, out of 13,438 elementary-school children, 6·4 per cent were found to be left-handed, the proportion of boys being nearly twice as large as that of girls.

Kenneth L. Martin (*Journal of Educational Research*) put the incidence of left-handedness in mental institutions as high as 16 to 30 per cent, and a survey of idiopathic epileptics revealed nearly 15 per cent to be sinistral.

Very little testing of the deaf, blind and dumb has been carried out, but in one report by Gertrude Hildreth in 1951, the incidence was 3 per cent for deaf girls, 4 per cent for deaf boys, 11 per cent for blind girls and 10 per cent for blind boys. The investigator suggested that left-handedness is an accompanying symptom rather than a causal factor.

IV

THE CLUE OF THE CAVES

It has often been said that the habits of primitive man can provide the clue to hand-preference.

At some stage, almost certainly in the Bronze Age, man developed his "tool-sense", and this use of his hands, guided by the brain, alone distinguished him from the lesser animals, the animals he learned to hunt and kill with the weapons he had fashioned. The age of the arrowhead had begun, as Longfellow noted in verse:

> "At the doorway of his wigwam
> Sat the ancient arrow-maker
> In the land of the Dacotahs,
> Making arrow-heads of jasper,
> Arrow-heads of chalcedony . . ."

Thomas Carlyle had written: "I wonder if there is any people barbarous enough not to have this distinction of hands; no human cosmos is possible to have begun without it." Dr Cunningham added: "So far as history takes us, right-handedness would appear to have been a common birthright of mankind."

But was Palaeolithic man necessarily right-handed? His comparatively recent evolution from the admittedly ambidextral ape would argue that he was probably to some extent ambidextral himself. Experts examining cave-drawings over the past century have agreed that some show signs of having been drawn with the left hand. One of the proofs could be discerned from a profile: if it faced left as it usually did, it was likely to be a dextral drawing: if to the right, a sinistral. This is in the case of a single figure. But primitive artists would often, as in the later case of the Egyptians, make up a "mirror" pattern for two or more figures. There was, moreover, no recognised code, as Daniel Wilson points out:*

"Every man did what was right in his own eyes. Some handled their tools and drew with the left hand. A larger number used the right hand, but as yet no rule prevailed. In this, the arts and habits of that period belonged to a chapter in the infancy of the race, when the law of dexterity, as well as other laws, was begot by habit, or more convenience. Conventionality had not yet found its place in that unwritten code, to which a prompter obedience is rendered than to the most absolute of royal or imperial decrees. . . . The more the subject is studied, it becomes manifest that education, with the stimulus furnished by the necessities arising from all combined action, has much to do with a full development of right-handedness."

Many implements have been found which could, obviously, have been used by either hand. Those cut in flint, including arrow-heads, which have reversed bevelling, are equally obviously the work of primitive left-handed craftsmen. Dr Brinton, in his study of North American Aboriginal Art (1896) gave the remarkably high proportion of one-third as the extent of sinistrality among the tribes, and being a believer in its hereditary nature, he foresaw a reason for its continuation.

There is a curious reference, quoted by Wile, to South America before the Spanish conquest. Among the Incas, it was said, left-handedness could be a happy augury, and one of the Inca chiefs, a man renowned for his good deeds, was called Lloque Yupanqui—which means left-handed.

Among Stone Age tribes showing a marked degree of left-handedness, or at least ambidextrality, Wile quotes Australians, Africans, Hottentots, Bushmen, Bantus and Pygmies, among others. Early Neolithic tools found in England are frequently shaped as if for left-hand use.

But for the majority of primitive human beings, in earlier

* *Left-handedness*: Nature Series, Macmillan, 1891.

centuries, the majority rule must have gradually taken shape. As soon as man developed a sense of environment, he must inevitably have looked for some kind of conformity. Assuming the theory of cerebral dominance, that majority must soon have been assured. Assuming, in addition, the theory of a cultivated hand-preference, that majority must also have been approved, and as with animals, the censure of a primitive human tribe would be strongest against the minority, whose hand-practice did not fit the pattern. Tribes choose a chief—and if the chief be right-handed, so must be his most trusted followers.

During the Bronze Age, right-handedness must have assumed a physical dominance. Later it was to assume a physiological and social dominance. "There arose," says Wile, "not so much a decline in the hereditary presence of left-handedness but rather a suppression of it under the demand for adaptation to changing principles of social organization, preservation, and advancement."

The French anthropologist, Paul Sarasin, made a major contribution to our knowledge of hand usage in the Stone and Bronze Ages. In the area of Moustier, he studied many Stone Age implements, finding that some of the wedge-shaped stones and hatchets were sharpened on the left and others on the right. He came to the conclusion that handedness during the entire Age showed no marked preference. It was a matter of chance, and this he confirmed with further researches in two other French areas.

His findings among Bronze Age tools, however, prove how dextrality gradually asserted itself. This was shown not only by the effects of wear on the cutting edges of sharp instruments, but in the important single instance of the sickle. To this day there is no such thing (unless it be specially manufactured) as a left-handed sickle or scythe, and even back in the Bronze Age, the method of making them was predominantly for right hand use. Already the preference for a dextral tool was becoming, not solely numerical or biological, but social—preferred, that is, by custom and not merely by instinct. Wile comments: "Whether the hand that ought to be preferred was under the influence of an anatomical superiority of one side of the brain, or a belief in magic, cannot be disregarded, and possibly both were important."

Abram Blau makes the point that a primitive Bronze Age tool took a great deal of time and trouble to make, and it was therefore imperative for operators to use it with the hand for which it was constructed. In other words, the inventor or maker could decide the side of usage, while the user had little choice. Ehud the Benjamite made his own dagger, fit for the deed he had to do, left-handedly, but his was a special case. Moreover, tools were precious and held in high regard, being handed down from generation to generation. Blau adds: "A one-sided orientation in relation to skills holds many advantages. It makes for economy in development for special capacities; training concentrated on one side is more intensified than when divided among two sides. The sustained hand preference promotes strength, deftness, endurance, and growing capability. The cultivation of an habitual approach fosters speed and accuracy, whether applied to the tools of peace or war. All in all, with the coming of tools there appeared many essential and practical reasons for a one-sided orientation."

The handing on of a tool, say, from father to son would also preserve this one-handedness, for the boy would have to be taught how to use the instrument. Any conscious society eventually demands a series of codes. Some may be ethical, others physical, and the more primitive the society, the more intolerant its attitude to the man whose habits or beliefs run counter to the main stream. The discovery of smelting copper, in about the 5th century B.C., not only gave primitive craftsmen a whole new range of instruments and weapons: it began the acceptance and later domination of the right hand which later was to be exalted in worship, to the detriment of its unworthy opposite member.

One aspect of sidedness, if not actual handedness, completes the story of primitive man, emerging as a thinking creature. Sun-worship was undoubtedly the earliest form of worship, an instinctive turning to the source of light, which would influence all succeeding kinds of worship. To quote Wile, that ardent student of the sun:

"There can be little doubt but that with the development of reason, and the rebirth of emotions under the impact of a conscious self-environment, in which curiosity, wonder, fear and awe, must have elicited sharp reactions, man began to orient himself. Then perhaps he grasped the significance of those fundamentals which formed the basis of his religious formulations. Trees and serpents may have had their early worship, but slowly there came a consciousness of dependence upon the magnificent sun, yielder of light, warmth, vegetation and life. With the daily advent of that orb, man felt more safe, and he was grateful. Thus began a new homage, and man faced the east, his anxious eyes following through its course via the south to its glorious extinction in the west. . . . If there were a sun cure in those primeval days, man would have been made right by turning himself to the right, ever in the course of the sun.

"This, of course, applies only to those who lived in the northern hemisphere, but they have always been greatly in the majority."

Wile received a critical question on this point, from a reader who wrote: "If earth's rotation has much to do with handedness, it would seem that people like the Australian savages, who have lived for untold generations in the southern hemisphere ought to be much more left-handed than those who have lived similarly in the northern hemisphere." Some research showed that this was probably the case, but in such primitive areas it has been difficult to obtain reliable statistics.

V

IS HANDEDNESS HEREDITARY?

We have considered the many theories as to the origin, in man, of the preferred or dominant hand. Perhaps it is necessary to recapitulate, in more detail, on the question most frequently asked in connection with left-handedness. Is this minority trait hereditary or acquired? Does the undoubted fact that most left-handers have sinistrality in the family, of whatever generation, prove the hereditary theory?

The issue is joined among the experts. Dr Cunningham's celebrated Huxley Memorial Lecture put him firmly among those supporting the theory that it is transmitted from parents to children. Von Bandeleben (1910) agreed with him. Frank H. Crushing, witing in the *American Anthropologist* in 1892, stated: "The hand of man has been so intimately associated with the mind of man that it has moulded intangible thoughts no less than the tangible products of his brain. So intimate was this association during the very early manual period of man's mental growth that it may be affirmed to be, *like so many other hereditary traits*, still dominantly existent in the hands of all of us."

The writers Woo and Pearson, who place the proportion of natural left-handers as high as 25 per cent were convinced that they inherited this—as recessive, opposed to dominant characters—according to the Mendelian law of heredity. The findings of Gregor Mendel, the formidable Austrian biologist who became a monk, and experimented with flowers in the monastery garden, have affected everyone's theories about human heredity, not least those faced with explaining the incidence of left-handedness.

H. D. Chamberlain, who examined a total American population of 12,000, the equivalent of a small town, in 1929, learned that, in families where one or both parents were left-handed, 17 per cent of the children were sinistral also; in families where both were right-handed, only 2 per cent of the children were left-handed. So he came down on the side of the inherited trait, but did not ascribe it to the Mendelian recessive.

F. Ramaley, in the *American Naturalist* of 1913, had already advanced this theory, based on 610 parents and 1,310 children. He estimated left-handers as numbering up to one-sixth of the population. Another approach to the hereditary theory was made through the examination of twins, it being considered that twins should have a "mirror-effect" between left and right, rather like Tweedledum and Tweedledee in *Through the Looking Glass*. But in an enquiry into twins, Sir Cyril Burt found, in a group of eighty-four, only four instances where both twins were left-handed (they were identical twins) and only one where a single twin was sinistral. H. H. Newman, in the *Journal of Heredity* (London, 1920) accepted the view that left-handedness was an inherited recessive trait, but admitted discrepancies between one twin and another.

Of the famous Dionne Quins, only one, Marie, was left-handed. She proved the brightest and cleverest of the five, but died when comparatively young.

J. Mark Baldwin* was in no doubt about the inheritance of handedness:

"It is likely that right-handedness in the child is due to differences in the two half-brains, being always associated with speech, that the promise of it is inherited, and that the influences of infancy have little effect upon it. . . . This inherited brain one-sidedness also accounts for the association of right-handedness, speech, and musical faculty."

Opposing this, two years later, G. M. Gould of Philadelphia:†

"Heredity has, directly, nothing whatever to do with the

---

* *Mental Development in the Child*: Macmillan, New York, 1906.
† *Righthandedness and Lefthandedness*: Lippincott, Philadelphia, 1908.

existence of the 94 per cent of right-handed and 6 per cent of left-handed."

Ira S. Wile believes that changes during the Bronze Age argue against the hereditary theory. But, conversely, he agrees "there is no reason to doubt that handedness is transmitted from parent to child, and hence that it is, to some extent, hereditary. If left-handedness has deviated from a primary potential half-use or preference, there must be some reasonable explanation."

The explanation, he thinks, is that the left-hander is indeed a Mendelian recessive, and he urges his point by the references to primitive man in the Bronze Age, to the protection of the heart on the left side, where it was supposed to reside, and to the social pressure.

"There arose, now, not so much a decline in the hereditary presence of left-handedness, but rather a suppression of it under the changing principles of social organisation, preservation, and advancement."

Abraham Blau comes down firmly against the heredity explanation in his monograph *The Master Hand*. "Nature versus nurture", as he calls it, has long been an academic conflict. On this subject of handedness, the protagonists could be divided into the "hereditarians" and the "environmentalists".

The theory of hereditary transmission of sidedness, he believes, not only offers no adequate solution, but stops up many subsequent avenues of research, by over-simplifying the problem. "To say that right-handedness is hereditary presumes that it is foreordained and predetermined in the nervous system of the child, so that at the proper time it will use its right hand for cutting, writing, throwing a ball, &c. It is a neat theory . . . but it collapses when we consider that so far absolutely no proof has been mustered for it."

He makes the point that, in the west, the preferred direction of gaze is from left to right. If this were instinctive, it would mean that children would be born, for instance, prone to write from left to right. But what of these Semitic or Oriental writers who write the other way? Handedness, in other words, cannot be geographic or racial if it is hereditary. It is, in Blau's view, the psychologist's job to determine how much can be classified as hereditary, and how much acquired. "Many activities which were once accepted as inherited, now appear under closer analysis to be dependent on environmental or learning influences."

Blau cites another example, an experiment in which a sparrow was reared in a nest of canaries. It lost its own native chirp, and began to imitate the canaries' song, which it did with an amazing capacity to learn. Back in the sparrows' nest, it resumed its chirp. Back among humans, he admits that the inherent human structure which leads to preferred dextral handedness is based fundamentally upon hereditary factors. "But," he adds, "heredity is involved only to the extent that it is a valuable reservoir waiting to be exploited. The particular choice, direction and nature of the skill finally achieved are quite outside the province of the germ plasm."

Much of the exploitation can be made as the result of the local human culture which the child, maturing much more slowly than animals, eventually acquires. "The experience of animals disappears with each generation. . . . But where the horizon of the animal is narrow, man's is infinite. Culture represents the combination of past social experience and mass learning. . . . Each human infant takes over this culture where the previous generation left off. In a literal sense, man's experience becomes immortalised and part of the property is transmitted to his heirs." Blau quotes technical accomplishments from the telephone to television as "excellent examples of the culture . . . made ready for future generations".

This is a powerful plea for acquired laterality—the side being the right, or Master side; and, as we shall see, in considering Blau's work further, the left represented the unnecessary rebellion against the main stream of culture. "As soon as we are born, society steps in and says: 'Thou shalt use thy right hand not thy left hand!' . . . One-sided preference is thus firmly ingrained in the human constitution."

Burt quotes Sir Thomas Browne as one of the early school of

anti-hereditary thought, with his dictum that right-handedness of the majority is a sane and serviceable convention. "It is most reasonable for uniformity and sundry respective uses that man should apply himself to the constant use of one arm. Dextral pre-eminence"—and this is one of Browne's most celebrated pronouncements—"hath no regular or certain root in nature."

The most important line of investigation, Burt declares, is the well-nigh universal nature of the right-handed tendency in every country and race. It is not merely a convention, like the rule of the road in driving. He considers the view that in the dextral man, the bones of his right arm are longer and stronger, and finds this proved in 75 per cent of the population. The opposite would appear to be true with the sinistral man, but he may number only 9 per cent of the population. At birth, the length is said to be almost identical. Therefore is to the use and skill of the preferred hand that one may attribute the length and strength. "Man, by his right hand," as Crichton-Browne quoted, "hath gotten himself the victory." Burt reports that the earliest known London man and the earliest ape-man (Pithecanthropus) were both right-handed, and that semi-erect apes show a dextral preference. A tendency towards right-handedness has therefore been handed down from prehistoric times, and becomes marked, as we have seen, by the usage of tools and implements in the Bronze Age.

But if right-handedness be innate or inherited, is left-handedness to be regarded likewise? This, says Burt, does not follow. It may be due to some interfering factor.

Finally, he refers very insistently to the process of imitation, whereby left-handers may watch how the majority perform their tasks or sporting practices, and fall into the majority habit, without coercion; also to the practice of nursing, and the assumption, which even Plato held, that the hand that rocks the baby, as distinct from the cradle, not so much rules the world, but rules the handedness of the baby. Obviously, if a baby is habitually held on the left arm—to give the mother or nurse freedom of action with the right hand—its own right arm will be thrust against the body, and freedom of movement will be afforded only to the left arm—freedom to stretch out at any passing object. This is the factor which operates at about the time when most children develop a preference for one hand above the other.

The right-handed hold seems to be orthodox, and taught in modern nursing institutions, many years after Plato's day. But Cyril Burt, who is the most tenacious of enquirers when he feels interested in a problem, says how he made "a peripatetic census in the streets of poorer districts, where mothers take their infants with them when they shop". He found that in seventy-three cases the child was carried on the left arm and in only twenty-seven on the right.

Pursuing this idea, Burt examined many representations of the most famous image of mother and child—the classical paintings to Mary and the infant Jesus.

"I examined a hundred well-known pictures of the Madonna and Child, and find that fifty-nine have the child on the left and only forty-one on the right: with the earlier painters, in particular, the left position becomes commoner."

Burt sums up: "I find it incredible that the various facts I have summarised can be interpreted in terms of habit-formation only, without invoking the influence of some innate and inheritable factor as well." But he adds: "The inherited bias must in most instances be comparatively slight, otherwise it would not be so difficult to substantiate; and secondly, there must be numerous instances, more or less exceptional, which cannot be explained by heredity at all. With any individual child, therefore, other factors must be cautiously ruled out before any innate tendency can be safely presumed."

Professor Henry M. Halvorsen describes the beginning of "motor development".*

"Although it is generally believed that infants fail to show hand preference during the first few months of life, asymmetry of posture is indicated at birth by the prevalence of the tonic neck reflex attitude. This postural reflex, as is well known, has a pronounced effect on the position of the arms, but it also affects

* *The First Five Years of Life*: edited by Arnold Gesell: Methuen, London, 1954.

the position of the other extremities. The lateral position of the head during the first few months predisposes the infant to regard the activities of the hand which he is facing. Thus, in the first step in the co-ordination of hand and eye-movements, indications of the preferred hand may already be present."

Professor Halvorsen believes that dominant sidedness begins with the greater use of the small muscle groups of one side or the other, or it may, in later years, be indicated by the preferential use of one hand in spontaneous activity as well as in reaching. This means going back to the sort of test in which you throw a ball unexpectedly at a child, and see which hand he instinctively puts up to catch it. Hand preference makes its appearance mainly during the second six months of a child's life, and may become more marked after eighteen months or two years. Halvorsen's survey gave more credit to right-handers than left-handers in the matter of bodily poise, reach, and grasp, as with making a tower of cubes.

Ambidextrals do not appear to shine in these early stages, and show tendencies of being retarded in speech development. It is obvious that the child is in fact striving towards the use of one hand, instead of two, even though the second hand may be employed in an auxiliary role—one hand to reach out, the other to steady the body against a chair or a wall. Furthermore, even the very young child begins to realise that he can, by twisting and stretching his body, reach farther with one hand than with two, and reaching out is surely the favourite habit of any infant.

"The determination of handedness in childhood is at best a very complicated problem", writes Professor Halvorsen, obviously not wishing to commit himself to any definite theory, out of the many propounded. "Whether handedness is innate or due to factors in antenatal or postnatal life is not known. However, the problem is of such importance that it should be made part of every clinical examination. . . . Tests which place a premium on skill or precision of movement rather than on frequency of use or amount of activity may be most revealing for the early detection of handedness."

Experiments in footedness were also made by Halvorsen. We know from observation how animals walk or trot, and what difference there is between the preferred foot. The marching of soldiers is "by the left" and that is an agreed order with a purpose behind. But what of the instinctive preference of children stepping on to a walking-board?

The children were divided into age-groups of 4, 5 and 6 years. Out of 24 children in the first group, 29 per cent always led with the right foot and only 4 per cent consistently with the left, but there were many variations. At 5 years old the left-handed preference rose sharply to 17 per cent, with 19 per cent of those who used the left foot at least 2 times out of 3. At 6 years the proportion had dropped slightly to 14 per cent. The total number of times each foot was used came to:

Right   420   Left   303

This results in a high proportion of left-footed children in the whole test.

Another test in an American clinic by Dr Burton Castner, in which eyedness was added to handedness and footedness, showed a marked increase in the number who were left-eyed, as opposed to the proportions with hand and with foot. The results, writes Halvorsen, point to a higher relationship between hand and foot than eye and hand, or eye and foot. The greatest changes in laterality between the ages of 3 and 7 occurred in the instance of the hand.

VI

THE LANGUAGE OF THE LEFT

The original of the English word "left" is not as simple as we might expect: nor is it unbiased. Though Webster's *Dictionary* connects it with the verb "to leave", that is probably not the meaning when applied to the left hand or side. The *Oxford Dictionary* definition begins:

> LEFT (Middle Eng. *left, lift,* Old Eng. *left* . . . the primary sense, "weak, worthless" is represented also in East Frisian *luf*, Dutch dialect *loof*, and the derived sense (left hand) in Middle Dutch and Low German *luchter, lucht, luft*, and North Frisian *leeft.* ct. further (though the connection is very doubtful) Old English *lef*, weak.

Burt adds that the Anglo-Saxon *lyft* means weak or broken, "akin to lopt or lopped and possibly the German *licht* and *leicht*, in the sense of fragile". There is a further line of connection with the Latin *laevus*, an archaic word meaning the shield or left hand: but in this sense there is nothing derogatory, and at that early stage the odious comparison between right and left had not been made (indeed, with the early Roman augurs, the left was the lucky side.) The Greek word for left, *aristera*, also meant "the best" (as in aristocrat) although the Greek augurs faced north, and favoured the right. It is all rather contradictory.

The word *sinister* for left is of later origin. It is, literally, the pocket side, from *sinus*. The pocket in a toga was always on the left. But again, it had no "sinister" meaning until the Romans adopted the Greek method of augury.

Another Latin alternative, *scaevola*, means a left-handed

person. It was the surname of Caius Mucius, who made his way to the camp of Lars Porsenna, with the object of killing him, and having failed, burnt off his own right hand. The word had its variants, *scaevus*, left, towards the left side, and *scaevitas*, awkwardness or clumsiness, but survives only as a family name. Quintus Mucius Scaevola was the most famous jurist in Cicero's time.

The *Oxford Dictionary* sums up four meanings of the adjective left-handed, two of them classed as obsolete:

LEFT-HANDED, a.
1. Having the left hand more serviceable than the right; using the left hand by preference.
2. *fig.* a. Crippled, defective, Obs. B. Awkward; clumsy, inapt. (cf. Latin *laevus*, French *gauche*.) c. Characterized by underhand dealings. Obs.
3. Ambiguous, doubtful, questionable. In medical language: spurious.
4. Ill-omened, inauspicious, sinister. Of a deity: unpropitious Obs.

But the prejudice still exists in English. Roget, whose monumental *Thesaurus* is sometimes affected by its compiler's severe and traditional views, contains this entry:

Unskilfulness: clumsy, awkward, *gauche*, gawkish; stuttering, stammering; tactless, indiscriminating; lubberly, unhandy, all thumbs, butter-fingered, thick-fingered; left-handed. . . .

Names in other languages for left, left hand, and a left-hander have nearly always contained at least one derogatory meaning, either "weak", or "clumsy", or sometimes downright evil. About the only language where the epithet cannot be applied, is, oddly enough, English, as we have seen. But the subsidiary meanings in other dictionaries show that this is merely a temporary respite.

Here, taken at random, are some of the language equivalents of the Left:

French: *gauche*: awkward, clumsy; the meaning which has been taken over bodily by the English language, as in Lord Chesterfield's, "Mr —— is *gauche*; it is to be hoped he will mend with keeping company." (1751) or: "The known *gaucherie* of our cabinet in all sorts of Continental interference." (Edinburgh Review, 1823.)

Russian: *lievaia ruka*: can this be an echo of the Latin *laevus*? *Levja* is the name for a left-hander.

Italian: *mancini*: this word can mean not only crooked but even maimed (mancus). Italians do not overlook the fact that a famous criminal figure of the 1930's was called Mancini. But there have been several famous, honourable families with the same name.

Hebrew: *zeroa*: only used in conjunction with the word *yad*, which means hand, when both are used in one sentence. *Yamin* means right hand.

Turkish: *solak*: there are, in modern Turkish, in the Roman alphabet, phrases like *Solcu* (left-wing politician) and "*sol tarafin-dan yalmak*" (to get out of bed on the wrong foot, i.e. left side).

The Turks are remarkable as a people whose method of writing was "switched" by Kemal Ataturk to Roman alphabet letters, written from left to right in western style, instead of in the traditional Muslim way. The psychological and speech upsets were not nearly as great as might have been expected.

Portuguese: *Canhoto*. Also has the connotation of weak and perhaps mischievous.

Dutch: *Links*: Links houden—keep left.

German: *links*: *linksjer*, a left-hander: the language as in other European equivalents, has phrases for morganatic or left-handed marriage (a German speciality), the left-handed compliment, and the rope coiled anti-sunwise on a ship.

Danish: *kejten*: *kejthandet* (which has a similarity to the English provincial "cat-handed").

Norwegian: *keivhendt*:

Finnish: *vasen*: *vasenkattinen* (a left-hander).

Polish: *lewy*, the left hand. *Leworeki*, left-handed. *mankut*, a eft-hander.

Czech: *levy, levak,* similar to Polish. *Levoruk,* left-handed.

Rumanian: *Stang: Stangaciu,* left-hander.

Spanish: *zurdo* (including the translation "malicioso"). *Azurdas* means to go the wrong way: *no ser zurdo* means to be very clever, i.e. not to be left-handed!

Hungarian: *bal: bolkez- balodalt,* a left-hander.

Irish: *coitag* (kithogue). In the traditional Manx language of the Isle of Man it is *kiuttagh.*

Gaelic: *clith-lanihach: ciotach* (an obvious comparison).

Cornish: *cledhec* (from which comes the Cornish slang variations on click-handed, clickety-handed, etc.)

Maltese: *xellugi.*

Malayan: *kidul.*

Hindu: *khabbalabra.*

Chinese: *yung tso show teih* (there are many different forms with subtle changes relating to leftward movements, etc.).

Romany: *bongo* (which also means "crooked, evil". This word was made popular in England some years ago in a book and play by Mr Wolf Mankowitz, *Expresso Bongo,* but it is not clear if the author knew the meaning of the word.).

Japanese: *hidari (hi-sun: dari-on,* the horizon). The Emperor faced south on all ceremonial occasions, hence the sun rose propitiously on his left.

In Britain, there is a rich profusion of regional words to describe the left-hander. They vary in authenticity and popularity, and many are variants of each other.

Perhaps the best known, and often used in normal conversation by people who have no idea of its origin, is "cack-handed". Some say it is of Scottish origin, and derived from the variant "car-handed". But "car" is itself a variant of "keir" meaning left (Gaelic—caer). "Cack" is colloquial for excrement, which leads us straight to the Muslim belief in the clean and unclean handed. Partridge quotes:*

"*Cack-handed:* cack; cacky; left-handed, clumsy. From Cack —excrement. Used by children and women. Colloquial."

* *Dictionary of Slang and Unconventional English:* Oxford, London.

"Cat-handed" is a Devonshire version; "Ca pawed" (keaw-pawed) can be localised to the Bolton area of Lancashire: "Cork handed" occurs in Derbyshire: "Gallock-handed" in East Yorkshire: "Bang-handed"—Tyne-Tees area: "Keggy" in Castle Bromwich, near Birmingham; "Wacky" in Evesham, Worcestershire; "Spuddy-handed" in Gloucestershire; "Scrammy" in Bristol; "Kefty" in West Somerset; "kay-fisted" in Fylde, Lancashire; "Corrie-pawed" or "corrie-fisted", in various parts of Scotland; "Kithogue" (ciotag) Irish, but not necessarily slang.

The ancient Cornish word, "cledhec", for the left-handed, has given rise to the local "click" or "clicky" hand. In Devonshire, according to Dr Capener, local resident and expert on Leonardo da Vinci, the expression is "couchie", supposed to be a corruption of "gauche".

The word "gawky" has usually been associated with the same word, but the experts don't all agree. The Yorkshire "gallock"-handed has been shortened to "gawk"-handed, but there the resemblance may end, for the Scottish "gawk", which meant a cuckoo, or a foolish man, derives from the Latin *cuculus*, with derivatives following—the Anglo-Saxon *geac*, Icelandic *gok*, Danish *giog*, and Old High German *gouch*.

It is indeed an etymological maze, sorting out these meanings, but there is no lack of them in the English tongue, whatever their derivation, and most of them, typically, are terms of mild contempt. The American slang term "Southpaw" entirely derives from the fact that a left-handed pitcher in baseball faces south, and will be dealt with in the chapter on sport. In Australia, a left-hander is a "molly-dooker", derived from "molly", an effeminate man, and "dukes" the slang word for hands.

One remarkable omission is of any known nursery rhyme addressed to, or describing, a left-hander. In Peter Opie's exhaustive enquiry into the folklorique of children's jeers and jingles, there are references to almost every peculiarity except that of the Odd Child Out—the "cack-hander".

Phrases applied to left-handed people or objects include:

the Northern Irish Protestants' "left-footer", meaning a Catholic; "left-hand rope", a rope coiled anti-sunwise, i.e. from left to right—this expression occurs in many languages, testimony to the superstitious nature of seamen; "left-hanging Judas", a rope left dangling over the port side; "left-handed marriage", the morganatic kind referred to in many languages; "left-handed compliment", amounting to an insult; "left-handed spanner", or "flannel-hammer", an imaginary tool left behind by a workman, as an excuse to return; "left-handed wife"—the third in rank among the Kaffirs; "left-handed gun", first mentioned in the *Newgate Calendar* of 1825.

The origin of the political meaning has been explained by H. L. Mencken.*

"Left, in the sense of a radical faction, was introduced by Carlyle in his *French Revolution* in 1837. It comes from the French *côte gauche* (left side). In the French Assembly of 1789, the conservative nobles sat to the presiding officer's right, the radicals of the Third Estate to his left, and the moderates directly before him."

The *Oxford Dictionary* gives, as its first known use of a non-parliamentary application, the mutiny of Communist sailors at Kiel. "Matters," reported the *London Daily Chronicle* (Dec. 2nd, 1918) "are going to the left. . . ." A connection between left-handedness and left-wingedness is reflected in the title of the play by Clifford Odets, *Waiting for Lefty*. In this, Lefty was a political figure: originally, the term merely meant a sinistral.

The sole geographical term is the township of Left Hand, West Virginia, quoted by Mr Mencken.

* *The American Language*: Knopf, New York, 1948.

VII

AUGURY

"Swallows have built
In Cleopatra's sails their nests; the augurers
Say they know not, they cannot tell."

Julius Caesar

"We defy augury; there's a special providence in the fall of
a sparrow."

Hamlet

"Quod di omen avertant."

CICERO: *Philippic III*

When he said: "May the Gods avert this Omen," Marcus
Tullius Cicero, Roman author, orator, politician and philosopher, spoke with some authority, for he was also one of that
select band of sixteen chosen men, an Augur. This office is
worth examining in some detail, since although prophecies and
omens had been known since the days of Empires long before
the Greek or Roman, the Roman practice had a direct bearing
on the Good and Bad Luck preference between Right and Left
—and, of course, gave the Latin word sinistra its present
unhappy meaning.

In the early days of Roman augury, the situation was the
other way round. The priest, or augur, faced south when
watching for the portents, and the left was the lucky side.
Among the Greeks, the augurs faced north, and since the east,
with its rising sun, was a favourable omen, the right hand
became the fortunate one. Cassandra, Priam's daughter,
prophesied first by auguries (perhaps in her happier time of

life). Odysseus received wine from the Gods from the right direction. Homer's Ajax spoke of the Trojans thus: "For their success, Jove thunders on the right." Calchas prophesied the number of years of the Trojan war by the number of sparrows flying from the right.

Cicero, who, in his long treatise on the subject, *De Divinatione*, concludes with the view that augury and prophecy had fallen into disrepute, and that divination was compounded of "a little error, a little superstition, and a good deal of fraud", was in no doubt about its early history and high calling. The man who, according to Juvenal, could exclaim: "O happy Rome, born when I was Consul!" was not known for his modesty or taciturnity. In the dialogue of the *De Divinatione* with his brother Quintus, the latter says: "How trustworthy were the auspices when you were augur! At the present time, Roman augurs neglect auspices, though the Cilicians, Pamphylians, Pisidians and Lycians hold them in high esteem. . . ."

These tribes relied mainly on the flight of birds, as did the Carians (who numbered among them the famous Heraclitus, the "dear old Carian guest"). And it is the blend of bird-flight and thunder which gives Cicero his first two major examples from the early history of Rome, indeed from its very foundation, for both Romulus and Remus were augurs, and rivals, not only for the city, but for its very name.

> "Then Remus took the auspices alone
> And waited for the lucky bird; while on
> The lofty Aventine fair Romulus
> His quest did keep to wait the soaring tribe:
> Their contest would decide the city's name
> As Rome, or Remora. . . ."

The rest of the augurs gathered on the Capitoline Hill, to await the outcome. At dawn, a bird appeared, flying to the left.

> "Then Romulus perceived that he had gained
> A throne whose source and prop was augury."

The left was therefore still lucky, and so it was in 86 B.C., when Gaius Marius, seven times elected consul and driven out of Rome, awaited his return after the revolt with Cinna. The bird he looked out for was an eagle, and eventually it appeared.

> "When Marius, reader of divine decrees,
>   Observed the bird's auspicious, gliding course,
> He recognised the goodly sign foretold,
>   That he in glory would return to Rome;
> Then, on the left, Jove's thunder pealed aloud
>   And thus declared the eagle omen true."

Eagles were one of the favourite birds for augury by flight. An eagle, Cicero notes, once warned King Deiotaurus to discontinue a journey. Other birds judged by flight were the hawk and osprey. They were the *Alites*. Those judged by voice were the *Oscines*—the raven, crow and owl. Of these the raven has remained the most popular. Hamlet may have defied augury, but Lady Macbeth was highly susceptible:

> "The raven itself is hoarse
> That croaks the fatal entrance of Duncan
> Under my battlements."

An interesting sidelong note is the way Lady M. says, even at this early stage, "*my* battlements". Othello felt the same dread foreboding influence of the bird:

> "O! It comes o'er my memory
> As doth the raven o'er the infected house,
> Boding to all."

John Gay, in the 18th century, in one of his fables, wrote:

> "That raven on your left-hand oak
> (Curse his ill-betiding croak)
> Bodes me no good."

Edgar Allan Poe, whose Raven brought forth the ridicule of James Russell Lowell, was under no doubts as to the inauspicious character of the bird.

"Ghastly grim and ancient raven wandering from the
    nightly shore—
Tell me what thy lordly name is on the night's Plutonian
    shore!"

"Prophet," said I, "Thing of evil—prophet still, if bird or
    devil!
By that heaven that bends above us—by that God we both
    adore."

"Take thy beak from out my heart, and take thy form from
    off my door!
Quoth the Raven, 'Nevermore'."

As for owls, there is one memorable postscript to add before
we return to Cicero. Max Beerbohm wove part of the plot of his
Zuleika Dobson around a telegram received at Oxford by the
undergraduate Duke of Dorset:

"Deeply regret inform your Grace last night two black owls
came and perched on battlements remained there throughout
the night hooting at dawn flew away none knows whither
awaiting instructions Jellings."

The Duke, a fatalist in the classic tradition, wired back:

"Prepare vault for funeral Monday Dorset."

Owls and Ravens. . . . They have made their dismal appear-
ances through many ages of history. Sir Thomas Browne noted
that, when Alexander the Great entered Babylon, so many
ravens were seen that they were thought to "pre-ominate his
death". When an owl appeared before the battle between
Crassus and the Parthians, it meant defeat and death for the
Roman General.

Cicero seems to have escaped any calumny by taking a sort
of elder-statesman look at divination and augury. He is careful
to distinguish between the Greek augury and the Roman, the
one named after *furor*, or frenzy (perhaps today we should call it
euphoria) and the other *divi*, after the Gods. "A really helpful

and splendid thing it is," he says of Roman augury, "If only such a faculty exists—since by its means men may approach very near to the power of the gods. . . ."

He knows his ritual. The augur's staff is the equivalent of the magic wand which marks out the *templum*, or quartering, a space within which the augur could operate (reflected later in the magic circle of the alchemist and wizard). "This staff is a crooked wand, slightly curved at the top, and because of its resemblance to a trumpet, derives its name from the Latin word meaning 'The trumpet with the battle charge is sounded'."

He can quote an early example of an augur, Attus Navius, whose lord and master, Tarquinius Priscus, simply said to him, "I am thinking of something. I won't tell you what. Tell me if it can be done." The augur replied that it could be done. "It" was to cut a whetstone in two with a razor, and tradition has it that Tarquin succeeded in doing so—no doubt much to the relief of Attus Navius. Cicero also realises how ancient is augury —how the Persian Magi assembled regularly, in a sacred place, for consultation, and how, among the Ancients, the men who ruled the state also had control of augury, "for they considered divining, as well as wisdom, becoming to a King".

But he was already unhappy about the situation. "We Roman augurs," he wrote, "are not the sort who can foretell the future by observing the flights of birds and other signs." There was futility in certain auguries—such as those divined from the droppings of food from the sacred chickens, who were overfed so that, inevitably, they should drop food here and there from their beaks. "If we are going to accept chance utterings," he added, "we had better look out when we stumble, or break a shoe-string, or sneeze!" These were prophetic words, for such chance happenings came into the good-and-bad luck category for many years to come, and maybe are still with us.

A Touch of the Devil: from
Joseph Glanvill's *Saducismus
Triumphatus* (1689).

Le Diable: sword in
left hand. One of the
Tarot pack of cards.

Apparition of the *Grand
Cabbala*, the Unclean Spirit,
with left hand outstretched.
He has been summoned
from the magic circle, with
the black hen already sacrificed.

Edward Kelly summons a Spirit from the Dead, in the Church-yard of Walton-le-Dale, Lancashire. His companion may have been the famous Doctor Dee, who was adviser to Queen Elizabeth, and cast royal horoscopes.

VIII

CIRCUMAMBULATION
or, *The Right Way Round*

"And ye shall compass the city, all ye men of war, and go round about the city once. Thus shalt thou do six days."

JEHOVAH TO JOSHUA BEFORE JERICHO

"Round about the cauldron go."

WITCHES IN *Macbeth*

"The Earth moves in a circle round the sun" is one of the first positive statements taught, in these enlightened times, to children at school. Moreover, the Earth, to those facing the magnetic north, itself revolves from left to right, and therefore the sun rises in the east. The sun, being light itself, was the earliest object of worship, from pagan times to the first chapter of the Gospel according to St John, which attributed the gift of light to God himself.

From these simple, primal facts has emerged such a wealth of ritual and superstitions that it would need an entire book to enumerate them all. From the earliest times, to go *with* the sun's course was not only lucky, but compulsory, to combat the evil spirits. This is why Joshua's procession, with the priests bearing the ram's horns and the trumpets, would have gone from left to right, while the witches' course would have been "widdershins" (*wiederschein*, against the sun, and anti-clockwise).

The importance attached to circumambulation is seen in the ritual of nearly every religion, though an anti-clockwise ambulation was sometimes recommended, the theory being that to adopt the Devil's method was to defeat the Devil's purpose. Nevertheless, the way to summon an Unclean Spirit involved marking out a magic circle, with the left hand, widdershins. The word itself became popular through the Scots corruption of the original German. There are many variations on it, and the leading authority on Scottish superstitions, Sir John Dalyell, spelt it "widderschynnes" in his book.*

"The sun was the grand object of pagan adoration," he wrote. "That a glorious luminary, so obviously the source of life and nutrition, so replete with benefits to mankind, should have received veneration, is far from reproachful to the earlier generations. . . .

"Motion or progress, in correspondence with the sun's apparent course, is accounted natural—perhaps involving a religious act in following it with the gaze from below. But to move in the opposite direction, against the course of the sun, inferred respect for Satan, and became an attribute of necromancers."

Dalyell referred to inhabitants of Colonsay who, before undertaking any enterprise, would walk "sunways around the church" (a favourite good-luck promenade in many places), and he added that the Shetland fishermen, like the Icelandic, would only turn their boats with the sun. A Highlander from Elgin, with his bride, approached "in observance of the sun's diurnal course". Herdsman danced three times "southways" (i.e. to the right, when facing east). Funeral processions in Iceland passed round the north side of the church if the burial was to take place at the south. From various trials for witchery and sorcery, Dalyell collected some choice examples of how to go wrong by going left. One Thomas Grieve attempted to cure illness in a family by carrying an animal "widderschynnes" three times, and afterwards burning it alive. One Jonet Forsyth, being refused some corn "went to the barne, and faddomit ane of the best stakis in the yarde about, contrair to the sunis cours"—and the grain was ruined. One Elizabeth Bathcat was denounced as a witch because she was seen "rynning widderschynnes" round the mill where she worked. It was unfortunate for her that mills were popularly supposed to be favourite meeting places for witches.

* *The Darker Superstitions of Scotland*: Griffin, London, 1835.

The examples pile up. A boy under twelve years of age was arrested for sorcery since, by pronouncing some words and turning himself "widdershin" he had caused a horse to break loose from the plough: a man who walked three times "witherwardis" round his neighbour's house caused his wife's breasts to refuse milk (a favourite accusation) and she fell "deadlie seik". These might better come under the chapter on Luck except that it is not so much the left hand or side itself which is of ill omen, but the actual sinistral movement.

The Scots seem to have paid great attention to the "right-hand turn" (*deiseal* in Gaelic). Drinking the waters of a consecrated fountain meant approaching the place in the appropriate pattern of the sun's motion. Sir James Frazer notes that when the dead are buried, the mourners go around in the same manner, and toasts to the bride at a wedding mean that the loving-cup must revolve clockwise.

"The rule is *deiseal* for everything. This is the manner in which screw-nails are driven, and is common with many for no reason but its convenience. Old men in the Highlands were very particular about it. The coffin was taken *deiseal* about the grave, when about to be lowered. . . . When putting a straw rope on a house or corn-stack, if the assistant went *tuaitheal* (i.e. against the sun) the old man was ready to come down and thrash him. On coming to a house, the visitor should go round it *deiseal* to secure luck on the object of his visit. The word is from *deas*, right-hand, and *iul*, direction, and of itself makes no reference to the sun."*

That acute observer of the Scottish scene, Sir Walter Scott, knew all about *deiseal*, and in *Waverley* describes how a Highland doctor approached his patient.

"He observed great ceremony in approaching Edward, and though our hero was writhing in pain, would not proceed to any operation which might assuage it until he had perambulated his couch three times, moving from east to west according to the course of the sun. This, which was called 'making the deasil', both the leech and his assistants seemed to

* J. G. Campbell, *Superstitions of Scotland*: Glasgow, 1900.

consider as a matter of the last importance to the accomplishment of a cure."

Two more examples, and then we will have done with *deiseal*, though not with the subject, which has wider issue in other cults and countries. It was related of the island of Eigg, that on the consecration of a holy well to St Katherine, the priest led the inhabitants, each carrying a candle, round the well sunways, "all of them making the deasil". This action sanctified the well-water, which was not thereafter allowed to be used for household or cooking purposes.

On the island of Lewis, according to Sir James Frazer, there was an old custom whereby a man would light a torch and carry it in his right hand, clockwise or deasil, round his house; and in the same manner, they would carry fire round a woman after child-bearing and before churching. This upset some of the midwives, but others agreed with the charm, believing that "fire-around was an effectual means to preserve both the mother and the infant from the power of evil spirits".

But the Gaelic customs, though ancient and well authenticated by local and contemporary reports, were not the only circumambulations practised on a globe fast spinning from left to right. The same ritual was found in Ireland, when Saint Patrick came to the sacred site at Armagh, and walked sunwise round the appointed place.

A dramatic example in Roman times was the conduct of the Gallic chief Vercingetorix, after he had been trapped and besieged by Julius Caesar in the hill-fort of Alesia, in what is now the Cote d'Or region of France. The Gauls resisted bravely. Vercassivelaunus, a brother chieftain, tried unsuccessfully to raise the siege. Caesar's ramparts stretched a full ten miles round the beleaguered hill, and in the end privation led to surrender. But it was noted that the defeated Vercingetorix, before delivering himself up, was allowed to make a threefold circumambulation of Caesar's tent, sunwise, perhaps in the hope that whatever gods he trusted in would eventually come to his aid. No doubt the Romans kept a close grip on their weapons as the Gaul made his symbolic gesture: certainly they had no doubt about what to do with Vercingetorix, who was later exhibited at Caesar's triumph in Rome, before being put to death.

But the list could be extended to many cults, religions, and periods of history. The Buddhist prayer-wheel, the Wheel of Life, revolved from left to right, and the priests, with their left hands bristling with uncut fingernails, made their appearance and obeisance in that direction. The Whirling Dervishes of Turkey, that remarkable sect of marathon dancers who still perform their interminable rotation for the benefit of tourists, always whirled with the sun. And the Muslim pilgrims arriving in Mecca walk round the sacred Kaaba shrine from left to right, keeping their right hands towards the object of their devotion.

When the Brahmans offered sacrifices to their ancestors, the officiating priest began by moving three times round to the left, followed by three turns to the right. The first movement indicated that he "went away" with three of his ancestors: the second, that he returned to his own world. A similar ritual was followed at the Roman funeral rites for the son of Lycurgus. The poet Statius describes in his *Thebais* how soldiers marched three times round the pyre by the left, with their standards reversed as a sign of mourning. After this, the augur, obviously the proper authority to arrange the ceremony, ordered them to proceed thrice in the opposite direction—a dextral movement, to efface their mourning and the "sinister" unlucky omen. Homer describes how Achilles made a threefold circuit round the body of Patrochis, but does not include the second sinistral movement.

Marriage customs in many countries abound in these superstitious ambulations, and often the house of the bride or groom had a central pillar, round which the pair walked, and perhaps the guests too. Evidence for this has been found in places as far apart as Italy and Japan. The Laws of Manu (Brahman) demanded that the bride alone should pass thrice round the ancestral hearth, and once she made the seventh step forward, the union was held to be irrevocable. A curious baptismal rite occurred in Estonia, where at one time the father of the baby had to run, not ambulate, round the church.

There are probably few countries or religions which do not include this superstitious movement. Around the Stupas, the Buddhist tombs of holy men, circular galleries were sometimes built, so that pilgrims could more easily make the propitiating walk. Some of these still exist in India, Tibet and Japan. An Indian who wished to build a house was first advised by the priests to walk three times round the plot of land, sprinkling it with water as he went.

To sum up, Count Goblet d'Alviella, in a scholarly contribution to Hastings' *Encyclopaedia of Religion and Ethics*, adds:

"When once the regular march of the sun was identified by circumambulation by the right, it was natural that the reverse should be identified with the reversing of the normal course of nature, and in consequence, should be associated with the idea of malign influence and death or evil, like all the ceremonies of the Liturgy, when they are executed backwards. . . . Here, then, is a rite which, devised by our distant pre-historic ancestors, is still celebrated before our eyes in official liturgies and in popular customs, after having passed through at least three successive religions."

In Yorkshire, it was said that if you walk round the room "widdershins" at midnight, in perfect darkness, and then look into a mirror, you will see, leering out of it at you, the face of the devil.

In Ireland, in mediaeval times, the O'Donnells possessed a "battle-book" which was always borne three times round the army before they engaged the enemy, to ensure victory.

IX

WIDDERSHINS AND WITCHES

"Michel Udon and Pierre Burgot confessed that they rubbed their left arms and hands with a certain powdered ash, and that when they touched an animal, they caused it to die."

BOGUET: *Examen of Witches*

"It is rating one's conjectures at a very high price to roast a man alive on the strength of them."

MONTAIGNE

"Berald, Beroald, Balbin, gab gabor agaba; arise, arise, I charge and command thee."

EXORCISM CHARM

It cannot be proved, and it has never been explicitly stated in words (though often in illustration) that the Devil was left-handed. But what other assumption could right-handed and right-minded men make? It is worth while considering the tragic history of witchcraft as it affected England and the continent of Europe, and to consider some of the methods adopted by latter-day wizards and exorcists, as well as the superstition that a leftward movement, whether ritual or involuntary, was somehow connected with the powers of darkness, and the Devil. After all, it could be argued, no less a person than Jesus Christ had given approval of dextrality. It is not being fanciful to suppose that His vision of Judgment helped to justify certain aspects of persecution, paralleled, in our own day, by the anti-semite persecutions of Hitler and the Nazis. True, Christian and Hebrew ritual, in common with nearly every religion in history, would have been dextral anyway but it was the converse which did the damage; that if the sheep going on the right side were due for heaven, the goats on the left were due for damnation.

The history of witchcraft has a horrid fascination for many of us today, and not only for those who like to read of death and torture. The bizarre details of witchcraft trials, the absurdity of the evidence, the capacity not only for yokels but for wise men, legal men, medical men and royal personages, to be deceived, are all an extraordinary chapter in the history of mankind. He destroys what he fears; he punishes those who are unusual; his reason is suspended. Modern authors such as Arthur Miller, whose play *The Crucible* was based on the case of the Witches of Salem in Massachusetts, and Aldous Huxley, whose *Devils of Loudon* described demon possession of Ursuline nuns, have given an accurate picture of the effects of hysteria and extrasensory perceptiveness which can turn a humdrum or religious community into a bear-garden. In particular, Huxley's rational and scientific approach makes a valuable comment on such events and such cruelty.

Witches, he decided, after regarding the whole of their lamentable history, were held to be responsible for three main disasters to mankind; the raising of tempests and floods, the bringing-on of diseases, whether personal or communal, and the deprivation of the sex-impulse in man as well as woman. This corresponds very well with the innumerable accusations from the records of witch-trials, and the apparently sober but obviously biased accounts, such as the monumental *Malleus Maleficorum* of the Dominicans Jakob Sprenger and Heinrich Kramer (1486)* which was quoted down the ages by the witch-hunters. The campaign which created such a blood-bath on the Continent was merely a continuation of the Catholic Inquisition attack on the Albigensian Heresy. Another victim—another scapegoat—was demanded, and in witchcraft it was ready to hand.

Aldous Huxley examines in detail the question of the well-known physical attributes of a witch, as alleged by her accusers.

---

* *Malleus Maleficorum*: Introduction by Montague Summers: John Rodker, London, 1929.

On examination—and this took place, sometimes, disgustingly, in court—the witch would be found to have on his or her body (and it was almost always hers) the witches' teats, which were supposed to suckle her Familiars, the odd brood of creatures which ranged from frogs to cats. Huxley comments: "Since 9 per cent of all males and a little under 5 per cent of all females are born with supernumary nipples, there was never any shortage of predestined victims. Nature punctually did her part: the judges, with their unexamined postulates and first principles, did the rest."

There were some forthright and courageous critics of the gullible witch-hunters. The first counterblast, by Reginald Scot, was one of the most remarkable, both for its uncompromising opposition and biting style.* Scot declared himself to be "appalled by the assumption that works done by the almighty power of the most high God and by Our Saviour, His Only Son Jesus Christ Our Lord, should be referred to a baggage old woman's nod or wish". Scot is not an entire disbeliever in the supernatural, nor does he entirely excuse the witches. "These miserable wretches," he thinks, "are so odious unto all their neighbours, as few dare offend them, or deny them anie thing they ask: whereby they take upon them, yea, and sometimes thinke, that they can doo such things as are beyond the abilities of human nature."

Of the public, he says they are "assotted and bewitched by the jesting or serious words of poets, by the inventions of lowd liers and couseners, and by tales they have heard from old doting women, and with whatsoever the grandfoole their ghostlie father or any other morrow Masse Priest had informed them.

"Sometimes observers of dreames," he continues, "sometimes soothsayers, sometimes the observers of the flieng of foules, or the meeting of todes, the falling of salt, &c. are called witches. But as for our old women, that are said to hurt little children with their eies, or lambs with their looks, or that pull down the Moone out of heaven, or make so foolish a bargain,

* *The Discoverie of Witchcraft*: London, 1584.

or doo such homage to the Divell; you shall not read in the bible of any such witches, or of any such actions imputed to them."

Back came the subject of the Scriptures, on which the authority of the witch-finders ultimately relied. Scot obviously had to raise the incident involving the most famous witch of all time, who was exorcised by King Saul at En-Dor. He ridicules the idea that the prophet Samuel actually appeared, garbed in his own habit. This was to become a popular example for argument, particularly when Joseph Glanvill took it up in his *Saducismus Triumphatus* a century later.* Glanvill, it is surprising to learn, was able to be a member of that eminent scientific body, the Royal Society, and at the same time a believer in witchcraft and possession by devils—a parallel case with Sir Thomas Browne.

"Yea, the verie Phrase, hath a devil," he wrote, "or, the devil's in him, applied to those that act furiously and un-advisedly, doth imply that there is such a real Thing as a diabolical Possession, to which madness and extreme folly are resembled." Of the detractors, he said: "If they deny Witches, it is plain that they are anti-Scripturists, the Scripture so plainly attesting the contrary."

This was the trump card played by the witch-hunters. Scot's book, published only twenty years after Queen Elizabeth's Act on Witchcraft, raised the wrath of the new Scottish King, James, who in turn published his own book,† a sort of left-handed compliment in itself. One of the plates in Glanvill's work, which has often been reproduced shows, among other things, a fully-winged and clawed Demon in the traditional style, putting out his left hand to touch a woman at a witches' coven.

Other sceptics rallied to Reginald Scot's cause, notably John Webster, a non-conformist clergyman who became a doctor, and who held in his *The Displaying of Supposed Witchcraft* (1677) that the existence of angels or spirits and the existence of witches

---

* *Saducismus Triumphatus. Or A full and plain Evidence concerning Witches and Apparitions*: London, 1689.
† *Daemonologie*: Edinburgh, 1597.

were two entirely different things, and that the Bible made no mention of compacts between the Devil and witches. An earlier critic had been Samuel Harsnett, whose *Declaration of Egregious Popish Impostures* (1605) made a deep impression. The author later became Archbishop of York, and at one time succeeded in exposing the fraudulent exorcist John Darrell. This was the law as laid down by Queen Elizabeth.

"Those who shall use, practise or exercise any Witchecrafte, Enchantment, Charme or Sorcerie, whereby any Person shall happen to be killed or destroyed . . . shall suffer paynes of Death, as a felon or felons."

ELIZABETH I. *Act of Witchcraft* (1563)

The Queen's Act was a strengthening of the Act passed by Henry VIII, and was later to be given further clauses by James I, whose interest in demonology exceeded that of any English monarch. He even wrote a best-seller on the subject. It was the age of fortune-tellers, astrologers, alchemists and sorcerers. Bishop Jewel, in a sermon before the Queen, complained that "Witches and sorcerers have marvellously increased within Your Grace's Realm. Your Grace's subjects pine away unto death. Their colour fadeth, their flesh rotteth, their speech is benumbed, their senses are bereft."

During the reign of Mary, many Protestants had taken refuge on the Continent, where witch-hunting went on with unparalleled ferocity. It was therefore to be expected that English Protestants would somehow manage to connect Popery with Paganism, though the Continental Catholics were the most assiduous witch-hunters. Elizabeth was encouraged to produce her Act after several supposed attempts had been made to influence her by the Black Arts. For this, the Countess of Lennox and the Pole Brothers, Arthur and Edmund, were thrown into the Tower. The latters' sorcery was, of course, held to be part of a plot to place Mary Queen of Scots on the throne.

But the Queen, like most of the Elizabethans, was very interested in Magic, and received at court the famous Dr Dee.

Eric Maple, in his study of witchcraft,* describes him as "Queen Elizabeth's Merlin".

"He was very learned, having studied at Louvain and Cambridge, where he attained eminence in mathematics, philosophy, astrology, and alchemy, but his intense intellectual curiosity lured him into a study of magic, and this earned him the undeserved reputation of being a wizard. He was in trouble in Mary's reign for casting a horoscope of the Queen at the request of someone close to the Court, but was found not guilty of plotting against the royal life, and acquitted."

Dr Dee, who wrote altogether forty-eight books on the subject of magic, may have had royal patronage, but his choice of colleagues was not so auspicious. For a time he associated with the magician Edward Kelly, perhaps the most celebrated of the hocus-pocus purveyors of the time. The two men indulged in the practice of raising spirits, it was alleged, and later travelled through Europe, where, as Mr Maple points out, it was something of a miracle that they were not burned by the Inquisition.

One avowedly authenticated case of Kelly raising a spirit from the dead has come down to us through the ages, both in a written report and in a drawing which has been reproduced in a number of books on magic, to show how the magician and his accomplice went about their work. Several chroniclers, including Eric Maple, say that the second figure in the illustration is Dr Dee himself, holding the torch with his left hand while Kelly describes the magic circle anti-clockwise, also with the left hand. But Ebenezer Sibly, in his book on magic,† identifies the associate as one Paul Waring. Dee, he says, had already broken off the association and Kelly had "degenerated into the lowest and worst species of the magic art for the purposes of fraud and avaricious gain.

"Many wicked and abominable transactions are recorded of him," Sibly continues, "which were performed by witchcraft, and the mediation of infernal spirits. . . ." Weaver, in his *Funeral Monuments*, records that Edward Kelly, with one Paul Waring,

---

* *The Dark World of Witches*: Robert Hale, London, 1962.
† *Illustration of the Occult Sciences*: London, 1769.

who acted in capacity of companion and associate in all his conjurations, went together to the churchyard of Walton le Dale, in the County of Lancaster" (a county famous for its witches) "where they had information of a person being interred, who was supposed to have hidden or buried a considerable sum of money, and to have died without disclosing to any person where it was deposited. They entered the churchyard exactly at twelve o'clock at night and . . . exorcised the spirit by magic spells and incantations, till it appeared before them, and not only satisfied their wicked desires and enquiries, but delivered several strange predictions concerning persons in that neighbourhood, which were literally and exactly fulfilled."

Maple adds that Kelly was sent to the pillory for this deed, and that afterwards, he and Dee set up house together, having everything in common, and even exchanging wives. Sibly would not divulge full details on how to enter into compact with familiar spirits, in order "not to put a weapon into the hands of the blood-thirsty or revengeful". But he described the magic circle in detail. It had to be nine feet square, with an inner circle inside which the magician and his associate stood, ringed round with sundry crosses, triangles, and holy names of God. The circle was held to be the principal fort and shield of the magician, and he stepped outside it at his peril. The example was quoted of Chiancungi, the Egyptian fortune-teller who, with his sister Napala, achieved great fame in England, but once, on raising the Evil Spirit Bokim, stepped outside the circle, and, according to reports, was killed within moments by the monster.

Exorcism also comes within Ebenezer Sibly's recommendations. If this should take place by an *open* grave, with the body lying there, the magic wand and torch are held with the *right* hand. After touching the body three times, the magician intones the magic words, "Berald, Beroald, Balbin, gab gabor agaba; arise, arise, I charge and command thee." He adds: "If the body has been hanged or drowned or is a suicide, the Exorcist has to bind to the top of his wand a bundle of St John's wort, with the head of an owl."

A pretty business, this exorcism. But it is still practised by church authorities, under a recognised religious formula, when there is evidence of a poltergeist, or other unidentified presence in a house. The existence of a spirit world is by no means ignored by the churches of today. It could hardly be otherwise, if the Son of Man be credited with the casting out of demons. The ritual is right-handed throughout.

The traditional appearance of the Unclean Spirit in the form of a goat has a variant in a creature called The Grand Cabbala. E. W. Waite describes how this hybrid should be summoned.*

"Its success will depend on a recollected and devotional spirit on the part of the operator, together with a clean conscience otherwise, in place of commanding the evil spirit, the latter will command him. This understood, the process is simple. You have merely to secure a black hen which has never been crossed by the male bird, and to do this in such a manner that it shall not cackle. . . . You must repair to the high-road, walk till you come to a cross-way and there, on the stroke of midnight, describe a circle with a cypress rod, place yourself in the midst thereof and tear the bird in twain, pronouncing three times the words, *Euphas, Metahim, frugativi et appellavi*. Next turn to the East, kneel down, recite a prayer and conclude it with the Grand Appellation, when the Unclean Spirit will appear to you in a scarlet surcoat, a yellow vest and breeches, of pale green. His head will resemble that of a dog, but his ears will be of those of an ass, with two horns above them; he will have the legs and hoofs of a calf. He will ask for your orders, which you may give as you please, and as he cannot do otherwise than obey, you may become rich on the spot and the happiest of men."

Despite his mixed physical appearance, it is obvious that the Grand Cabbala is dressed in the height of 18th-century fashion, and will greet you with his left hand outstretched like any Boy Scout.

Witch-cults and covens were credited in various parts of Europe, but few examples are represented by anything but

* Edward Waite, *The Book of Black Magic*: London.

hearsay and rumour. Henri Boguet, in his *Examen of Witches*, describes how they could afflict with the left hand.

"Witches cause hurt and injury by a touch of the hand. . . . Michel Udon and Pierre Burgot confessed that they rubbed their left arms and hands with a certain powdered ash, and that when they then touched an animal, they caused it to die."

In Guazzo's *Compendium Maleficarum*, evil spirits are seen proffering the left hand to human beings, and in the Devil's Baptism the Fiend is pouring water (which would probably be urine) left-handedly over the head of the new convert to the evil practices.

Dr Margaret Murray, in her researches, learned much about the witchcraft supposed to be active in the Basque country during the 17th century. The *Basses-Pyrenees* have always been a strange, withdrawn part of the world, part French, part Spanish, but in loyalty entirely faithful to the Basque tradition, which is one of the oldest in Europe, and boasts a language which is compounded from many sources. Dr Murray has reproduced the old French in quoting from the diabolical practices of the region.*

Witch-masses were presided over by a Queen of the Sabbath. In 1609, it was reported that one could "en chasque village trouuer une Royne du Sabbat, que Sathan tenoit en délices comme une espouse privilegiée". Those who believed in witchcraft would approach the scene and acclaim the Queen, "luy baisent la main gauche, tremblans avec mille angoisses, et luy offrent du pain, des œufs, et de l'argent". Apparently these offerings were well received, for "La Royne du Sabbat les recoit, laquelle est assise a son costé gauche, et en sa main gauche elle tient une paix ou platine, dans laquelle est gravee l'effigié de Lucifer".

So far, so good—or rather, so bad—but the Witch Queen is, after all, only there because she is summoned by Satan himself. The Devil appears and makes his mark. "Il les egratigné tous

* *The Witch-cult in Western Europe*: Oxford, 1921.

avec le bras gauches, et les ongles de la main sinistre." So, to be scratched by the Devil's talons was the mark of honour. The other marks were made on the left eyelid, the left shoulder and the left thigh.

The Satanic tradition knows no frontiers, and not long after this date, Dr Murray noted a devil's mark found on a suspected witch in Scotland, Isobel Crawford of Irvine. It was described as "the devill's mark, quhilk was lyke ane braid dyn spott, in the inner syde of hir left thie . . .".

Dr Murray describes how an Essex witch, Rebecca Jones, condemned in 1645, met Satan, who apparently called at her front door, like any travelling salesman. She admitted "a very handsome young man, as shee then thought, but now shee thinks it was the Devill: who asked this Examinant how shee did, and desired to see her left wrist: and then he took a pin from the Examinant's owne sleeve, and pricked her wrist twice, and there came out a drop of bloud, which he took off with the top of his finger."

To have intercourse with the Devil was, in the opinion of the Church and the Law, one of the primary desires of witches. Any psychiatrist could have explained this, but it was not the age of the couch and the thesis and the Freudian interpretation. Some of the deluded women in Boguet's *Examen* described their sexual experiences in detail. It was, they all agreed, a most unpleasant one, since although Satan is credited with living in a very hot climate, his physical presence on earth seems to have been exactly the opposite. He was a cold lover, in fact, and one witness asserted that his Member was not only very chilly to the touch, but narrower than mortal man's.

Most of those accused of witchcraft were women. Why was this? It may have something to do with the female sex being held to be the weaker one (Adam behaved badly but not as badly as Eve) and therefore the "left" sex—"That cursed Left", as one man described his wife, accused of child-murder. It may also be the animal instinct which ostracises and then persecutes the odd one out, the minority. "Who mobbed the kestrel out of the air?" asked W. H. Auden. But the witches could not be said to be the victims of envy. In his study of the Black Arts, C. L'estrange Ewen describes their pitiable state.

"We may picture most of the English witches as poverty-stricken women, old, ugly, decrepit and diseased, unkempt and dirty, muttering and mumbling as they hobbled about, begging their livelihood, feared by many of their neighbours, hated by others who blamed them for their misfortunes, gibed at by urchins, often spurned and harshly treated by their betters, and scratched and beaten by anyone who had an unusual ailment."

There is an irresistible parallel between the treatment of witches and the treatment, through the ages, of the Jews, and it is significant, perhaps, that it was in Germany that the persecution of both rose to its greatest height, in different centuries. The whole thing was inspired, in each case, by fear—fear of the unknown, and dislike of the unusual, coupled with the necessity of finding a scapegoat (and the luckless animal was first condemned by the Jews) for whatever had gone wrong.

The Goat deserves an honoured place in the dishonourable history of Demonology. "The lust of the Goat is the bounty of God," wrote William Blake, but few would have agreed with his candour, any more than they might have desired, in a wife, "What in whores is always found—the lineaments of gratified desire." Since the Book of Leviticus, the goat was condemned to bear the sins of the world (later this was to be replaced, in religious ritual, by the Lamb of God).

"And Aaron shall bring the goat upon which the Lord's lot fell, and offer him for a sin offering.

"But the goat, on which the lot fell to be the scapegoat, shall be presented alive before the Lord, to make an atonement with him, and to let him go for a scapegoat into the wilderness."

It was not long before the goat's cloven hoof became associated with the Devil (though it was also linked with the Great God Pan) in the celebrated Judgment of the Sheep and the Goats. A theory could be devised that this was partly due to the practical problem, in countries such as Egypt and Palestine, of the goat's grazing habits. Once the region of Galilee was, we are told, like a luxurious garden. Now, except for the kibbutz settlements and farms, it is dry and barren, and visitors will be told that this was because the Muslims did not tether their goats, but let them eat as they wished, and scratch the ground with their cloven hoofs.

The National Archives of Paris contain an official copy of the trial of Joan of Arc. (Since the French completely abandoned their heroine, it might be argued that the British Museum would have been a more suitable place for it.) Sketched in the margin of one page is a contemporary portrait of the Maid. She is wearing a skirt, not the infamous male apparel, and her unsheathed sword is in her left hand. There does not seem to be any other evidence for the sinistrality of Joan, but since she was burnt for witchcraft, she may have been said to have followed the familiar pattern ascribed to witches and their ways.

Dr Margaret Murray has pointed out* that Lorraine, the area from which Joan came, had been described by the Synod of Treves as containing "all kinds of magic, sorcery, witchcraft, auguries, superstitious writings, prognostics drawn from the flights of birds and similar things, observation of the stars in order to judge the destiny of persons born under certain constellations, the illusions of women that they ride at night with Diana or with Herodias and a multitude of other women".

A century after the Maid's death, women in Lorraine were being put to death as witches by the hundred. It was certainly no help to Joan, before the English court, to have heard "Voices" under the Fairy Tree at Bourlemont. Nor, in another sense, was it a help that she chose as her protector the notorious Gilles de Rais, for he was to desert her, and later to be condemned himself for many outrageous crimes, from sodomy to sorcery. Chroniclers and playwrights, from Gilles himself, who staged a big Passion Play in her honour soon after her death, to Bernard Shaw and Anouilh, have reflected the various reasons for her condemnation. In Dr Murray's own view, she was a Victim God, successor to William Rufus and Thomas à Becket, and succeeded by Gilles de Rais himself. But the ultimate trial was an English one, in a secular court, conducted

* *The God of the Witches*: Sampson, Low, London, 1933.

by the Earl of Warwick and the Duke of Bedford, and it is clear that she was condemned, not as a heretic or a masquerader in men's apparel, but simply as a witch. The only difference lay in her sentence; in England she would have been hanged, not burnt.

"A damning fact," concludes Margaret Murray, "was that she had held communication with 'evil spirits' under the Fairy Tree; in fact, like John Walsh in Dorsetshire, Bessie Dunlop in Ayrshire, Alesoun Peirson in Fifeshire, and many others, her connection with the Fairies was proof positive that she was not of the Church." Whether left-handed or not, Joan of Arc would have been suspected of many of the sinistral habits of the witches' Coven and the Sabbath, where Satan greeted and was greeted "avec le bras gauche".

The witch-trial at which Sir Thomas Browne gave evidence is worth mentioning in detail. It seems remarkable that the learned doctor of Norwich, whose longest work deflates the *Vulgar Errors* believed in by mankind, and gives the first valuable observation on left-handedness, could have come down on the side of the prosecution in such a lamentable case. The trial has something in common with the celebrated Witches of Salem case, described by Arthur Miller, in that the younger witnesses were always going into fits in court, and in the English case, they would not speak or behave rationally until the two suspected women, Amy Duny and Rose Cullender, had been found guilty.

Sir Matthew Hale, a distinguished legal figure and Lord Chief Baron of the Exchequer, presided over the Assizes at Bury St Edmunds, on March 10th, 1664. Complaints about the two old women, who had both been previously accused of witchcraft, were made by members of two local families, the Durents and the Paceys. Evidence was given that Amy suckled the infant of Mistress Durent, and that the child "fell into fits". Soon afterwards, a great Toad was found in the room which, being thrown in the fire, caused a big explosion. At the same time, a neighbour corroborated that he had passed Amy Duny's cottage, and seen her nursing a severe scorch. She had prophesied, "The child will not live long", and it did not. Other members of the family complained of similar fits.

The same troubles afflicted the Pacey family, after Rose Cullender had been refused any herrings by Pacey's wife, and had gone away cursing. The fits, it was alleged, were not all alike; some were on the left side, some on the right. Evidence was also given of the familiar habit of vomiting nails and pins, some of which were produced in court. (This was one of the oldest pieces of counterfeiting in the history of witchcraft, and even a child without conjuring experience could be taught how to conceal them in the mouth till the right moment.) The two women were subjected to the usual degrading physical examination, and extra teats were found on their bodies.

This was enough for conviction, but the scene in court was becoming highly melodramatic as the "bewitched" children screamed or were obstinately silent. Only when Amy Duny was ordered to touch them (presumably with the right hand) did their shrieking stop. But an "ingenious person" in court declared that the children might have counterfeited, and one of them, being blindfolded, continued to scream when touched both by the witch and a bystander. Among eminent persons present, Mr Serjeant Keeling was unsatisfied by the evidence. Then the great Dr Browne's opinion was consulted. He merely happened to be in Bury on that day, and had attended purely out of interest. He came down strongly on the side of the prosecution, declaring that the said women were indeed bewitched by the Devil, adding that on a recent journey in Denmark, he had come across several instances of this vomiting of pins and nails.

The Jury, directed by the Judge, took only half an hour to reach a verdict, and the women were hanged, confessing nothing.

Another aspect of magic concerns Lewis Carroll, that allegedly shifted Sinistral. He may have had access to a strange 18th-century book entitled *Witchcraft Detected*, by a Member of the School of the Black Arts in Italy. The anonymous writer quotes Reginald Scot's bad-luck symbol of the left shoe on the right foot, from the 16th-century *Discoverie of Witchcraft*, and goes on to quote the example of Augustus Caesar himself, translated from Pliny's original Latin by Samuel Butler, in *Hudibras*.

> "Augustus, having by oversight
> Put on his left shoe for his right
> Had like to have been slain that day
> By soldiers mutinying for pay."

It was the White Knight in *Through the Looking Glass*, who referred to one who might "madly squeeze a right-hand foot into a left-hand shoe".

If this were the only comparison, we could assume that this old tradition was fairly common knowledge. But in *Witchcraft Detected*, the author also gives instructions on how to change the colour of a rose from red to white, with a sulphuric prescription. This is precisely what the Queen of Hearts wanted done in *Alice in Wonderland*, and Alice found the gardeners trying to paint them, to avoid losing their heads.

·The Student of the Black Arts has several references to handedness. For instance: "Some will hold fast their left thumb in their right hand when they hickup; or else will hold their chin with the right hand while a gospel is sung."

But his most ambitious recipe—one which does not occur in the Lewis Carroll books—is How to Make Yourself Invisible. The instructions are precise, and involve water running widdershins.

"To go invisible, put fair clean water that running against the East, on the fire, and wash yourself, going about the fire three times, saying Panthon, Craton, Muriton, Bisocogneton, Siston, Diaton, Maton, Tetragrammaton, Agla, Agarion, Tegra, Pentassaron, Tendicata. . . ."

After this incantation, the suppliant who wished to make himself scarce had merely to call on the Sisters of three Fairies. Their names were Milia, Sibylia, and Achilia. "When they appear," reports the enraptured Student of the Black Arts, "one of them puts a ring on the finger, and you go away invisible with them."

It sounds an enthralling experience.

In his book *Magick** Aleister Crowley, a notorious authority on the Black Arts, has described in detail the Office of the Black Mass, which is less horrific than that apparently practised in France, with Madame de Montespan as the naked Priestess, but which has interesting sidelights on left- and right-handedness. It would be impossible to go into all the details of the Temple (in this case, incongruously situated on the south-eastern shore of Loch Ness in Scotland, famous later for other monsters) or with the ceremony in detail. But the participants are the Priest, bearing the sacred Lance, the Priestess (who should be *virgo-intacta*—but could also be specially dedicated to the Great Order), the Deacon with the Book of the Law, and two children, clothed in white and black, one positive one negative, one bearing a pitcher of water and a pillar of salt, the other a censer of fire and a casket of perfume.

The Deacon, before the congregation and facing west, declares the whole purpose of this peculiar Law:

"Do what thou wilt shall be the whole of the Law. I proclaim the Law of Light, Life, Love and Liberty."

He prays to Chaos, the sole vice-regent of the Sun upon Earth: and to Babalon, the Earth and mother of all.

The Virgin Priestess then enters, with the children on either side of her, and it is then possible to see how handedness comes in. She holds the Chalice in the left hand, and the Paten in her right.

"The Priestess, the negative child on her left, and positive child on her right, ascends the step of the high altar. . . . With the children following her, the positive next her, she moves in a serpentine manner involving $3\frac{1}{2}$ circles of the Temple (deosil about altar, widdershins about font, deosil about altar and font, widdershins about altar, and so to the Tomb in the west)."

It is thus, as with the Greeks and Romans, an alternate right and left movement. The rest of the office has no significance for handedness, in Aleister Crowley's version, but it is a

---

* *Magick in Theory & Practice* by the Master Therion. Printed for private subscribers at the Lecram Press, Paris, 1929.

splendid display of sexual significance, mumbo-jumbo, and strip-tease, nevertheless, and has provided a cheap thrill for the ignorant and the orthodox over the ages. During the Priest's prayer to the Circle of Stars, and, more particularly, to the Queen of Space, the Priestess has divested herself of her robe, and invokes love:

"I love you! I yearn to you! Pale or purple, veiled or voluptuous, I who am all pleasure and purple, and drunkenness in the innermost sense, desire you. Put on the wings, and arouse the coiled splendour within you: come unto me!"

The Love Duet which follows is reminiscent of a mock-religious *Tristan and Isolde*, but it ends with nothing more outrageous than the Priest presenting the Priestess with the symbolic lance (which she kisses eleven times) and kissing her knees—she has meanwhile resumed her robe.

X

LUCK AND THE LEFT HAND

"My nose bled at the left nostrill about 4 h.p.m. I doe not remember any event."

JOHN AUBREY, *March 25th, 1675*

"Sir, it is no matter what you teach them first, any more than what leg you shall put into your breeches first."

SAMUEL JOHNSON, *July 26th, 1763*

"The left hand of a dead man dipped in a milk pail causes cream."

IRISH SAYING

Ever since Judas spilled the salt (as he is depicted in Leonardo da Vinci's "Last Supper"), and indeed for many centuries before and after, all manner of physical movements and twitchings and sensations presaged good luck or ill luck, riches or poverty, birth or death. Even today some people, having spilled the salt—that commodity so highly regarded among more primitive races—will follow the tradition of propitiating Satan by throwing a little salt with the right hand over the left shoulder, i.e. in the Devil's direction. So many of the superstitions are connected with either right or left that a separate study of them is necessary. It is not the same process as Augury or Circumambulation since these are more deliberate and ritualistic and follow certain rules. It is more the involuntary movement, such as the twitching of an eyelid or the passing of a threshold with the wrong foot, which account for good or bad fortune.

"Luck, and the lack of luck," writes Dr Wile,* "refer to possibilities outside of man. They deal with Nature and the

* *Handedness: Right and Left*: Lothrop Lee & Shepherd, Boston, 1934.

forces behind it. Man is still superstitious; his mental processes have not altered greatly despite the enormous increases of his factual knowledge. . . . Belief in the operation of chance and the effective powers of visible and invisible beings has never been completely relinquished. In the early days of all-pervading supernaturalism, the idea of luck came into being, and sinister ideas of luck began to cluster about the left hand. . . . The idea of luck, and a belief in it, accounts for the unaccountable and explains the unexplainable. Then the luck idea seizes all human activity, and every moment, action, achievement has meaning and portent and every happening brings up the question: 'Is it an omen of good or evil?' From man to his contactual world is but a broadening of this idea and now that all that occurs in nature possesses a personal meaning—whether the cracking of a twig, the singing of a bird, the flash of a meteor or the movement of the sun. Everything depends upon luck—and luck is bound up in the when and the where and the how."

John Aubrey's left "nostrill" had significance for him even in the comparatively enlightened 17th century.* And though Dr Johnson pooh-poohed the idea of luck in putting on your breeches in Scotland, he observed the habit of entering or leaving a house with right foot foremost, because: "to enter the house with the skir or left foot brings down evil on the inmates." The Scottish custom of "first-footing" is a famous one, and has its own laws of luck. Sir John Dalyell in his *Darker Superstitions of Scotland*, adds a further note of the habits of the Jews.

"Some (of them) take care, in their dressing in the morning, to put on the left stocking and the right shoe first, without tying it: then afterwards to put on the left, and so to return to the right, that they may begin and end with the right side, which they account to be the most fortunate."

No mad cramming of left-hand foot into right-hand shoe for them!

* Sir Thomas Browne believed in ghosts, and Aubrey records the celebrated appearance of an Apparition at Cirencester. "When asked if it were a good ghost or no, it made no answer, but disappeared with a curious perfume and a most melodious twang. Mr W. Lilly believes it was a fairy."

Dalyell adds, still on the question of luck:

"Organs on the right and left had their particular mystic virtues. In Scotland, salt is thrown over the left shoulder to avert strife. A witch directed a person to give his left hand to his brother in silence, for effecting an evil purpose. Pulling a plant, while resting on the right knee, was an ingredient of divination. In Mexico, it is said, a patient will enquire whether medicine is to be taken with the right or the left hand: if with the former, the liver will benefit: if with the latter, the kidneys. A wasp or beetle, caught with the left hand, or the heart of a living snake, extracted thus, was employed medicinally by the ancients."

If we survey mankind from China to Peru, we shall find a proliferation, and often a repetition, of these local minor superstitions. Birds occur in many of them, as in the days of the Romans. The Scandinavians considered the magpie to be as bad as omen as a raven, but Wile notes that, in some parts of Devon, a man will spit over his right shoulder three times, to put off the ill-luck, and in Ireland, "to see three magpies on the left hand when on a journey is unlucky; but two on the right hand is a good omen".

Luck and sneezing are connected in Roman times, by Sir James Frazer. Sneeze to the right, good fortune: to the left, ill omen. The itching palm is another favourite, and the phrase has existed to this day. But not all the signs agree. In some countries, to have an itching left palm means that you will give money away or lose it: in others, that you will receive it. The majority, however, condemn the left palm, which is only to be expected.

Feet come into the lucky dip, and not only as legs into breeches or boots over thresholds. The rule that soldiers march with the left foot first, to the command, "By the left, quick march!" is capable of several interpretations. It is noticeable among animals that quadrupeds usually lead with the right limb, and bipeds with the left. (This they presumably do by instinct, and not under command.) But it has been argued that, since the left leg is regarded as the weaker, if it ventures forth and is injured, the result is not as serious as if it had been the right leg. A more probable explanation is that, since the right arm holds the sword or spear, a left-foot forward action will give the necessary momentum for the weapon to be in action after only two paces. Obviously it would not be lucky for a Scottish soldier to cross a local threshold left-right. With Egyptians, however (a people credited with certain left-handed tendencies), it has sometimes been regarded as lucky to enter a house by the left foot first—especially if it is supposed to be haunted. A hare's foot is an emblem of good luck in England, but there seems to be no preference as to which foot it should be. For the English hare, an American superstition substitutes the rabbit, and specifies the left hind foot—the sort of charm Tom Sawyer might have carried round with him. A dramatic instance of this is quoted by John H. King,* taking his example from the *Journal of American Folklore*.

"At an execution in America, as the body was cast off a rabbit was roused from a hedge, then a chase of all present ensued until the animal was caught, when Judge Winn offered five dollars for one of the feet to keep it as a talisman of luck." No doubt, with his victim still swinging, he felt the need for some charm to guard against misfortune—and the foot would have been the left hind one.

Paws of lions and bears were lucky in more outlandish countries, and the sign of the "Bear's Paw" reached England as a tavern sign.

Albertus Magnus, in the 13th century, advised a husband whose wife had rejected him, to wear the marrow from a wolf's left foot, "and she will love none but you". Marcellus declared that, to ensure a wife's fidelity, she should be touched by the tail of a lizard, cut off with the left hand. Equally important for good or bad luck was the eye.

> "What immortal hand or eye
> Can frame thy fearful symmetry?"

William Blake wrote this of his *Tyger, Tyger, burning bright*, but it is a reminder that the hand and the eye are regarded as

* *The Supernatural*: Williams & Norgate, London, 1892.

the significant parts of the body, and it is usually the asymmetry in which the significance lies. The right hand is the hand of power, a theme repeated monotonously in the Bible. The left eye is usually the Evil Eye. A remarkable example was found by F. T. Elworthy in his book on this "Ancient and Widespread Superstition".* It is one of the marble amulets at Woburn Abbey, the most spectacular of Britain's Stately Homes, where the present Duke of Bedford casts a benevolent rather than an evil eye on his many thousands of visitors.

"There is a framing, and it is usually thought to have been built into a wall, as a house-decoration, but still more as a protection. The centre is a human eye, and, as Jahn says, 'the left, which may be considered a special feature of its sinister intention, and moreover the pupil is strongly marked'."

The eye is being attacked by various creatures—a lion, a snake, a stork, and a scorpion. On the right is the figure of a gladiator, stabbing at the eye with a trident held in the right hand. In his left hand he holds the gladiatorial *fuscina*, or short sword. But it is the figure on the eyelid above which commands most attention, a man in a Phrygian Cap, who has pulled up his shirt and is squatting down with naked buttocks in an attitude which Elworthy tactfully describes as "one of the utmost contempt".

"Eat not thou the bread of him that hath an evil eye," advises the Book of Proverbs. "If thine offend thee, pluck it out," declares Jesus. Back to the very earliest and therefore most superstitious times goes the belief that certain people possessed this malignant quality, and that those who were "overlooked" would suffer for it. It was not necessary for an unpopular old woman to be seen kissing a goat's backside or suckling a "familiar" or describing a circle widdershins. A Look might be enough to bring her before the judges, as a witch.

But would the Evil Eye be necessarily the left eye?

This raises the very complex question of Ocular Dominance, which is dealt with elsewhere in this book. One authority,

---

* *The Evil Eye*: John Murray, London, 1895.

Beaufort Sims Parson, claimed: "The right eye governs the movement of the limbs on the right side, and the left eye the movements of the limbs on the left side of the body. This ancient harmony of function survives in man at least to the extent that right-eyedness accompanies right-handedness, and left-eyedness accompanies left-handedness, all this notwithstanding man's possession of binocular vision."* Parson went further than most in finding a close connection between eyedness and the preferred hand—that is, between ocular dominance and cerebral dominance. And yet, it is generally acknowledged that the brain controls the opposite side of the body, and vice versa. Eye tests are today a common way of determining handedness in children —a far cry from the traditional days of the Evil Eye, whose critics would admit no tests.

Amulets containing a single eye were common among the Egyptians, Phoenicians and Etruscans, as well as later with Greeks, Turks, Arabs and Nubians. There are many examples which also contain groups of creatures and symbols similar to those in the Woburn amulet, but sometimes with the addition of a phallus (similar to those seen on walls in Pompeii, to indicate the location of brothels), a lizard, thunderbolt, crab, dog, elephant, stag, owl, and many others. Later the charms became popular with the seafaring people of Naples and Malta. To bring the amulet picture right up to date, lucky cameos with an eye as design can be bought in shops today.

Many of the hand-shapes outlined on walls by Muslims and others are coloured red. The superstition of the red or bloody hand is, of course, a very old one. If you dipped your hand in the blood of a ceremonially sacrificed animal and pressed your palm on the wall, you would be warding off the Evil Eye. The "red right hand" was mentioned first by Ovid, and from him Milton borrowed the phrase, when Satan told his followers of the attacks they might expect from the hosts of Heaven:

"What if the breath that kindl'd those grim fires
Awak't should blow them into sevenfold rage

* *Left-handedness*: Macmillan, New York, 1924.

> And plunge us in the flames? Or from above
> Should intermitted vengeance Arm again
> His red right hand to plague us?"*

The most famous red hand is the Bloody Hand of Ulster. The arms of Northern Ireland consist simply of a shield argent, and upon it an outstretched hand gules. There is no apparent connection between the colour and the sanguinary history of Ireland, but the hand is determinedly dextral.

A hand has been described, in various slang phrases, as "a bunch of fives", and in the Middle East, the phrase "five in your eye" would be followed by an outstretched palm held before the face of one suspected of the Evil Eye. If the left hand is used as well, Westermarck has noted, the phrase in "Five and Little Five". But the right hand was ever the lucky one and the mighty one. Virgil gave it the highest praise when he refers in the Aeneid to "*Dextra mihi deus*"—"my right hand was a god to me".

Cicero believed the Evil Eye to originate from a sense of envy, *invidia*. (The Latin verb *invidere* means "to look at closely", and, victims of the eye were "overlooked".) His belief was taken up by Sir Francis Bacon, in his essay "Of Envy".

"There be none of the affections which have been noted to fascinate or bewitch, but love and envy. They both have vehement wishes. . . . We see, likewise, the Scriptures calleth envy an Evil Eye, and the astrologers call the evil influence of the stars evil aspects. So that there still seemeth to be acknowledged, in the act of envy, an ejaculation or irradiation of the eye."

Sir Thomas Browne, believer though he was in witchcraft and sorcery, had no belief in the power of the Evil Eye. Continued fear of it, he ascribed to such failings as "the common infirmity of human nature", credulity, supinity, and "adherence unto antiquity authority". But the fear continued.

The power of the hand was long connected in men's minds with the eye, since evil could be communicated by touch—even

* *Paradise Lost*, Bk. ii.

a Royal touch. An instruction in the Book of Proverbs means, says Elworthy, "avoid his presence, lest you come into contact with him; he may be blind, but his touch is malignant. Great as may be the power of mere personal presence, such as the rubbing of shoulders with one possessed with the terrible faculty, the effect is tenfold greater when there is the actual and intentional touching by the baneful person." By the same token, a touch by a holy person, such as Jesus, could have exactly the opposite effect. Many of the Miracles are described as being wrought by the touch of Our Lord's hand, or the smiting of the Rock by the hand of Moses, or victory in battle being assured by the raising of his hand.* The Benediction has always involved the raised right hand.

Evidence of witchcraft laid great stress on the consequence of the witch not only "overlooking" but touching her intended victim. Boguet's *Examen of Witches* devotes a whole chapter to this practice, in which the hand is usually the left. It is not surprising, therefore, that the hand became as important a symbol as the eye, both as the object of fortune-telling and chiromancy, and as a good-luck charm in itself. Hand amulets go back, as do the eye amulets, to the days of the Phoenicians and Etruscans, and indeed further, to Moses and the Children of Israel.

Great importance was later attached to the position of the fingers and thumb, but over archways and doorways in Muslim countries, an open right hand, with all fingers extended and palm outward, was the conventional pattern. Though Muslims have always objected to images, the hand seems to have been an exception, since it implied hospitality. It was to be seen over the great gate of the Alhambra in Spain, where the Caid dispensed justice in oriental fashion. In Tunis, many examples have been found over doorways, or drawn on walls. In the great Mosque of Santa Sophia in Turkey, a freak formation of marble on one of the columns resulted in the lifelike and life-size image of a human right hand. For a long time this was regarded as the manifestation of the hand of the prophet and to pray near it was

* *Exodus Ch. 17*. Whenever Moses lowered his hand, the Amalekites began to win.

to receive protection from the Evil Eye. In Hebrew, the word *Yad*, originally Arabic, meant not only the hand, but the Hand of God, and the later corruption *Yamin* was applied to the tribe of Ben Yamin, or sons of the Right Hand. But Hebrew words were sometimes capable of two meanings:

yamin:	right or south
kedem:	front or east
semol:	left or north
achor:	behind or west

There have been occasions when this double meaning could have remarkable consequences.

Hand-gestures have a history all their own, and they have been capable of many interpretations. "Do you bite your thumb at me, Sir?" demanded a Montague of a Capulet. "No, Sir," was the guarded reply, "but I bite my thumb." The famous Winston Churchill "V" sign has its contemptuous counterpart if the two fingers are given an upward thrust. The Freemason's handshake has its own significance and, in previous ages, the position of the thumb and fingers, whether in an amulet or in company, could have a variety of meanings. Perhaps the most famous is the *mano fica*, or "fig-hand", in which the thumb is protruded between the index and middle fingers. In one sense it was a guard against evil spirits. Elworthy quotes one Dean Ramsay who "remembered how in Yorkshire he and his school-fellows, from 1800 to 1810, used to put our thumb between the first and second finger, pointing downward as the infallible protection against the evil influences of our particular witch".

The antiquity of this hand position may be gathered from the fact that a "fig-hand" amulet in Oxford's Ashmolean Museum dates back to Phoenician times. In the Roman age it was considered the height of indignity: Dante mentioned it twice, the French adopted the phrase *faire la figue* from the Italians, and it gave rise to the contemptuous English expression "I don't care a fig".

Another celebrated hand-gesture was the *mano cornuta*,

A KISS FOR THE DEVIL

Since everything was in reverse—widdershins, the Lord's
Prayer backwards—the theory about the Witches' Coven was
that His Satanic Majesty (who appeared in the form of a Goat)
should be greeted by a kiss on the backside. Three of the
followers of Satan hold torches in their left hands. The wood-
cut is from Guazzo's *Compendium Maleficarum*, a 17th-century
book on witchcraft.

AUGURIES
A Roman sacrificial offering before a war (sculpture from Trajan's Column). Axes and horns are held both left and right-handed.

STRICTLY FOR THE BIRDS
Romulus (foreground, on the Capitoline Hill) and Remus, compete, by divination of birds' flight, for the honour of founding Rome.

in which the index and the little finger were extended to make two horns, i.e. to suggest cuckoldry. Again, this piece of manual manipulation was well known in all European countries, and finds its way into a number of plays, "Cuckledom being," Addison complained, "the basis of most of our modern plays."* Miniature amulets made with sharp horns could also be used to give a suspected cuckold an unexpected prick. There were no regulations, and no apparent significance as to which hand was portrayed.

Chironomy, defined in the dictionary as "the art or science of gesticulation, or of moving the hands according to rule in oratory, pantomime, etc.", was a practice of great antiquity. Numa Pompilius, successor to Romulus in Rome, is said to have made use of the hands as a means of counting, and Greeks may have begun this method even earlier. Each hand was employed, the folding or bending of each finger signifying the number. The left hand indicated the figures first from 1 to 10, then from 20 to 90: the right hand took up the hundreds, up to 900, using the same patterns, but with ten times the value. For thousands, the right hand copied the left hand's positions indicating one to ten. The whole process looks very like the present deaf and dumb alphabet, though it only employs fingers and thumbs. No connection between the two systems has been traced.

The variations on the "left-handed" compliment as a derogatory phrase, and other sinistral connections with bad luck and misfortune, extended to many human activities beside the first-footing and the morganatic marriage, the left-handed blessing and other manifestations. Drinking habits were one source of prejudice. It was always considered bad luck to pass the wine with the left hand, or to circulate the bottle or wine jar anti-clockwise, and since men who believe in the phrase *in vino veritas* are apt to be upset at any alteration in their routine, great ill-temper could arise during drinking bouts, and feuds could arise.

An instance of the Left-Handed Toast, meaning ill-will, is

* *Spectator*, No. 446.

recorded among documents discovered at the stately home of the Marquis of Bath, Longleat, which put on record the feud between the family and retainers of one William Hartgill, and those of Lord Stourton, an enmity which lasted for nearly twenty years, between 1540 and 1557. R. Thurston Hopkins takes up the story.*

"Over a hundred closely printed pages of the Wiltshire Archaeological Magazine, July, 1864, deal sketchily with the large number of letters and official documents giving the full story of the Hartgill-Stourton feud ... Some days after Lord Stourton had 'falled utterly out' with William Hartgill, he was with a number of his retainers, local landowners and farmers round the council table at Stourton House. His Lordship finally rose, and held up a glass of wine. 'Gentlemen,' he said, with eyes blazing, 'the toast is the Hartgill family— left-handed.' With enthusiasm they seized their glasses with their left hands and emptied them, indicating that they drank to the Hartgills' downfall. . . ."

In the Middle East, the relative position of master and servant, in the geographical rather than social sense, can still be highly important, and to ignore it is to court disaster. British diplomats have usually been highly sensitive to this, and have a long record of discreet and correct behaviour. There is an example concerning Ibn Saud of Arabia which is worth recalling for two reasons: one, the degree to which Winston Churchill was rated above normal rules of procedure; the second, the degree to which his local officials could let him down.

During the Second World War, Churchill and Roosevelt met King Saud together. Roosevelt, a chain-smoker, tactfully put his cigarettes away in the Royal presence. Churchill, according to the biographer of Saud, David Howarth,† said to the interpreter, "If it was the religion of His Majesty to deprive himself of smoking and alcohol, he must point out that his rule of life prescribed an absolutely sacred rite of

---

* *Adventures with Phantoms*: Quality Press, London, 1946.
† *The Desert King*: A Life of Ibn Saud: Collins, London, 1964.

smoking cigars and also drinking alcohol before, after, and if need be during all meals and in the intervals between them."

King Ibn Saud graciously accepted the position. Princely gifts were exchanged. The Arabian King's were much the most costly, but Roosevelt promised an aeroplane, and Churchill the gift of "the finest motor car in the world, with every comfort for peace and every security against hostile action".

The archives of the Rolls-Royce company contain no record of a car being delivered to Arabia at this time, but Mr Howarth's researches discovered that the Ministry of Supply had discovered one, which was sent to the British Legation in Jidda, after receiving their advice on structural refinements and coachwork. The Legation had been uninformed on one important matter, which became obvious as soon as the car was inspected at Riyadh. King Ibn Saud was full of admiration for the vehicle, but pointed out that it had a right-hand drive. Nobody had remembered that the King sometimes sat in the front seat of his cars, especially when out hunting, but that to sit on the left of his chauffeur would be an intolerable oriental humiliation. Ibn Saud therefore gave the car to Abdullah, his brother.

A minor incident of one-sidedness, but in its way a significant one for any western diplomats wanting to win friends and influence people. The Rolls-Royce company recently designed a new type of luxury car intended solely for Heads of State and other types of Potentate. They would not be likely to allow such a mistake to occur again.

Muslim countries provide the best examples of hand-preference and superstitions. Valuable information in the case of Morocco has been provided by the Swedish anthropologist, Edward Westermarck, in a monumental work resulting from several years' stay in that sunlit country.* Almost every action seems to arise from consideration of either the right or the left side. To summon the *djinn* or evil spirit, women had first to put on their veil with the left hand, and hold it up with that hand. The left eye was painted with antimony. The One Who

* *Ritual and Belief in Morocco*: Macmillan, London, 1926.

Charmed Away the evil spirit (*neddara*) put her left hand on the patient's head while muttering her incantation. If a Moroccan suffered from fever, he made seven knots in a palm leaf (the tying of knots always held great significance) and drank seven times from a spring; both operations had to be made with the left hand. If a child suffered from whooping-cough, it could be placed, at sunset, on the dunghill of the household, and a left-handed man (*azermad*) would tie a string of fresh palm leaf round its neck, and then cut the string with a sickle. Evidently there were some uses for the left-hander in Moroccan villages! Indeed, to summon the good spirits, the formula was still the seven knots in the palm leaf, but again tied with the left hand.

Ritual in death has always been followed in tribal countries with the greatest discipline. Instructions for the washing of the Loved One in Morocco were precise. Some parts of the body were to be washed with water, others with soap and scent. The one who performed the rite had to say his prayers, the *bismillah*, before doing so, and all parts of the body were to be washed with the left hand. No doubt all this was to propitiate the *djinn*. A ring of silver or copper worn on the left hand was held to be a charm against the evil ones, who were thought to attack on the left side, this being the weaker one. The Evil Eye also came into the picture. The measuring of grain was done either after sunset or at daybreak, to prevent it being affected by the eye. "The man who is going to work it," writes Westermarck, "moves a shovel once round the grain from left to right, picks up some of the grain with his left hand and slowly pours it into his right hand, then throws it in the direction of the Evil Eye." This is the exact equivalent of the spilling-the-salt routine. The twitching and itching followed the same accepted pattern. Twitching of the right eyelid meant that a member of the family would come back to you; of the left, that a relative would die, or some other sorrow. Itching of the big toe of the left foot was a presentiment of death. If your beard itched, and you scratched it with your right hand, you would receive something; if with your left, you would give something away. The same was held to be true about the well-known itching palm, which Westermarck also credits to Germany, Norway and "The West Highlands", but he might have added almost as many countries as are now in the United Nations. In Tangier, strangely enough, he found exactly the opposite rule prevailed. But Tangier has always been a highly individual place.

Note on the word "Yemen"

Early expeditions into this part of the Middle East, on the Red Sea, were led by one Peter Forsskal of Denmark. Later explorers, Von Haven and Niebuhr, encountered unexpected opposition from the local Arabs, and much of the trouble arose through a mistranslation of a word. "Yemen" in early Arabic and Hebrew meant "the right hand" or "the right side". Since Arabs regarded the left hand as unclean and the left side— carrying the heart—the weaker, "yemen" became synonymous with "fortunate" or "beneficent". Hence the name given to the country by the western pioneers: *Arabia Felix*. But to the Arabs, who faced the east for all their prayers and prophecies, Yemen had merely come to mean "the land to the South", i.e. to the right. It is the European custom to take all bearings facing north, the Point of the compass, which would place Arabia Felix on the westward side. Any suspicion that this might imply a leftward connotation would have had a profound effect on sensitive Arabs—as it indeed proved. Among the reasons for the failure of the expedition, Carsten Niebuhr lists the failure "to live more in conformity with Oriental custom", which in effect meant knowing your right hand from your left, and letting one know what the other was doing.

XI

AMBIDEXTERITY

"Descended from apes, my dear?" a Bishop of Killaloe is supposed to have exclaimed to his wife, on first hearing the Darwinian theory. "One hopes that it is not true: or if true, that it does not become too widely known. . . ."

Alas for the Bishop and his kind. It became, not only widely known, but widely accepted, and consideration of the habits of our ancestors eventually led to new theories about Handedness, culminating in the founding of the Ambidextral Culture Society by one John Jackson, whose "argument for two-handedness and two-brainedness" emerged in a complete book,* with an introduction by Baden-Powell.

Visit any zoo, and you will find that gorillas, monkeys, chimpanzees are completely ambidextral in all their hand actions. "There was a time," declared an anonymous writer in the *Cornhill Magazine* (1881), "when man was practically ambidextrous. Why and how has he become lop-sided and one-handed?"

The various theories about this have already been described in detail, and though Jackson sets out these theories in his early chapters, for him this is not enough. The natural, ambidextral state of apes, and primitive man, becomes a sort of *belle sauvage* existence towards which modern man might with benefit return. The author's style is explosive and loquacious, with as many underlinings and exclamation marks as in a journal by Queen Victoria (whom, incidentally, he claims as being ambidextrous herself, but who never gave royal patronage to the Culture Society). The clarion call in his campaign goes like this:

* *Ambidexterity*: Kegan Paul, London, 1905.

"It may confidently be predicted, that,
SO FAR AS IS KNOWN—
There is no advantage, but there is every disadvantage,
in our being unidextrous: whilst—
There is no disadvantage, but every advantage, in our
being truly ambidextrous!!
Why should not perfect Ambidexterity be possible now?
WHY CANNOT MAN BE AMBIDEXTROUS AGAIN?"

So, with this vision of a Golden Age, Mr Jackson takes
his two-handed vorpal sword in both hands, and proceeds to
lay about him with great gusto, quoting evidence in support
of his campaign from eminent men, including as remarkable an
example as Sir John Adcock, Physician-in-Chief to the Shah of
Persia, who described His Imperial Majesty, the King of
Kings, as being, like many of his staff, adept at the use of either
hand. One Dr Humphrey of Cambridge declares: "In all
persons, I believe, the left hand may be trained to as great
expertness and strength as the right." Sir Daniel Wilson is also
quoted: "I use the pen in the right hand, and the pencil in the
left hand, so that were either hand disabled, the other would be
at once available for all needful operations."

The name of the divine all-rounder Leonardo is, of course,
prominently quoted, together with other alleged ambidextral
artists like Holbein, Durer, Mozzo of Antwerp, and Landseer.
But the most forceful testimony comes from a soldier.

Baden-Powell was at that time a Major-General, a Commander of the Bath, and a hero of the Ashanti wars. The
historian Hilary St George Saunders has related how, in the
campaign of 1896, Baden-Powell greeted a defeated chieftain
by holding out his right hand. The chief replied: "The men in
my tribe greet the bravest with the left hand," and they shook
on it that way. From this incident eventually came the famous
"southpaw" handshake of the Boy Scouts.

Baden-Powell was a convinced ambidextral, and signed the
Introduction to Jackson's book with both hands, reproduced in

facsimile. It was his contention that to train the human body completely and symmetrically was an obligation. It could only be accomplished by equal attention to both sides of the body. "This two-sided growth," he went on, "can alone be promoted and matured by educating our two hands equally, each in precisely the same way, and exactly to the same extent. It is hardly possible to lay too much stress upon this bimanual training, or to attach too much importance to the principle."

Then he added, as a soldier, "There is no doubt that the value of Ambidexterity from a military point of view is immense. I do not consider a man is a thoroughly trained soldier unless he can mount equally well on either side of his horse, use the sword, pistol and lance, equally well with both hands, and shoot off the left shoulder as rapidly and accurately as from the right."

The question of gunmanship is dealt with elsewhere, and is a vexed one, but apart from this, it is doubtful whether Major-General Baden-Powell ever succeeded in convincing either the War Office, or the men under his command, that this two-sided conclusion was either desirable or practical. He, however, went ever further in support of Jackson's discovery that fully ambidextral people could perform two tasks simultaneously.

"The heavy pressure of my office work makes me wish that I had cultivated, in my youth, the useful art of writing on two different subjects at once. I get through a great deal extra —it is true—by using the right and left hand alternately, but I thoroughly appreciate how much more can be done by using them both together."

Fighting a war on two fronts had, therefore, no terrors for General Baden-Powell. Jackson adds a number of illustrated examples of young people (all are girls) learning to write sentences and whole pages simultaneously with each hand. He is cautious about claiming too much for this intricate process of divided mental and physical attention, but asserts, in bold capitals:

"IT IS NOT FOUND! AND IT HAS NEVER BEEN FOUND, THAT SUCH SIMULTANEOUS WORK, ALTHOUGH CONTINUED DAILY FOR A LIFETIME, HAS EVER EXERCISED A DELETERIOUS EFFECT UPON THE MENTAL OR PHYSICAL STRUCTURE, FACULTIES, OR FUNCTIONS OF THE INDIVIDUAL!!"

"*Ergo*," he concludes, "simultaneous Ambidextral work must be harmless and healthful, as well as expedient and necessary."

Apart from Baden-Powell, his principal witness is none other than Sir Edwin Landseer, celebrated painter of "The Monarch of the Glen" and other animal studies. Landseer's fame brought him into contact with the Royal Family, and he taught both Victoria and Albert the rudiments of drawing and etching. (Since both he and the Queen were ambidextral, it would be interesting to know if they ever discussed the subject.)

Many artists have been credited with dexterity in both hands. Michelangelo, prone on his cradle high up in the Sistine Chapel, is said to have been able to switch brushes from one hand to the other to avoid cramp and exhaustion. Leonardo is the classic example, but his habit of mirror-writing may have been as much a gimmick as a genuine economy in physical expenditure. So too, Landseer used his ambidextral ability as a *tour de force* rather than an integral part of his technique. His biographer, Frederick George Stephens, has described a remarkable example of the artist's simultaneous work:*

"A large party was assembled one evening at the house of a gentleman in the upper ranks of London 'society', crowds of ladies and gentlemen of distinction were present, including Landseer, who was, as usual, the lion; a large group gathered about the sofa where he was lounging; the subject turned on dexterity and facility in feats of skill with the hand. No doubt the talk was ingeniously led in this direction by some who knew that Sir Edwin could do wonders of dextrous draughtsmanship, and were not unwilling to see him draw, but they did not expect what followed. A lady, lolling back on a settee,

* *Memoirs of Sir Edwin Landseer*: George Bell, London, 1874.

and rather tired of the subject, as ladies are apt to become when conversation does not appeal to their feelings or their interests, exclaimed, 'Well, there's one thing nobody has ever done, and that is to draw two things at once.' "

The lady had reckoned without Landseer. He immediately replied, "Oh, I can do that. Lend me two pencils and I will show you." This he did, drawing, without hesitation, the profile of a stag's head with one hand, and of a horse's head with the other, simultaneously.

"Both drawings," says Stephens, "were quite as good as the master was accustomed to produce with his right hand alone; the drawing by the left hand was not inferior to that by the right."

Enlarging on his general theme, Jackson has his bounds of ambition set wider still and wider:

"Let any serious man sit down and estimate, if he can, the appalling loss in brain power, in inventive genius, in muscular energy, in effective fighting strength, in time and money, that our British Empire is suffering every day of its existence by neglecting to avail itself of this wonderful potency that is lying dormant in its very (left) hand."

He calls up evidence from ancient peoples such as the Scythians before the year of the Flood:

"PEOPLE WERE ENJOINED TO EXERCISE BOTH HANDS ALIKE, WITHOUT PARTIALITY EITHER FOR THE RIGHT OR LEFT."

He claims Plato as a champion of Ambidextrality (though, as observed earlier, Plato's main complaint was about holding babies so that their inferior arm was free). Greek soldiers, like those of King David at Ziklag, were said to be able to fight equally well with either hand. Coming to his own times, he cites the Japanese:

"That they stand at the very head of civilised nations will be conceded readily by anyone, but it is not equally widely known that they are the most Ambidextrous people on earth. They have been two-handed from the remotest antiquity."

His panegyric on Japan, ranging from painting and pottery

to lacquer and poetry, seems to stem from the celebrated Japanese Exhibition in London in 1862, which certainly started a Nipponese vogue, and inspired Gilbert and Sullivan to plan *The Mikado*. It was strengthened in 1904 by Japanese success in the current war against Russia, in which "they had proved themselves as distinguished in military prowess as they have been for centuries in artistic pre-eminence". What seems to be lacking is any detailed evidence of their ambidextrality.

Jackson's most seriously argued and, as it proved, successful field was in education, and he made numerous recommendations for teachers and physical-training intructors to make their pupils bi-manual. Indeed, after his book had appeared, and the Culture Society had been publicised, a number of educational authorities recommended bi-manualism for infant schools, and copy-books were specially printed for this end. Jackson's dream of getting it on the statute book of the House of Commons was, however, never realised.

In his peroration, the author declares:

"Deprive mankind of two-handed exercises, movements and functions: withdraw all these manual occupations that make up our work-a-day lives, and there will follow a reversion to primitive savagery!"

Since it was from primitive (ambidextral) savagery that his theory first arose, this point seems to fall rather flat. But the defence rests. . . .

Jackson had received messages of encouragement from men and women in many walks of life (except, it seems, Members of Parliament). The distinguished Dr Cunningham wrote: "Much more could be made of the left side in education, and I am in full sympathy with the efforts of your Society." The Rev. Dukinfield Ashley wished him, "All success in your crusade on behalf of the neglected left hand." Surgeon-General Bradshaw, Hon. Physician to the King, said: "I am very much in favour of encouraging the use of the left hand for independent action." Lord Charles Beresford: "The utility of teaching Ambidexterity goes without saying." The Countess of Jersey had "always thought that it would be a good thing if children could be taught to use both hands much more freely than they do now". The educational journal, *Schoolmaster*, added: "The great convenience of being able to use the left hand with equal readiness will strike us all, and the only wonder is that we have never seriously considered the question before."

The Ambidextral Culture Society was formed "for the promotion of Educational Reform and Two-handed Training".

President: E. Noble Smith, F.R.C.S. Edin.
Vice Presidents: Maj.-Gen. R. S. S. Baden-Powell, C.B.
                 W. H. Cummings, Mus. Doc.
                 Sir James Sawyer, M.D., etc.
Hon. Secretary: John Jackson, F.E.I.S.
Secretary: J. Alf Jackson.

The Committee numbered more than fifty.

Beliefs: 1. That two perfect and equally dextrous hands are better than one.
         2. That the left hand *can* be cultivated to a much higher degree of dexterity.
         3. That such an increase in dexterity will be fraught with great benefit to the person and with many blessings to the public.

"JUSTICE AND EQUALITY FOR THE LEFT HAND!"

This plea for manual *liberté and egalité* was not long left unanswered. If Jackson had been able to consult augurs, they would have predicted thunder from the right. In the *Boston Medical Journal*, one Dr. G. M. Gould wrote of "ambidextral cranks, sillies and mongers". James Shaw, writing in *Knowledge*, is in favour of hand-preference, and declared that, if Ambidextrality were achieved, we would need "two handles to every door, two methods of winding-up every watch, Janus-shaped benches, gauges, and duplicate sets of screw-nails, scissors and scythes".

Jackson is shrill in his reply to this "mixed medley of gratuitous assumptions":

"Ambidexterity does not mean *two left hands*—no one, save possibly himself, has ever contemplated making people AMBISINISTROUS!!—it means *two right hands*."

But the main attack came from a famous surgeon, Sir James Crichton-Browne, lecturing in 1909 on "Dexterity and the Bend Sinister". This reasoned, pro-dextral discourse was regarded by Jackson as an attempt to kill his Culture Society. As "the English Goliath of Lopsidedness" he was "fired with a holy zeal to destroy the new Crusade". The main points Crichton-Browne in fact made were that, since we had been primarily right-handed for a long while, right-handedness seemed to be a terminal form of evolution, and that to make a "feverish attempt" to undo dextral pre-eminence was to fly in the face of evolution.

Whatever happened to the Ambidextral Culture Society, which, sixty years ago, caused such a stir? By claiming to be a national panacea as well as an essential element of human development, it obviously claimed too much, and seems to have passed away unwept and unsung. Interest in Ambidexterity did not, however, cease. In the 17th century, Sir Thomas Browne had said that he did not know a "distinction in nature" between left and right, but the distinction and preference was already beginning to become clear, once man became a biped, and lost the additional mechanical use of his toes.

The emergence of dextral preference has already been considered. What, therefore, explains the continuation of ambidexterity in a small minority of people, and is their bimanual ability really an asset? Sir Cyril Burt declares that this depends to a large extent on whether each hand has true dexterity, i.e. skill, and not just equal strength. Dr Margaret Clark adds: "Some investigators declare that there is no such thing as true ambidexterity, and that the people we are inclined to call ambidextrous are merely instances of changed left-handers . . . asymmetrical behaviour is the normal mode of adjustment: therefore ambidexterity is abnormal."

It is perhaps just as well that John Jackson did not live to hear such a judgment. Enough for him that he heard Crichton-

Browne quoting Holy Scripture by saying: "Man's right hand hath gotten him the victory."

Perhaps the whole Ambidextral Campaign of 1905 was but a storm in a tea-cup, stirred alternately clockwise or "widder-shins". Certainly there are a number of individual advantages in being ambidextrous. Dr Norman Capener has described the value to a surgeon of being able, in an arduous operation, to slip the scalpel from one hand to the other and continue, without altering his position. Leonardo, we know, found it useful. Ambidextral tennis champions such as Mrs Beverley Fleitz and Pancho Segura have the advantage of two forehand drives, and the majority of left-handers have learned to perform some functions with the right as the dominant member. To some extent, therefore, most sinistrals are in some measure ambidextral, but it is to a large extent an unconscious and unimportant changeover, undertaken in anything but the zealous spirit of John Jackson's Crusade.

XII

THE TRIBE OF THE HAND

"Ben Yamin" means, literally, "Son of the Right Hand", and therefore the tribe of Benjamin could be expected to be firmly dextral. Yet, strangely enough, the only complimentary references to prowess with the *left* hand in the Bible are associated with Benjamites. These are the "commando" group of left-handed slingers; the ambidextral survivors of the Battle of Mount Gilboa who rallied to the standard of David; and Ehud the Benjamite, who slew Eglon the King of Moab not only single-handed, but left-handed.

The tribe often seems to have been the isolated, "breakaway" group among the children of Israel and the left-handed slingers fought, in fact, against the other Israelites in the confusing civil war which broke out over an incident in the village of Gibeah.* It happened, apparently, "when there was no King in Israel", and from a trifling beginning arose a great conflict.

A certain Levite living on Mount Ephraim had a concubine who "played the whore against him" and went to her native town of Bethlehem. He persuaded her to return, and they journeyed as far as Gibeah, "which belonged to Benjamin". There they failed to find lodging, until an old man returning from his work in the fields offered them shelter in his house. There followed the same sort of incident as befell Lot, when he was sheltering the angels in Sodom. Benjamites surrounded the house, and demanded the Levite to satisfy their own unnatural lusts. The old man pleaded with them and offered his own daughter plus the concubine. The latter was thrust

* *Judges.*

out of doors among them, and they ravished her all night. Next day she was found, dead, with her hands "on the threshold". The Levite cut up her body into the traditional twelve pieces, and despatched them throughout Israel, to prove what had happened.

This pretty story had the effect of uniting and galvanising the Children of Israel "from Dan even unto Beersheba" in a campaign against the outcast Tribe of the Hand. They numbered 400,000. We are told that the Benjamites numbered 26,000, and that "among all this people there were 700 chosen men left-handed: everyone could sling stones at an hair breadth, and not miss". The men of Israel took their battle orders from the Lord, but the battle began disastrously for them.

At the first encounter, the Benjamites slew 22,000 Israelites. The Children complained to the Lord, and asked if they should fight again. Encouraged, they nevertheless lost 18,000 in the second battle. After this, they began to fast, and present burnt offerings and peace offerings, and after a running fight, in which the Israelites retreated several times, the Lord, true to his promise, delivered the Benjamites into their hand, and 25,000 of them were killed. But it is, perhaps, not unjustified they they should twice be described, in the account, as "men of valour".

The epic of the left-handed slingers might end there, were it not that in the very next chapter of the Book of Judges, there is the revelation that no Israelite daughter was allowed to marry into the tribe of Benjamin. The tribe had been well-nigh destroyed: the Children of Israel were very worried because they were unwilling to see the Benjamites disappear, but they had vowed a vow about their women-folk: "Cursed be he that giveth a wife to Benjamin."

So—and by now the story, if produced in Cinemascope, might recommend itself to Hollywood's Bible scriptwriters— the Israelites had to find wives for the men of Benjamin, and they must all be virgins. Four hundred such were found during the taking of Jabesh-Gilead, and handed over; but these were not enough. So the elders of the congregation got together, to see what could be arranged for the isolated Benjamites. There was, they discovered, an annual feast of the Lord at Shiloh, when the local women were wont to dance in the vineyards. Hide yourselves, they said to the men of Benjamin, and if the girls come out to dance, catch them and take them away, and we'll find some excuse for you. So the tribe of Benjamin was replenished, and restored to the tribes of the Children of Israel.

Saul had been slain on Mount Gilboa, for transgressing against the Lord, and David son of Jesse reigned. Part of his command were the Thirty, the chief captains, but he had these additional allies, from the army of the dead king.

"Now those are they that came to David to Ziklag, while he kept himself close because of Saul the Son of Kish: and they were among the mighty men, helpers of the war.

"They were armed with bows, and could use both the right hand and the left in hurling stones and shooting arrows out of a bow, even of Saul's brethren of Benjamin.

"The chief was Ahiezer, then Joash, the sons of Shemaah the Gibeathite; and Jeziel, and Pelet, the sons of Asmaveth . . . and Ismaiah the Gibeonite, a mighty man among the thirty, and over the thirty. . . . These are they that went over Jordan in the first month when it had overflown all its banks; and they put to flight all of them of the valleys, both towards the east, and towards the west."

There is so much name-dropping in the Book of Chronicles that the narrative tends to become obscured, but it is obvious that these ambidextral warriors were, once more, from the Tribe of the Hand.

What no one can apparently explain is, what was wrong with the Ben-Yamin, the Sons of the Hand? Why were they shunned? Was it because, like the seven hundred slingers, they were predominantly sinistral and therefore unpopular? Was it due to their consanguinity with Saul, that mysterious and luckless figure? Saul, the Benjamite, had consorted with wizards, and on one occasion, when the Lord would not answer, raised the apparition of the Prophet Samuel by consulting the witch of En-dor. The Hebrew word *se'mol* means left, and in the Zohar, the Jewish book of mysticism, Sammael, the Serpent, is represented as "the personification of evil, the other, or left side".*

Was like calling to like? Were left-handers, apart from Ehud, associated with sorcery and witchcraft? Another Samuel, of Nineveh, an astrologer, was criticised by one of the Hasidic leaders in the 12th century for dealing in witchcraft and having intercourse with demons, and Nineveh is the wicked city wherein, as the Lord told Jonah, were "more than six score persons, that cannot discern between their right hand and their left hand".†

---

* *Gerson Scholem*: *Major Trends in Jewish Mysticism*, p. 239: London, 1955.

† Compare the men of Gog and Magog, of whom the Lord said: "I will smite thy bow out of thy left hand, and cause thine arrows to fall out of thy right hand." *Ezekiel*, ch. 39.

XIII

EHUD

The James Bond of the Benjamites

The only known instance of a left-hander being chosen by Jehovah to help the children of Israel is the spectacular case of Ehud the Benjamite. The story reads like a thriller in the best tradition.*

The Israelites had been doing evil in the sight of the Lord— a not uncommon practice—"serving Baalim and the groves". Twice they had been rebuked, and it seems that one of their crimes was incest. The Lord therefore used a tactic often used before, to bring them back into the way of righteousness. He backed one of their enemies. "And the Lord strengthened Eglon the King of Moab against Israel." Moab marched against Jericho, "the city of palm trees", and took it, with the aid of the Ammonites and the Amalekites.

"So the children of Israel served Eglon the King of Moab eighteen years."

Moab was probably the name of a tribe rather than a district. They inhabited the area at the north of the Dead Sea, not far from the region where the famous scrolls were found: but though there is no scroll to describe the exploit of Ehud, the Old Testament story is detailed enough. When the Children of Israel repented, and cried again to the Lord, He relented, and chose a deliverer for them, Ehud the son of Gera, a Benjamite, "a man left-handed". Remembering the body of sinistral slingers among the Benjamites, it would be intriguing to think

* *Judges*, ch. 3.

that he was one of them, but the famous Seven Hundred are only mentioned later.

The plan was to send a present to the King, which meant, by custom, a large number of presents carried by porters. Ehud was to be in charge of the deputation. The author of Judges then gives an exact description of the weapon:

> "Ehud made him a dagger which had two edges, of a cubit length."

This dagger, known as a gomed, would be similar to a dirk, about thirteen inches long, a small but deadly instrument. In considering the case of Ehud, the psychologist Millais Culpin writes:

> "The emphasis of the story is upon his deliberate planning, his single-minded determination, his independence of all help, even to the making of his own dagger: and the result is a picture of the left-hander *in excelsis*."*

We are told that Ehud strapped the dagger under his raiment on the right thigh, and we can now see the wisdom of the Lord in choosing a sinistral for the deed of delivery. Every King of that time lived in perpetual fear of assassination, and, before the private audience which was to follow the presentation, guards would be bound to feel Ehud for a concealed weapon—but they would feel on the wrong side. The gifts were delivered to Eglon, "who was a very fat man". We can imagine Ehud waiting impatiently for the right moment to get the King by himself, and when he had dismissed the porters, "he himself turned away from the quarries that were by Gilgal, and said 'I have a secret errand unto thee, O King' ".

The Hebrew word for "secret" does not define whether it meant a private message or a divine one, but whatever was said, it had its effect. Eglon cried "Silence!" and those that were round about him left him. The King then retired to his summer parlour, "which he had for himself alone". The Dead Sea area is notorious for its heat and humidity (Sodom, 1,300 feet below sea-level, is the lowest point on earth) and

---

* *Mental Abnormality: Facts and Theories*: Hutchinson, London, 1931.

the King's chamber was no doubt a sort of roof garden. Ehud followed him, and then, according to the Bible account, he revealed that the message was from God. He rose from his seat and "put forth his left hand, and took the dagger from his right thigh, and thrust it into his belly".

The climax is well known, as one of the horror-stories of the Old Testament. In went the dagger so far that Ehud could not at first get it out, so fat was the King. The Benjamite presumably knew that the servants would become suspicious if the private audience went on too long, but that if he made his exit without a farewell from the King, suspicion would at once be aroused. The solution of this James Bond-type son of the Hand was to lock the doors and play for time.

"When he was gone out, his servants came; and when they saw that, behold, the doors of the parlour were locked, they said, surely he covereth his feet in the summer chamber. And they tarried till they were ashamed: and behold, he opened not the doors of the parlour; therefore they took a key and opened them: and behold, their lord was fallen down dead on the earth."

It was during the period of waiting that Ehud made his escape. He got through the quarries, and to safety. The Children of Israel were waiting anxiously to know how their divinely appointed hero had fared. A trumpet call came from the mountain top, the mount of Ephraim. It was Ehud's signal that the King was dead. The tribe gathered, and the Benjamite led them down from the hill, telling them that the Lord had delivered Moab to them, and urging them to attack. The Israelites "crossed the fords of Jordan towards Moab" and proceeded to defeat and massacre the subjects of the late King Eglon. It was not an impressive number, as these Old Testament massacres go: only 10,000 men, "all lusty, and all men of valour", but none of them escaped.

Eighty years of peace followed, and presumably Ehud the Left-Handed continued to enjoy the favour of the Lord and the admiration of his people. His successor, Shamgar the son of Anath (no connection with the curse of anathema) was cast in the same heroic mould. He slew six hundred Philistines with an ox-goad. Modern supermen of the Bond type cannot compete with the heroes of the Scriptures.*

The interesting part of the Ehud-Eglon story is that left-handedness was so much a part of the plot. There have been, apparently, no subsequent thrillers in which much use is made of sinistrality, with the exception of *The Trial of Mary Dugan*, which is a far cry from the *Book of Judges*, or *Murder in Moab*.

* Two chapters later in the Book of Judges, the "stars in their courses" fought against Sisera, killed by Jael the wife of Heber. Her course, readers will remember, was to give him milk when he asked for water, and "bring forth butter in a lordly dish". After this, she drove a nail into his head, but she wielded the workman's hammer in her right hand.

XIV

CHRISTIANITY AND THE LEFT

Christian ritual is predominantly dextral, in all its aspects; that is, in addition to the clockwise and sunwise circumambulatory movements of the priests, with the altar facing the east. At Christian Communion, the most sacred of all the offices for Catholic and Protestant alike, the elements of bread and wine are carried from the altar by the priest to the right, and he (and his assistants if it is a large church) administer them to the communicants from left to right, with the wafer given in the right hand, and the chalice held similarly. The wafer has to be taken by the communicant with the right hand uppermost, supported by the left, and is conveyed thus to the mouth. The chalice must be grasped with the right hand first, with the left hand lower in support.

There is obviously a necessity to have some uniformity in such a ritual, but equally obviously it stems from the dominance of the right hand. Similarly, the sign of the cross is made dextrally, and the last movement is from left to right. More important still is the Benediction, which is always made with the right hand. In countless paintings, the right hand of Jesus is raised in blessing, with the two first fingers raised. To give a blessing sinistrally was blasphemy, and part of the Black Mass. What would the faithful think if there were such a person as a left-handed Pope, who gave the Easter blessing *Urbis et Orbis* sinistrally? This dextrality has become an instinct, and left-handers do not object. But it is also an order.

When a Bishop performs the act of Confirmation, he may have to use both hands if the numbers are large and have to be presented to him two by two. But there are superstitions—one is quoted from Dorset—which say that a child confirmed with the left hand will always be unlucky.

The handedness of the Christian marriage service is well known, though there are variations. In England the bride, who stands on the left of the groom in the church, has the wedding ring placed on the traditional "third finger, left hand". There are several theories about this choice. One is that this finger has a particular relation to the heart, although Sir Thomas Browne, had, in the 17th century, denounced "this common conceit, that the heart was on the left side".

Another is that, no matter which finger is used, the left hand is the weaker hand, just as woman, created from one of Adam's left ribs, is the weaker vessel. A third is that this finger has a magical charm which protects from witchcraft, a superstition going back to the days of Ancient Egypt.

The French, however, order it differently. When General de Gaulle visited London in April, 1960, an astute evening newspaper* noticed that Queen Elizabeth was wearing her wedding ring on her *right* hand, and put it down as a compliment to Madame de Gaulle and French custom.

Just as the bend sinister meant bastardy, so the *mariage à main gauche* meant a union unsanctified by the church. The other word, known in British circles since at least the reign of King George IV, is "morganatic".

Bend Sinister

This has nothing to do with the Black Magic of Morgan le Fay and Merlin, but is a German word derived from "morning

* *Evening Standard.*

gift". It occurs in many languages under the name "morgan-atica", and though it was originally applied mainly to titled German families, its meaning has become widespread. An 18th-century King of Sweden "marryed the King of Den-mark's daughter by a left-handed wife (as they are there called)". Horace Walpole in 1788 wrote: "The children of a left-handed alliance are not entitled to inherit." Southey remarks of Cowper: "His mistress, now considered as his left-handed wife, was united to him by moral ties." It was left to Thackeray, in *The Four Georges*, to remind his readers of this German habit: "They contracted left-handed marriages after the princely fashion of those times."

At such ceremonies, the bridegroom offered his left hand to the bride, which would normally be a token of shame. But there were those who, like Mrs. Fitzherbert, were prepared to suffer this insult, and at the time of the crisis over King Edward VIII and Mrs Simpson, the morganatic marriage was can-vassed in certain quarters.

A woman morganatically wedded, however, would, as Walpole pointed out, have none of the legal rights of the lawful bride. This problem roused the interest of the redoubtable Mary Wollstonecraft in her *Vindication of the Rights of Women*:

"The necessity of polygamy, therefore, does not appear; yet when a man seduces a woman, it should I think, be termed a *left-handed* marriage, and the man should be *legally* obliged to maintain the woman, and her children, unless adultery, a natural divorcement, abrogated the law."

These were bold words in those days, but it is a procedure which is only even now being considered seriously, without reference to morning gifts or handedness.

In the Book of Genesis, there was a real mix-up when the old man Israel blessed his grandsons, Ephraim and Manasseh, brought to him as he was dying, by their father Joseph. Israel laid his right hand on the head of Ephraim, and his left hand on the head of Manasseh, who was the elder son, and who should, presumably, have been honoured by the major hand.

"Bless the lads", said Israel (a curious Authorised version phrase), but this action had upset his son Joseph.

"When Joseph saw that his father laid his right hand upon the head of Ephraim, it displeased him: and he held up his father's hand, to remove it from Ephraim's head unto Manasseh's head. And Joseph said unto his father, Not so, my father: for this is the firstborn: put thy right hand upon his head. And his father refused, and said, I know it my son, I know it: he also shall become a people and he also shall be great: but truly this younger brother shall be greater than he. . . ."

The old man had his way, and Ephraim was preferred before Manasseh. It was all part of a very difficult family life for Joseph.

There are precise instructions in the Book of Leviticus about the cleansing of lepers, and these were some of the instructions Moses had to give the priests:

"The priest shall take some of the blood of the trespass offering, and the priest shall put it upon the tip of the right ear of him that is to be cleansed, and upon the thumb of his right hand, and upon the great toe of his right foot: and the priest shall take some of the log of oil, and pour it into the palm of his own left hand: and the priest shall dip his right finger in the oil that is in his left hand, and shall sprinkle of the oil with his finger seven times before the Lord. . . ."

This elaborate ritual ends up with the oil being put on exactly the same dextral places on the leper as the blood of sacrifice. The whole description is repeated in the case of a leper who cannot afford the requisite two lambs as an offering, but only one. The interesting additional offering is of "two turtledoves", but for those who remember their Christmas songs there is no mention of a partridge in a pear tree.

The largest proportion of references to the Hand in all its aspects is contained in the Psalms. Here is the complete list:

Psalm 16, v.11
Thou wilt shew me the path of life: in thy presence is fulness

of joy; at thy right hand there are pleasures for evermore.

16, v.8
I have set the Lord always before me: because he is at my right hand, I shall not be moved.

17, v.7
Shew thy marvellous loving kindness, O thou that savest by thy right hand them which put their trust in thee.

18, v.35
Thy right hand hath holden me up, and thy gentleness hath made me great.

20, v.6
Now know I that the Lord saveth his anointed; he will hear him from his holy heaven with the saving strength of his right hand.

44, v.3
For they got not the land by their own sword, neither did their own save them; but thy right hand, and thine arm.

45, v.4
Thy right hand shall teach thee terrible things.

63, v.8
My soul followeth hard after thee: thy right hand upholdeth me.

72, v.23
Nevertheless I am continually with thee: thou hast holden me with thy right hand.

74, v.11
Why withdrawest thou thy hand, even thy right hand? Pluck it out of thy bosom.

45, v.9
Kings daughters were among thy honourable women: upon thy right hand did stand the Queen in gold of Ophir.

80, v.17
Let thy hand be upon the man of thy right hand, upon the son of man whom thou madest strong for thyself.

89, v.42
Thou hast set up the right hand of his adversaries; thou hast made all his enemies to rejoice.

98, v.1

O sing unto the Lord a new song; for he hath done marvellous things; his right hand, and his holy arm, hath gotten him the victory.

108, v.6

That thy beloved may be delivered; save with thy right hand, and answer me.

109, v.31

For he shall stand at the right hand of the poor, to save him from those that condemn his soul.

109, v.6

Set thou a wicked man over him: and let Satan stand at his right hand.

110, v.1

The Lord said unto my lord, sit thou at my right hand, until I make thine enemies thy footstool.

110, v.5

The Lord at thy right hand shall strike through kings in the day of his wrath.

118, vv.15, 16

The voice of rejoicing and salvation is in the tabernacles of the righteous: the right hand of the Lord doeth valiantly. The right hand of the Lord is exalted; the right hand of the Lord doeth valiantly.

121, v.5

The Lord is thy keeper: the Lord is thy shade upon thy right hand.

137, v.5

If I forget thee, O Jerusalem, let my right hand forget her cunning.

139, vv.9 10

If I take the wings of the morning, and dwell in the uttermost parts of the sea;
Even there shall thy hand lead me, and thy right hand shall hold me.

144, vv.7, 8

Send thine hand from above; rid me, and deliver me out of

great waters, from the hand of strange children; Whose mouth speaketh vanity, and their right hand is a right hand of falsehood.

Apart from the Psalms, and the specific cases in which handedness plays a part in the story (such as with the tribe of Benjamin) there are numerous scattered references from the Scriptures which reinforce this favour towards the right.

The tactics of Gideon when advancing on the hosts of Midian are well defined:

"And the three companies blew the trumpets, and brake the pitchers, and held the lamps in their left hands, and the trumpets in their right hands to blow withal: and they cried the sword of the Lord, and of Gideon."

Not always was the left hand despised. In the praise of wisdom, the Book of Proverbs (ch. 3) declares:

"Length of days is in her right hand; and in her left hand, riches and honour."

Jews used phylacteries—small leather boxes containing old Hebrew texts—attached to the arm or the forehead, as the equivalent of the amulet, a guard against evil. The phylactery was placed on the left arm, since it was believed that the heart was on the left side and that the arm, if bent, would protect it. Dr Wile reports on a further Jewish custom at Succoth, The Feast of Tabernacles:

"The worshippers wave a *lulab* in the right hand and hold an *etrog* (a citrus fruit known as 'Adam's apple') in the left hand. The *lulab* consisted of a palm branch, to the lower end of which was tied a piece of myrtle on the right side, and a piece of willow on the left side. The procedure is thus described: 'Facing east, holding the *lulab* in the right hand and the *etrog* in the left, the worshipper shook the former in the direction of east, south, west and north, up and down, forward and back, in acknowledgment of God's sovereignty over nature.' One notes the importance of the right hand, facing east, Creator of all, the source of light and life."

Wile adds that the symbolism of the fruit in the left hand may well have an affinity with the "forbidden" fruit of the garden of Eden, and be associated with Eve, who represented the left, female, inferior side which has always distinguished Hers from His.

XV

OTHER RELIGIONS

To recount equivalent stories and customs from religions other than Christianity would involve a great amount of duplication, since the myths as well as the facts have a distinct similarity. We might, however, choose one or two religious customs where, apart from Circumambulation which has a story to itself, handedness or sidedness plays its part.

The poet and moralist Edward Carpenter has classified religious fervour into three main categories—heavenly phenomena (the movements of the sun, moon, stars, etc. and the awe they created), the changing seasons, including growth of vegetation and food: and the mysteries of sex and reproduction.*

In Dr Wile's view, the basic element was sun-worship, which had been all over the world, in Japan, India, the Antipodes and South America as well as Europe and the Middle East. He can quote from the Assyrians, from the Zoroastrian faith of Persia, which regarded Mithras as the adjudicator between the powers of light and darkness, or left and right, from the Egyptians, and from the Hindus and Brahmans. In southern India, particularly, there were two opposing castes, the Right-Hand sect and the Left-Hand sect. The dextral form of worship, Dakshina, is rival to the left hand, known as Vami or Vamachari. It has even been asserted that battles took place between the two sects—a unique case, apart from the slingers of the Benjamites, who were only a tiny minority of their tribe.

The Aztecs and the Inca were some of the most fervent of sun worshippers: it became, in fact, the recognised state religion. The way of worship was to touch the soil with the

* *Pagan and Christian Creeds*: Harcourt, Brace, New York, 1920.

middle finger of the right hand, and touch the lips with some of the soil. Aztecs also faced east, as do Muslims facing Mecca, or Christians facing the altar.

In Japan, Shinto worship at one time devoted greater prominence to the eye than the hand. In the legends, the Sun-Goddess, Ama-terasu, was created out of the left eye, and the Moon-God, Tsuki-yo-mi, out of the right eye of the general Creator, Izanagi. Wile comments: "One strongly suspects that the era of this tale dates back to a period when the Japanese court faced south, and the sun arose on its left; but the increasing influence of the sun led to its dominance and power when later Japanese court position found the rising sun on the right side."

In Egypt, the idea of the left was associated with the setting sun. The god Set had once been popular, but was then denounced and dethroned, and deemed to be a devil. He was replaced by Osiris, and later by Hor, the symbol of the rising sun.

These two symbols, sharply contrasted, one meaning death and darkness, the other life and light, were characterised by the left eye and the right eye respectively. The eye of Hor, or Horus, became popular as an amulet.

The Roman cult of Mithras came into startling and dramatic prominence in England in 1954, with the discovery of a Mithraic temple in the heart of the City of London. While workmen were digging out the foundations for a large block of City offices, experts and volunteers were feverishly working against time among the bulldozers, to unearth treasures, including a perfectly preserved head of the God himself, a God particularly popular with men of the Roman legions, whether at home or, as in this case, on colonial service. Mithras has been, strangely enough, associated with the left hand, since certain bas-reliefs have shown him laying his left hand on a figure symbolising the sun. There can surely be little evidence for this: most standard portrayals of the God show him slaying a bull, and this he invariably does by placing his left knee on the bull's back, and cutting its throat with a dagger held in his right hand—an action picture which Roman legionaries could understand and applaud.

A Roman augur practising fortune-telling (right-handedly)
with a cock in the centre of the magic circle. The grains of
corn are seen on the perimeter of the circle, and the bird's
selection of them determines the secret word.

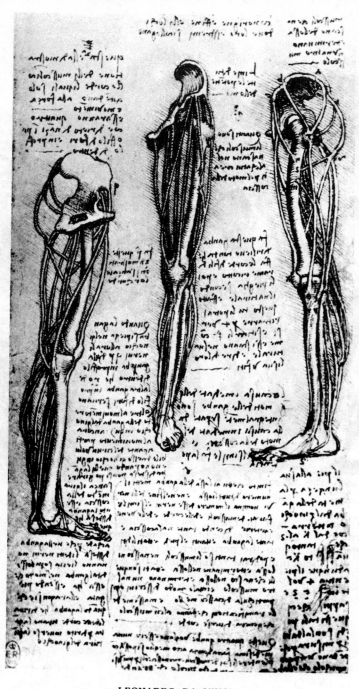

LEONARDO DA VINCI
Anatomy of the left leg, with notes added in the left-
handed mirror-writing which Leonardo always adopted.
From the collection in the Royal Library, Windsor Castle.

Yang and Yin

The Buddhists, whose prayer-wheels always rotated clockwise, believed in two cosmic principles, the Yang and the Yin. Yang was the guardian of the south, with a bird as its symbol. Yin, symbolised by the tortoise, was the opposing principle, and the guardian of the north. Augury was interpreted by these two, in terms of left and right, and there were the two usual labels—Yang, active, male, representing light and life and the right hand, Yin, passive, female, representing earth and darkness. The union of these two was the ultimate truth in a circle, the Tao, which is the supreme Chinese symbol.

The teaching of the Buddha has been variously interpreted, particularly in recent years, but the "way of life" as recommended by the Master has followed a familiar path, one towards a cross-roads. This was summed up very recently by E. B. Schnapper in his book on the Buddhist "way".*

"In the same way as the traveller through the wilderness is threatened by fearful beasts, so the follower of the Buddha's teaching, if he wants to cross to the farther shore, has to brave a monster-teeming sea, 'with devils and fearsome waves impassable'." Upon further request, the Buddha reveals something about the journey which must be taken towards Nirvana, the level ground which is the journey's goal.

"First, he makes clear the paramount need for non-clinging to all that is impermanent. Then he tells a parable: he tells of two men, one skilled, the other unskilled in wayfaring. The

* *The Inward Odyssey*: Allen & Unwin, London, 1965.

unskilled man asks the way and is told by the skilled man that after a little stretch the road will divide. The left-hand one is to be avoided, the one on the right is to be followed. This will lead successively to a thick forest, a marshy swamp, a steep precipice, and eventually to a delightful stretch of level ground (Nirvana)."

Then the Buddha himself explains the meaning. The skilled man represents an enlightened being, while the unskilled stands for the mass of the people: the divided way is the state of wavering; the left-hand path is the wrong way of life; the right-hand path is the eightfold path recommended by the Buddha.

Another significant feature is the representation of the Boh tree, beneath which Gautama was found in meditation. On each side a male figure holds the tip of the tongue with the thumb and forefinger of the left hand, and bears a garland with the right hand. The Buddha is said to have descended, as a white elephant, to enter Queen Maya's right side without piercing it.

The Swastika is perhaps the most famous symbol in history, even more celebrated than the Cross. The name, coming from the Sanskrit, means good luck or fortune, and in its usual form, with the hooks on the cross-shape facing left to right, appears on remains found as far back as the Neolithic period, and in places as far apart as India, Egypt, Greece, Italy, Spain, America, Mexico, Brittany and Ireland. "We have a clear indication," declared Professor Max Muller, "that the Swastika was originally a symbol of the sun, perhaps the vernal sun as opposed to the autumnal sun, the *Suavastika*, and, therefore, a natural symbol of light, life, health and wealth."

We may consider it remarkable that tribes and countries and centuries, which had no connection with each other, should have produced this common emblem. Thus it existed among American Indian and Indian tribes long before there was any knowledge of existence between the western and eastern hemispheres. And yet, as a device, it is very simple to draw, and clearly indicates the lucky movement from left to right.

In his book on Signs and Symbols, Albert Churchward gives

it an important place.* It becomes a directional sign, as with the Egyptians, who used it to indicate that ritual processions should proceed from left to right. One might almost think of it as a traffic signal:

KEEP RIGHT—ONE WAY ONLY

But Mr Churchward also recognises the existence of the Suavastika, in which the hooks on the cross are facing from right to left. He gives examples from Ireland and Scotland. The largest number of these sinistral swastikas, however, has been found in Southern India, where at one time there lived a left-handed sect.

This Suavastika was adopted by that lover of India, Rudyard Kipling, and decorated all his books. It is a symbol as familiar as the Moorish design adorning the works of the late Somerset Maugham—a design to ward off the Evil Eye.

But history will recall that one man, more than any other, is associated with the right-handed Swastika, and gave it a significance (whether as a symbol of good luck or sun-worship doesn't seem to be clear) which at one time tormented Europe and the world. His name was Adolf Hitler, who adopted the Hackenkreuz as the symbol of the Nazis.

This would seem enough to bring the history of the Swastika to an abrupt close. Unless the Suavastika acquires new popularity, the hooked cross is unlikely to reappear as the trademark of any group of men.

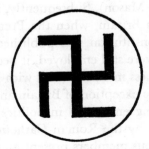

Swastika
(Hitler's emblem)

Suavastika
(Kipling's emblem)

* *Signs & Symbols of Primordial Man*: Allen & Unwin, London, 1910.

XVI

"THE LEFT KNEE BARE BENT"

The Freemasons, a famous cult with a powerful patronage in high places through the centuries, dates its origin to one of the major building projects of the Old Testament, the Temple of Solomon. The description of the Temple at Jerusalem takes up several chapters in the Second Book of Chronicles, and it is minutely described, measurements and all. Most important, from the Freemasons' point of view, were the two pillars erected in front of the Temple. The one on the right was called Jachin, the one on the left Boaz. So, the circumambulation of the Senior Deacon at the initiation must lead off with the left foot, advancing from west to east with five steps, as if ascending a winding staircase.

This is no place to consider the history of the movement, which must have originated with working masons, and which obviously gave the language such masonic expressions as "on the square", "on the level", and "third degree" (the status of a Master Mason). Subsequently, it was given its modern form in 1717 in Britain, when the Premier Grand Lodge was formed (the constitution was published in 1723). Although building terms were still employed, it became a benevolent organisation of business men, extended with Lodges all over the world, and, with the exception of Britain and the United States, frequently becoming embroiled in politics and anti-clericalism. It is still banned by the Roman Catholic Church.

Famous members present an astonishing variety, if we compare Washington, Burns, Mozart, and Hogarth, in the earlier years, and the many members of the British Royal Family in later years. It has enjoyed the direct patronage of the throne for several generations, and the Duke of Gloucester is the present Grand Master.

But it is also strongly connected, in its ritual, with handedness, or rather, laterality generally. The traditional march of the soldier begins with the left foot, and the "by the left!" command is given because he bears his weapon on the left, and might lose balance if he began with the right foot. This, then, became the practice in military Freemason lodges, and was extended to the civil lodges. But it was in contradiction to the Roman superstition that it was unlucky to enter a house with the left foot first. The Mason was therefore permitted to step on the threshold of the symbolic Lodge with the left foot, provided his subsequent step, over it and within, was made with the right foot.

The great hero of the Masons, Hiram Abiff, was in the great tradition of the dying and resurrected God: Adonis killed by a wild boar, and living again, Osiris killed by Typhon, Orpheus slain by the Bacchantes, Pythagoras by the mob, Moses abandoned in the rushes, Jesus condemned by the Jews.

The ritual of the Freemasons, and the celebrated signs with which members greet and exchange information with each other, is supposed to be secret. In fact, the penalty for divulging these mysteries is the fearsome one of having the right hand cut off and slung with a string over the left shoulder, "there to wither and die". The punishment has never, as far as one can gather, been carried out: it is just as symbolic as casting salt over the left shoulder to propitiate the Devil. But it remains on the masonic books.

At the Initiation of an Apprentice, he is led before his superiors, blindfold, and with his left trouser leg torn open (considering how much masonic regalia is hired, the outsider might wonder whether trousers could also be hired, already torn). According to the Catechism of 1776, he is then asked:

"When you was made an Apprentice, why was your Left Knee bare bent?"

The reply to be given:

"Because the Left Knee is the Weakest Part of My Body, and an Enter'd Apprentice is the weakest part of Masonry."

This is laterality with a vengeance, and the various signs given secretly between full members are also based on the right and left hand, in a series of infinite variations.

Although he does not seem to have been punished by the supreme penalty for revelation of the signs, one calling himself "Disgusted Brother" published what he alleged to be a number of the Freemasons' signs.*

Most of them are so simple as to appear, to the initiated, accidental, and many concern pockets in the clothes. (It will be remembered that the original Latin word *laevus*, meaning left, indicated the pocket of the toga, which was on the left side.) The signs were indicative of the days of the week, and this is how "Disgusted Brother" read them:

Sunday sign: right hand in pocket of breeches, with thumb out, pointing to the left side.

Monday sign: left hand in left pocket, thumb out, pointing to the right side.

Tuesday sign: right hand in right waistcoat pocket, with thumb out, pointing left.

Wednesday sign: the reverse—left hand in left waistcoat pocket, with thumb out, pointing right.

Thursday sign: right hand in right coat pocket, with thumb and forefinger out, pointing downwards.

Friday sign: exactly opposite—for right, read left.

Saturday sign: putting the first three fingers of the right hand to that part of the right eyebrow next the ear, and so drawing it along till the 3rd finger touches the nose.

"Disgusted Brother" asserts, in the 18th century, that these signs "are observed exactly the same by all Masons throughout the Globe". He adds that a Brother meeting a Brother must first give the signs of the two preceding days, and then he returns

* *Secrets of the Freemasons*, printed by J. Scott at the Black Swan in Paternoster Row, London, 1759.

the 7th or Saturday sign. It would obviously be easier if they met on a Monday.

Another writer on Freemasonry is one Walton Hannah, whose alleged revelations were published nearly two hundred years later.* This enlarges on the hand signs, particularly as a form of greeting, and divides them into the Masonic degrees. Here are a few examples:

First Degree: Penal Sign

The right arm is held horizontal with the shoulder, with the elbow bent, and the hand held horizontally with the thumb, to the left of the windpipe. The sign is completed by drawing the hand across the throat and dropping it to the side.

The Grip: The thumb pressed into the first joint of the forefinger. Presumably right-handed. There seem to be variations on this.

Second Degree: The Sign of Fidelity

The right hand is placed on the left breast with the thumb pointing upwards.

Third Degree (The Master Mason)

Penal Sign: The right hand is held horizontally, palm downwards, with thumb at right angles to left of navel. It is then drawn across the body, to the left, then to the right.

Sign of Sympathy: Head bent forward, and the forehead struck gently with the right hand.

Sign of Horror:† dropping the left hand a little out from the body, with the palm facing outwards. The right hand is raised, its back to the face, and the head is turned over the right shoulder.

---

* *Darkness Visible*: Augustine Press, London, 1954.

† The Sign of Horror seems a favourite among Freemasons. Bernard Jones, in his *Freemasons' Guide* (Harrap, London, 1950) writes, "who has not noticed the look of horror on a guest's face when his left-hand neighbour at table has attempted to pour him wine with his left hand?"

Third Degree: at Closing Time of the Lodge

The Five Points of Fellowship between Junior Warden and Master are as follows:

Hand to hand, right foot alongside right foot, knee to knee, breast to breast, with the left hand over the back. The Master "locks up the secrets" with right hand on left breast.

Hannah gives the positions taken up by the chief officers in the Lodge as follows:

Senior and Junior Deacons to the right of the Grand Master.

The Junior Warden in the southward position—the sun in meridian.

The Senior Warden in the westward position—to indicate the setting sun, and the closing of the Lodge.

The Master in the eastward position—to open and enliven the day with the rising sun.

It will be seen from this that the whole aspect of Freemasonry is concerned with the motions of the sun and with the sun-wise circumambulation, as well as with the left and right hand. When the Apprentice is initiated, there are elaborate instructions, according to Hannah, which include the lead with the left foot, kneeling on the right knee with the left foot forward. If the initiation rite is broken, the penalty is said to be "the left breast torn open, and the heart given to the ravenous birds of the air". Again, there is mercifully no record of this ever having been performed, but the warning was at one time apparently there.

This Freemasons' Song is quoted by "Disgusted Brother":

> "The Grand Architect
> Whose word did erect
> Eternity, Measure, & Space,
> First laid the Fair Plan
> On which we began
> The Cement of Harmony and Place.
> Like Pillars we stand &c."

"Then let us unite
    Sincere and upright
On the level of virtue to stand:
    No mortal can be
    So happy as we,
With a Brother and Friend in each Hand!
    Like pillars we stand, &c."

"The World is in pain
    Our secrets to gain
But still let them wonder and gaze on:
    They ne'er can divine
    The word or the Sign
Of a Free and an Accepted Mason."

XVII

THE LEFT HAND IN LITERATURE

"Let not the right side of your brain know what the left side doeth."

BERNARD SHAW: *John Bull's Other Island*

There is no well-known Left-Handed Hero in history or in fiction. Possible candidates might be Ehud the Benjamite, or Leonardo da Vinci—or even Satan himself as described in *Paradise Lost*. Milton wrote of his prose style: "This manner of writing wherein knowing myself inferior to myself, I have the use, as I may account it, but of my left hand." But Satan emerges in the poem, not specifically as a left-hander, but with many heroic characteristics, shouting defiance against God's "red right hand".

One of the earliest references to the left hand in war is in a major work by the Welsh border priest Layamon, whose 12th-century poem *Brut*, a variation on the Arthurian legend, is in the curriculum of most university students of English:

"Ich igrap mi sweord mid mire leoft honde."

Langland, in the 14th-century *Piers Plowman*, repeats the Bible quotation: "Let not thy left half, our Lord teacheth ywite what thou dealest with thy right side."

With the Elizabethan dramatists, increase in the good and bad luck aspects begin to appear. They knew their Aristotle, who had said: "That is the right side, from whence the motion of the body beginneth, the active or moving side; but that the sinister which is the weaker or more quiescent part." So Shakespeare could make Hector cry to Ajax in *Troilus and Cressida*:

"This hand is Grecian all,
And this is Trojan; the sinews of this leg
All Greek, and this all Troy; my mother's blood
Runs on the dexter cheek, and this sinister
Bounds in my father's . . ."

Cassio, emerging from the brawl in *Othello*, exclaims: "Do not think, gentlemen, that I am drunk. This is my right hand, and this is my left!" Perhaps Shakespeare thought back to the Bible story of Nineveh, "that great city, wherein are more than sixscore thousand that cannot discern between their right hand and their left." Hamlet, in declaring "the hand of little employment hath the daintier sense" was no doubt referring to the left.

Beaumont and Fletcher in *The Captain* (1613) took the derogatory view:

"That thou mayst know him perfectly, he's one of a left-handed making, a lanck thing."

Philip Massinger: "I would not give up the cloak of your service to meet the splay foot of any leftey'd knight of the Antipodes, because they are unlucky to meet." The connection with the left and the southern hemisphere is interesting at this early stage.

John Donne:

"Although a squint left-handednesse
Be ungracious, yet we cannot want that hand."

Thomas Middleton in *The Changeling*: "I'll go up and play left-handed Orlando among the madmen"—a reference to the belief that left-handers were often mentally afflicted.

Ben Jonson in *The Silent Woman*, speaks of one "that would not be put off by left-handed cries".

Robert Herrick:

"God has a right hand, but is quite bereft
Of that which we do nominate left."

Lovelace:

> "That which still makes her mirth to flow
> Is our sinister-handed woe."

Thomas Fuller: "A good artist is left-handed to no profession."

Dryden:

> "And while Jove holds us out the bowl of joy
> 'Tis dashed with gall by some left-handed God."

It all adds up to the superstition of bad luck on the left, a legacy of classical augury.

In later years, more practical consideration of the sinistral is found. Richard Steele noted, in *The Tatler*, the habits of certain swordsmen: "They are all left-handed, and have always been very expert at single rapier." Boswell, in his *Journal* of 1775, refers to the table manners of the King Louis XVI, from personal observation with Dr Johnson (supposed to have been a shifted sinistral): "The King fed himself with his left hand, as did we." Bolingbroke writes: "There is need of that left-handed wisdom", and in Walter Savage Landor's *Imaginary Conversations*, we find the phrase, "Thou hast some left-handed business in the neighbourhood, no doubt", a sentiment echoed in Washington Irving's *Salmagundi* ("We are indebted to the world for little else but left-handed favours."). Morganatic or left-handed marriage is referred to elsewhere, but we can recall Horace Walpole's dictum: "The children of a left-handed alliance are not entitled to inherit."

More romantic is Fitzgerald's stanza in the *Rubaiyat of Omar Khayyam:*

> "Dreaming when Dawn's Left Hand was in the Sky
> I heard a voice within the Tavern cry
> Awake, my little ones, and fill the Cup
> Before Life's Liquor in its Cup be dry."

Charles Reade, humanitarian and author of *The Cloister and The Hearth*, had this to say in his pamphlet *The Coming Man:* "There is certainly amongst mankind a vast weight of opinion against my proposition that man is by nature as either-handed as an ape; and that custom should follow nature. The majority believe the left arm and hand inferior to the right in three things: power, dexterity, and dignity. Nor is this notion either old fashioned or new-fangled. It is many thousands of years old; and comes down by unbroken descent to the present day."

Benjamin Franklin, statesman, philosopher, author and inventor, a man of incredibly diverse genius, wrote what is perhaps the most encouraging letter the sinistral could ever hope to read. It may seem surprising that Franklin could spare the time from his activities as agent for the American colonies and inspirer of radical French thought, to pen a letter on behalf of the Left Hand. Yet it was a serious attempt to recommend ambidextrality to the teaching profession. It is called, "A Petition to Those Who Have the Superintendency of Education".

"I address myself to all the friends of youth, and conjure them to direct their compassionate regard to my unhappy fate, in order to remove the prejudices of which I am the victim. There are twins sisters of us; and the eyes of man do not more resemble, nor are capable of being on better terms with each other than my sister and myself, were it not for the partiality of our parents, who made the most injurious distinction between us.

"From my infancy I have been led to consider my sister as a being of a more educated rank. I was suffered to grow up without the least instruction, while nothing was spared in her education. She had masters to teach her writing, drawing, music and other accomplishments, but if by chance I touched a pencil, a pen, or a needle I was bitterly rebuked; and more than once I have been beaten for being awkward, and wanting a graceful manner."

So far, Franklin has merely voiced the prejudice of his time in dealing with left handers. But the Left Hand then postulates the question—what would happen if her right-handed sister were to suffer injury or disease?

"Must not the regret of our parents be excessive, at having

placed so great a difference between sisters who are so perfectly equal? Alas! We must perish from distress; for it would not be in my power even to scrawl a suppliant petition for relief . . .

"Condescend, sir, to make my parents sensible of the injustice of an exclusive tenderness, and of the necessity of distributing their care and affection among all their children equally. I am, with profound respect, Sirs,

"Your obedient servant,

THE LEFT HAND"

XVIII

LEONARDO AND THE LEFT

Leonardo da Vinci is the Patron Saint of the Sinistrals. Famous in his lifetime, his reputation has grown through the centuries. For one of his cartoons, the drawing of the Holy Family, £800,000 was raised, in order to keep it in London's National Gallery. At the end of the runway at Rome's latest da Vinci airport, a huge statue of Leonardo stands. Appropriately, it is his left hand which is raised in greeting to the visitors.

It was said of Leonardo, "he took all knowledge as his province". In his Introduction to the *Notebooks*, Edward McCurdy describes his many-sided activities as: "The working of the mightiest machine that perhaps has ever been in a human brain." J. P. Richter, presenting Leonardo's literary work, declares: "His genius is universally recognised as one of the greatest mankind has ever produced." Superlatives come easily when people write about Leonardo, and he deserved them all.

The young man who worked for a number of years in the studio of Verrocchio in Florence amazed his colleagues in the *bottegha* by the diversity of his interests and talents. No one was surprised when he set up an amateur dissection room next door to the studio. After a day's painting, he would write, always in that secret, mirror script which caused such confusion and hard labour for his chroniclers and translators. He wrote on a wide variety of subjects; art, poetry, music, philosophy among the humanities; biology, anatomy and many other medical matters; the nature of light, the pattern of the earth's geography, the meaning of religion. Among practical descriptions and inventions, he showed himself far ahead of his time; he could have been a Vauban, a Corbusier, a Hiram Maxim, one of the Wright Brothers. The drawings show an armoured car, an alarm clock, skin-diving and aqua-lung equipment, a parachute, two flying machines, a helicopter, a bomb exploding among soldiers, an oil lamp with its rays magnified by water in a globe, a submarine he designed for the siege of Venice, and a system of underground streets. Leonardo would have been very much at home in a world of astronauts and computers and television.

The largest book of mirror-writings in the world is divided into several sections at Windsor Castle, South Kensington, Paris, Bologna. But before we consider this phenomena of writing, let us consider the evidence on Leonardo's left-handedness, not only as writer, but in his more famous sphere as artist.

Vasari, a contemporary of da Vinci, described, in his *Life*, the disapproval of his grandfather at the use of the hand which was, in those days, associated with sorcery and wizards and the Black Arts. (Curiously enough, dabbling in Black Magic is one of the few things Leonardo seems to have avoided, and there is no drawing of a Philosopher's Stone in the *Notebooks*, and no recipe for the conversion of base metals into gold.) Vasari also noted the peculiar handwriting.

"He wrote backwards, in rude characters, and with the left hand, so that anyone who is not practised in reading them, cannot understand them."

Merejowsky, whose florid and sometimes fanciful account of Leonardo's life gives a vivid picture of the age, added a possible reason.

"Beltraffio noticed that he held his pencil not in the right but in the left, and reflecting: 'He is left-handed', recalled the strange rumours which were current about him; Leonardo was reputed to write his compositions in a reverse script which could only be read in a mirror—not from left to right, as we all do, but from right to left, as they write in the Orient. People said he did this to conceal his criminal, heretical thoughts about Nature and God."*

* *The Romance of Leonardo da Vinci*: Merejowsky, New York, 1928.

Another explanation is that Leonardo had the waywardness of a genius, and simply liked to mystify people with this *tour de force*. As Sir Cyril Burt put it:

"Leonardo's manuscripts may have been written with the left hand, to relieve an overworked right hand, just as he is said to have frequently changed hands when painting; but it is equally conceivable that, being of an eccentric turn, he delighted in the feat for its own sake—a motive occasionally found in brighter children."

There can be little doubt about the left-handedness itself. The earliest authority is the contemporary mathematician, Fra Luca Pacioli, who described Leonardo's left-handed line in drawing as having "an ineffable sweetness which has not been equalled since Albrecht Durer". Pacioli also noted the handwriting (*"Scrivesi allo rovescia e mancina"*). A modern authority, A. E. Popham, Keeper of Prints at the British Museum, is equally certain:

"One factor in Leonardo's drawings is constant, his left-handedness. He apparently never drew with his right hand, and the strokes of the pen or other instrument where they can be distinguished, slope down from left to right, not in the normal direction from right to left."

Popham adds that on the rare occasions when he adopted the normal mode of handwriting, he did it so that the result should be easily legible to others, as in marking the place-names on maps. After close examination, he concluded that there was no instance of a genuine drawing having been executed with the right hand.

It was Merejowsky who stated, without giving any definite proof, that while Leonardo drew and wrote left-handedly, his painting was done with the right hand. Many painters of the time seem, like Michelangelo, to have been ambidextral, so this is not at all unlikely. One important piece of evidence in support of this has been overlooked until this present work. A left-hander will instinctively, when folding his hands, place the left hand outermost, just as he will instinctively cross his left leg over the right. In the drawings made for Leonardo's most famous portrait, the Mona Lisa, the left hand can, in two examples at least, be seen to be placed over the right; but in the final painting of La Gioconda, the *right* hand is over the left. One can perhaps imagine Leonardo saying to himself, "There's something wrong here," and asking Mona Lisa to switch over hands, because, to a right-hander, it seemed more natural. The sittings with La Gioconda are well known to have been some of the longest on record, and were accompanied by musicians, whose airs would, Leonardo hoped, preserve that enigmatic smile. "All this," wrote Walter Pater, "has been to her but as the sound of lyres and flutes, and lives only in the delicacy with which it has moulded the changing lineaments, and tinged the eyelids and the hands." But no man knows which hand held the brush which painted her. The drawings from the Windsor Castle collection are not in doubt. The Sinistral can claim them.

There remains another mystery, perhaps the most interesting of them all. Was Leonardo da Vinci naturally left-handed, or did he adopt that hand as the result of an injury? If we accept cerebral dominance as the primary factor in handedness, the importance of the question becomes obvious.

The 500th Anniversary of Leonardo's birth (April 15th, 1452) was celebrated throughout the artistic world, and the Exhibition of his work at the Royal Academy in London was an event so popular that the queues were longer than those for a top West-End film. Many pages of the *Notebooks* were displayed, and the question of Leonardo's true sinistrality was raised again.

One of the best analyses of the subject came from a doctor, Norman Capener, F.R.C.S., writing in *The Lancet* a few days after the Quincentenary.

"Though it is, of course, true that Leonardo usually used his left hand," the doctor wrote, "I am not at all sure that he was properly a left-handed person. By this I mean, from the neurological viewpoint, he was not clearly a right-cerebral-hemisphere-dominant individual. . . . I believe there is reasonable doubt about this, and that to dismiss him as left-handed (as has so often been done) is to take too superficial a view of the matter."

Dr Capener found the evidence he was seeking in a reproduction of a drawing of the left hand with a drawing pencil. This was noted in the catalogue as evidence of left-handedness and mirror-writing. Dr Capener declares that, if Leonardo were drawing his own hand, he would have done so in a "speculum", or actual mirror. Looking closer, Capener notices that there is something peculiar about that hand.

It is "somewhat deformed by the middle finger being twisted and shortened. The presence of a pencil in the right hand does not surprise me. There are difficulties in using a pencil for the finer movements of shading and writing, which are largely phalangeal movements, without the support of the middle finger; and the middle finger of the drawing may well have got in the way. . . . I believe that for the more dynamic drawing of shape and structure Leonardo probably used his right hand, but for the contemplative aspects of shading and writing he used the left hand."

Was Leonardo's right hand crippled? This is the question which has several times been argued. Richter refers to the artist being involved in a brawl, and reporting "thank God for having escaped from murderers with only one hand dislocated". The quotation is in the Eastlake Library of the National Gallery in London. One of the criminals, the note adds, was beheaded. Additional evidence is contained in the Diary of one Antonio de Beatis, Secretary to the Cardinal of Aragon, who visited Leonardo in his old age at Amboise. The painter was living in the manor house of Cloux, the gift of King Francis I. He apparently showed his guest his paintings of John the Baptist, and the Madonna with St Anne, and the Secretary observed that paralysis had afflicted his right hand, "so that he could no longer paint with such sweetness, but still occupied himself with making drawings".

A final judgment will probably never be possible. "Better is a small and certain thing than a great falsehood", Leonardo wrote in his *Notebook*. The question of his sinistrality is no small thing, particularly for the apologists of the Left Hand. If they can claim such a mighty man as being right-brained, it is a powerful argument in favour of leaving left-handers alone, to pursue their own way of life. If, as Dr Capener argues, an injury to the right hand urged Leonardo to use his left, this may have resulted in an increased use of both spheres of the brain, the desired aim of the Ambidextralists.

XIX

THE LEFT HAND IN MUSIC

Playing the piano is a good example of the marriage of true hands, each one in balance and harmony with the other. No one could tell, from listening to a concert pianist or organist, from C. P. E. Bach to Cole Porter, that the player was sinistrous. Only when an accident happens to one hand is the marriage broken, and even then the accident need not have fatal results.

The case of the English pianist Cyril Smith is interesting. His life has been a triumph against obstacles. One example, his name. As far as the concert world is concerned, the reply to "What's in a name?" is "Quite a lot". In his autobiography* the pianist writes:

"It is a proud, bold achievement to be born a Yorkshire Smith, and to save me from becoming too swollen-headed about it, my parents gave me the undistinguished Christian names of Cyril James."

With everyone else dropping their Christian names and appearing as Niedzielski and Solomon and Horowitz and Cortot and even Liberace, it was difficult to see how the brilliant young pianist could be billed simply as "Smith", but as Cyril Smith he played his way into a very high rank of performance, specialising in duets with his wife, Phyllis Sellick. (The name Smith can, of course, lead on to fame and fortune, from F. E. Smith the lawyer to W. H. Smith the bookseller, and Ian Smith of Rhodesia.)

Cyril Smith had suffered one thrombosis, but continued to keep up an arduous annual round of international concerts. In

* *Duet for Three Hands*: Angus & Robertson, London, 1958.

May 1956, with his wife and several other well-known British musicians, he was in a plane flying from Kiev to Kharkov on a Soviet Union tour, when a second stroke took place. It was just as well that he was naturally right-handed, for the left side of his body was paralysed. "Where on earth is my left arm?" was his first thought as he came to, and the appalling truth dawned on him.

At Kharkov Hospital, weeks later, the truth was confirmed. The doctor said briefly: "He will never play again." But even while he was in Russia, his wife recalls that he said: "If we can't play with four hands, we shall play with three," and though, on his return to England, another doctor reconfirmed the Soviet verdict, Cyril Smith began to devise a three-handed technique which was to bring him back to the concert platform.

"There was no hope of my ever playing solo again," he wrote. "Some works have been written for the left hand alone, but none for the right. The right thumb is on the wrong side, as it were, to produce a satisfying performance one handed. It also occurred to me that with two right hands and one left, we might be able to produce a better balance than we had done with four. The great snag about four hands on one piano is that one hand is virtually playing the tune while three hands provide the accompaniment, and one of our greatest difficulties had been to get this balance right. We had often said, jokingly, that two left hands were a nuisance, and those left hands had had to do a lot of sketching in, scarcely articulating the notes."

He re-scored a Mozart sonata, and the unique duet began. At first he described the experience as "rather like running a three-legged race", and the way back was a long and difficult one, owing as much to his sense of insecurity as to technical problems. Cyril Smith adds: "In a way I was lucky. If my right hand had gone, I should have had to concentrate my energies on being a solo pianist, and this would have been far more difficult. I should have had to work alone. Instead, without even asking for it, I had all the help that was necessary."

Piano concertos for the left hand are not numerous, and seem to arise for some personal reason, such as affected Cyril Smith. When pianist Harriet Cohen cut her right hand badly on a broken glass, composer Benjamin Britten wrote a left-hand concerto in order to revive her confidence during the long period when her career was in danger of collapse. It was psychologically a turning point in her life when she finally agreed to play it on the concert platform, urged on by Britten's insistence, but it has also remained in the repertoire, and is a skilful exploitation of the left hand's potentialities. Prokoviev's Concerto of a similar kind does not, it seems, have a similar story behind it. The earliest and most interesting example belongs to that spectacular composer from the Basque Country, Maurice Ravel.

Ravel was born on the outskirts of St Jean-de-Luz, and his modest birthplace still stands among the cafés and restaurants along the sea-front. His life, like his music, is full of contrasts and colour. His biographer, Madeleine Goss,* describes how later he lived in a curious house, "La Belvedere", at Montfort L'Amaury, near Rambouillet, with his Siamese cat, Mouni, his mechanical nightingale, Zizi, and enthusiastic pupils who included Vaughan Williams.

Ravel also visited the United States twice. It was during the second tour that he decided to compose two concertos, employing jazz effects. The first, in G, followed the conventional pattern. The second in D Major, was written for his Austrian friend, Paul Wittgenstein, who had lost his right hand in the 1914–1918 war. It proved to be a challenge both to composer and performer, demanding tremendous technical virtuosity, and, with its use of *fortissimo* chords, has been compared with a Brandenberg concerto in modern jazz form. Madeleine Goss adds: "It is indeed quite dramatic. The solo part is devised so as to give the impression of a texture no thinner than that of a part written normally for both hands."

The concerto received its first performance in Vienna, on November 27th, 1931, with Wittgenstein as soloist. He found the part so difficult to play that he was at first unable to

* *Bolero, The Life of Ravel*: Henry Holt, New York, 1940.

undertake any future performances, and Ravel had to turn to the pianist Jacques Fevrier to demonstrate his virtuoso piece. The critics did not take kindly to it, and the concerto is not often played. As one of Ravel's last works, it was, in the words of the critic Gageure, "a witness to the pathetic struggle which had already been declared between his creative intelligence and implacable disease". By contrast, Frederic Bonavia declared: "It is not a curiosity, but as good and eloquent a piece of music as Ravel ever wrote."

Whatever its musical worth, the dedication which the composer wrote on the score shows that he, a right-hander, was sensitive to the prejudice against the Other Hand.

"This is not so much to show what the left hand can do, but to prove what can be done for the appendage that suffers from sinistral stigma."

Left-handers must include Ravel in their gallery of dextral heroes, along with Benjamin Franklin and Sir Thomas Browne.

It is to the contributor to Grove's *Dictionary* that we owe the knowledge that one of the sons of Bach—the great Johann Sebastian had eleven of them out of two marriages—was a sinistral. His second child, Carl Philipp Emanuel, became, in his lifetime, more famous than his father, and is still the second Bach we think of, though of his twenty symphonies, fifty clavier concertos and innumerable chamber and choral works, few are remembered today. To quote from Grove:

"The view that Johann Sebastian destined him for a learned profession is improbable. Though he was left-handed, and therefore impeded in the playing of all instruments except the clavier and organ, his musical precocity was remarkable."

There does not seem to have been a very warm relationship between the sinistral C.P.E. and his parents. He seems to have plundered his father's works considerably after his death, and though a celebrated and affluent musician, allowed his mother to end her days in an alms-house. Of his success there was no question. Mozart himself was proud to direct his oratorio "The Resurrection and Ascension of Christ" at Vienna in 1787, and

Haydn wrote: "Whoever knows me well must see that I owe a great deal to Emanuel Bach."

The left-handed son, by sticking to keyboard and choral music, had become a paragon, if an ungrateful one. It is a long passage of time to modern left-handed composers such as Cole Porter, Johnnie Dankworth, and Paul McCartney.

A musical instrument which can be affected by handedness is, of course, the violin. The instrument is invariably made, and strung, to be played from the left shoulder, with the right hand holding the bow. No Stradivarius or Guarnerius ever envisaged a sinistral fiddler. Today there is a very small but steady proportion of children who express a preference to play the other way round, and this can be done—at a cost.

A representative of the famous, century-old London firm of J. P. Guivier, whose founder left for the Franco-Prussian War in 1870, explained the process necessary. Not only would the strings have to be changed in order, with E on the far left and A on the right, but the pegs themselves would have to be switched and re-inserted. As far as the interior of the instrument is concerned, the wooden ridge (bridge-bar or bass-bar) would have to be removed from its position just right of centre, to the other side, or the interior sound-post would not transmit the correct vibration. Apart from these alterations, there is no reason why a left-strung violin should not be as effective as a conventionally-strung one. But the chin-rest is always made facing right to left, and Mr Wilks of Guiviers knew of no specially-manufactured rest facing the other way. In his view, there is no reason why a left-handed child should not be encouraged to play as a right-hander from the start. Children, he pointed out, don't pick up a violin instinctively, and try to play it, since they lack information about its use, and it is after all, a two-handed instrument, in which both hands are important.

A celebrated example of a left-handed violinist is Charlie Chaplin, who also composed most of the music for his later films. In his autobiography* he writes

* *My Autobiography* by Charles Chaplin: Simon & Schuster, 1964.

"On this tour I carried my violin and cello. Since the age of sixteen I had practised from four to six hours a day in my bedroom. Each week I took lessons from the theatre conductor or from someone he recommended. As I played left-handed, my violin was strung left-handed, with the bass bar and sounding post reversed. I had great ambitions to be a concert artist, or failing that, to use it in a vaudeville act, but as time went on I realised I could not achieve excellence, so I gave it up."

Chaplin resumed playing, however, in the film *Limelight* (1952) where he is seen making a tender solo performance of his main theme from the film, and playing it "widdershins". This caused some comment at the time, since cinemagoers thought there was *something* wrong about the performance, but couldn't at first place it.

For the sinistral fiddler, there is no place in a full orchestra. Indeed, the spectacle of a forest of first-violin bows sweeping in one direction, and a lone bow battling in the opposite direction is in itself a subject for a Chaplin situation, or an episode from a Marx Brothers film. Only in quartets can a left-hander take his place with his dextral colleagues.

This, according to James Barton, once a violinist with the international Allegri Quartet, can be an aesthetic advantage in the matter of position, quite apart from performance. The two violins can each face inwards, towards the remaining players, thus forming a visually harmonious group. Rudolf Kolisch, born in 1896 in Austria, and now living in retirement in Wisconsin, suffered an injury to his left hand, and was forced to hold his violin with the right and the bow with his left. This did not prevent him from forming, in 1922, a quartet, under his own name, which achieved a considerable reputation until it was disbanded in 1939.

Apart from classical quartets, the groups, usually in fours, which have dominated popular music in these times, contain the occasional sinistral. The most celebrated is Paul McCartney of the Beatles group (born 1942) who is both composer and performer on the guitar. Writing in an illustrated "Pop" Picture Book, he revealed: "When I was a kid I seemed to do everything back to front. I used to write backwards, and every time the masters at my school looked at my book, they used to throw little fits.

"I had difficulties outside school, too. I couldn't learn to ride a bike because I would insist on pedalling backwards and was quite convinced that mine was the right way, and everybody else's was wrong.

"I do everything with my left hand, and no matter how hard I try I can't alter the habit. A doctor once told me I shouldn't try to, because being left-handed is something to do with the brain."

It is a far cry from Bach to the Beatles, yet the small but persistent number of sinistral musicians does not look like dying out yet.

XX

ANIMAL LIFE AND THE LEFT

> "The centipede was happy quite
> Until a toad in fun
> Cried, 'Pray, which leg goes after which?'
> Which worked her mind to such a pitch
> She lay distracted in a ditch
> Considering how to run."
>
> ANON

Of all animal reactions to handedness, those of the ape, the gorilla and chimpanzee are the most important. Observation at zoos seems to reveal an almost complete range of ambidextrality. As an example of minor fieldwork, the author approached the cage in the London Zoo containing the immense, saturnine figure of "Guy", the giant gorilla from what used to be French Equatorial Africa. A popsicle was thrown at his feet. He picked it up with the left hand and delicately peeled off the silver-paper wrapping with his right before eating it. After a pause, another was thrown on to the same spot. This time, without hesitation, the gorilla performed the entire operation in the same manner, but with the hands (or paws) reversed.

"Neither instinct nor natural selection," writes Dr Wile, "appears to account for specialization. . . . It is not necessary to prove the descent of man's handedness from his ape-like ancestors who, admittedly, were ambidextrous and ambilateral. It is sufficient to study man's own evolution from the days when he began to depend on his brain rather than his teeth, and to rely upon his hands rather than upon his feet."

The most popular attraction at London's Zoo is the chimpanzee's Tea Party, and there one can see that cups and plates and food are handled indiscriminately.

The most celebrated experiment in the comparison between early behaviour and intelligence in ape and human was initiated in 1931 by the Kelloggs—W. N. Kellogg, Associate Professor of Psychology in the University of Indiana, and his wife. They matched Gua, a young ape born in Cuba, with their only son Donald, and brought them up together for a year, publishing the findings in book form.*

We are concerned here only with the subject of handedness, and on the assumption that all apes are ambidextral, some interesting divergences occurred. The Kelloggs began with that simplest of all tests: holding up an object, and noting which hand instinctively stretches out for it. For the start of a nine-month period of training, the ape Gua reached with her left hand rather than her right. But, within a few weeks the preference had shifted to the right hand, and there it remained until, at about a year old, the young ape went back to the left hand. Summarising, the Kelloggs made this table:

Total L hand reaches	107
Total R Hand reaches	110
Total with both hands	2

The boy Donald was not subject to as many experiments, but showed almost exactly the same proportion of preferences, namely:

Total L hand reaches	37
Total R hand reaches	36
Total with both hands	13

This might prove nothing, but the Kelloggs were interested to note the variations over the period, particularly to account for the reversion to the left hand in the second phase. The initial right-hand preference could easily be explained, since if, in feeding, the spoon was arbitrarily placed in the right hand, that hand would benefit from the practice, and become preferred.

* *The Ape and the Child*: Whittesley House, McGraw-Hill, New York and London, 1933.

The recurrence of left-handedness was not so easy to account for.

"Probably the most plausible explanation, is that each of the experimenters fell, quite without design, into the habit of carrying the subjects in their left arms. They themselves developed an incidental hand or arm preference. This had the effect of placing the subject's right hand either around the neck of the experimenter or upon his shoulder. As a result, when objects were approached for which the subject might reach, his left hand was more free to make the reaching reaction."

So, in clinical language of "subject" and "experimenter", the 20th-century Kelloggs repeated an explanation which goes back to Plato, who complained that nurses carrying children on their left arms encouraged them to become left-handed. There seems no limit, in time or country, to the debate on this matter of early handedness.

Since the Kelloggs were aware of the theory of cerebral dominance, they were in the position to make another experiment on the ape. If the dominant brain centre controlled not only the opposite hand, but the whole side of the body, how about giving Gua a *foot*-preference test, since her feet were grasping organs, like the human hand?

The ape was seated on a table with her legs spread apart at an angle of nearly 90 degrees, and her hands held or tied behind her. "A piece of orange used as a reward is placed in a position midway between the feet. She thereupon grasps it with the toes of one foot or the other and transfers it to her mouth. Curiously enough, the net result of the foot-preference tests shows a crude sort of relationship to the handedness tests. . . . There are more positive than negative indications that reaching with the foot tends to parallel reaching with the hands. Gua's choices during the early and middle months are for the most part towards the use of the right foot; and about at the age when she begins to manifest a left-handed tendency, the foot preference changes correspondingly."

It was not a conclusive test, but did argue some sort of transfer from one portion of the body to another on the same side. But in fact, it probably isn't necessary to experiment with apes to discover this. A left-handed footballer is also, in nearly every case, a predominantly left-footed footballer.

Another animal whose hand- or paw-preferences have given the experts much evidence is the rat, often used for human experiment.

With rats there seems to be a very definite partiality for the dextral side, and one estimate declares that 80 per cent of rats are right-pawed. There has been much study on laterality with this rodent, including the treatise by Tsai and Maurer.* Only a small number of the animals examined appeared to be ambidextral, and the preference for the right paw extended to more habits than mere reaching for food through the narrow neck of a bottle, although it was not consistent in all these activities. Indeed, the important discovery was made that the paw-preference could be reversed, by an operation, or the administration of a drug.

This, performed by Dr G. M. Peterson and described in the *Journal of Comparative and Physical Psychology*, consisted in removing part of the brain, or, in medical language, making "a circumscribed lesion in the contralateral precentral cortex", a specific area of the brain. The drug applied was Acetylcholine.

The importance of this experiment lies in proving that hand-preference is connected with one side of the brain without the development of speech, which had always been held by many to be a vital factor which separated human from animal handedness. Dr Margaret Clark has stressed the value of this discovery, describing it as disposing of the "primitive warfare theory" in which man first became selective, and seeing a connection in the pattern of behaviour between children and animals, before the activity of writing begins. Dr Clark quotes one writer describing the infant as passing through "a fleeting, simian phase, with rudimentary random handedness". (Perhaps from that came the expression applied to a child as "a little monkey".)

* "Right-handedness in Rats", *Science*, Vol. LXXII, 1930.

Apes and rats have therefore given help to experts in trying to trace the origin of our manual behaviour. Presumably the Peterson operation could be performed on a human being: but it hardly seems that the question of handedness is vital enough to justify such a piece of surgery, and few would be found so addicted to the other hand that they would be prepared to undergo it—not even a left-hander in Morocco.

A spokesman in London's Natural History Museum puzzled many by referring to a "left-handed whelk". He was referring, of course, to the whorls or spiral markings on the shell-fish, which, in the case of the whelk, would normally run from right to left. That observant writer Jules Verne notes a similar discovery of a left-to-right whelk in *Twenty Thousand Leagues Under the Sea*. Similar "left" formations have been found on snails, and are said by some authorities to be hereditary.

The left-handed whelk in question, discovered in a sea-food shop at Walton-on-the-Naze, Essex, was said to be "extremely rare", and one expert computed that only about one in five million would have the spiral from the left. But a local fisherman declared he had a collection of eighteen, and had found about two specimens a year on his stretch of the coast. The left-handed whelk also has the honour to be mentioned in Webster's *International Dictionary*.

Patient research by experts has resulted in many odd discoveries about the fish world. Nature, it seems, generally favours a sideways movement or pattern, and this is more commonly from east to west, following the course of the sun. In ancient times this movement was held to be of the highest significance, determining good or bad luck—even as we have seen in the case of the Roman augurs, an omen of success or failure in battle.

But Nature knows no such moral distinctions. Apes and monkeys, man's ancestors, are happily ambidextral, as anyone who has been to that Chimps' Tea Party at the Zoo will realise. It might be thought that the fish world would be the same, but this is not so. Wile has made an exhaustive study of the finny species, with some surprising results. He quotes

SIR THOMAS BROWNE
Doctor, of Norwich. First champion of
the sinistral.

BENJAMIN FRANKLIN
Wrote a letter on behalf of the left-handed.

LEWIS CARROLL
Lived in a stammering, looking-glass world.

SIR COMPTON MACKENZIE
Played cricket, fills his pipe, left-handed.

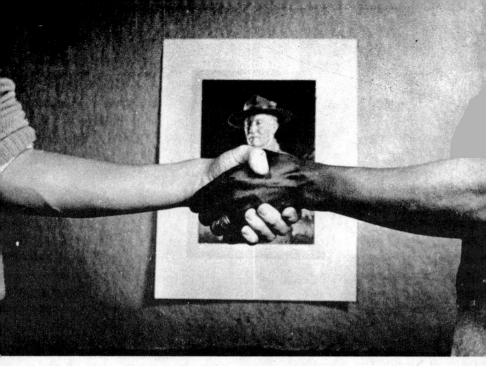

THE LEFT-HANDED HANDSHAKE

This is the custom of the Boy Scouts in every country. In the background, the ambidextral Lord Baden-Powell.

MICHELANGELO

Sinistral Michelangelo's Adam, from the Sistine Ceiling, receives life through his left hand.

Aristotle in noting that most lobsters have the right claw larger and more developed than the left, and this is the claw used to get their food. But the left-and-right difference becomes more marked in the case of the flat fishes. These have only one eye, and it is not always on the same side. "As flat as a flounder", is a popular phrase. But on *which side* is the flounder lying, on the bed of the sea? The side with the single eye uppermost, obviously, and in the case of the flounder, this is the right side. The same is true of the Dover sole and plaice. The halibut, however, is of the opposite persuasion, with its eye on the left. The United States Commissioner of Fishes reported, as long ago as 1886:

"As the tropical *Hippoglossinae* (Halibut) and the *Pleuronectinae* (flat fish) are sinistral species, the eyes and colour being on the left side of the body, it follows that the tropical flounders are nearly all left-sided species, while those of the arctic and antarctic waters are chiefly dextral species, the eyes and colour on the right."

One clue, then, is in the temperature of the seas inhabited by the fish. If the Dover sole be dextral, the sole species in the Mediterranean and Indian waters is sinistral. It cannot merely be light and the rotation of the sun, for the halibut is persistently left-eyed in both the northern and southern hemispheres. One cannot but admire the patience with which the experts have pursued the problem of the *Pleuronectinae* and sympathise with them for failing to reach any definite reason for the differences.

XXI

RIGHT-HANDED BATH-WATER?

One of the most popular "teaser" questions among ordinary people is to ask, "Does your bathwater go left or right?" The favourite immediate answer, without a test being made, is "right", with the qualification that if you were south of the equator, it would go left. The last time the author was presented with this reply, he made the test in his own bath-room, to find that the water went clockwise in the hand basin, and anti-clockwise in the bath. The basin faced north, the bath east, but that is not likely to have accounted for the difference, though the question is in some way connected with the movement of the earth.

An interesting reply on this point was made in the London *Daily Mail*'s "Problem Post" feature in 1965.

"In ordinary household baths what scientists call "the direction of the rotation of the plug-hole vortex" is a matter of chance. Variations in the surface and angle of the bath can affect it, so can the criss-cross of tiny currents set up in the water when we take a bath.

"Various scientific experiments have been carried out, however, on both sides of the equator, using containers which were absolutely symmetrical and water that had been allowed to settle to absolute stillness. Under those ideal conditions water north of the equator swirls away anti-clockwise, to the left; water south of the equator swirls happily away to the right. Reason: the effect of the earth's rotation."

So there is some sense in the trick question after all. Today we are so accustomed to thinking about getting off the earth and reaching the moon, that we may have lost any sense of

wonder or enquiry about the planet we inhabit ourselves. The
fact that we are rotating at a rate of about 89,000 miles an hour
fascinated Isaac Newton, and was reflected in Wordsworth's
memory of Lucy in her grave:

> "Rolled round in earth's diurnal course,
> With rocks and stones and trees."

Various chapters in this book show how this movement has
affected man, from his religious worship to his personal habits,
and this laterality obviously has some effect on handedness,
particularly in cases of the superstitious Circumambulation at
ceremonies. But we are here concerned with the physical
aspect, and the deflection which rotation must inevitably cause.
Tides are one of the clearest examples, whether they be
measured in the practical terms of an expert, or in the poetic
language of John Donne:

> "O more than Moone
> Draw not up Seas to drowne mee in thy Spheare."

If the sun had really stood still at the command of Joshua,
human history would have ended there, just as it nearly did,
in H. G. Wells's imagination, when his Man Who Could Work
Miracles ordered the earth to stop rotating. But man, and
animals and nature are all subject to external pressure due to
this rotation, and this pressure is generally to the right in the
northern and to the left in the southern hemisphere (which
seem to invalidate the bath-water experiment). This deflection
is at its greatest in the polar regions, and ceases altogether on the
equator. It is not a direct, centrifugal pressure, and any deflection experienced by a human being is unconscious. Nevertheless, observation of erosion, and currents in seas and rivers show
that it is there and acts in opposite directions according to the
hemisphere. The Baltic Sea, for instance, has had its deviation
calculated with a maximum of 25 degrees to the right, and rock
and valley formations follow the same pattern. Thus the valleys
of Long Island have steeper western slopes, and the coastal
valleys of South Carolina have been moulded by the right-hand

deflection of streams. Long ago Herodotus, as quoted by Dr Wile, notes the lateral habits of fish in the river Nile.

"When any of this sort of fish are taken on their passage to the sea, they are found to have the left side of the head scarred and bruised; while if taken on the return, the marks appear on the right. The reason is, that as they swim down the Nile seaward, they keep close to the bank of the river on their left, and returning up stream they still cling to the same side, hugging and brushing against it constantly, to be sure that they miss not their road through the great force of the current."

In North Polar Regions the explorer Nansen noticed that when an ocean current flows eastward, with the earth's own motion, it flows more rapidly than the earth moves, and its direction is towards the equator. A westward ocean current is slower, and flows away from the equator. Glacial drifts he also put down to the deflecting force arising from the earth's rotation. The spiral formations of trees and plants and even shellfish, also follows a pattern, but this, known as the tropisan theory, is more likely to be caused by the effect of light.

In the end, it all comes back to the sun, which is the earth's sole source of light.

"We are living in a predominantly right-handed world," says Ira Wile, "and the rotation of the earth about the sun, the relation of man's activities toward the return of the sun, and possibly, to a slight extent, the rotational deflective pressure towards the sun, all may have played a part in determining the dominance of the human right hand and its social values. The effect of the actual movement of the earth, the unappreciated impulse, permeating him and unifying him with his world, was more or less built into his neural being. It became organized in his sense of equilibrium and orientation, a factor in the achievement of a sense of balance through the interdependence of his eyes and hands."

Mathematicians have always been interested in problems of left and right, whether sidedness or handedness or movement. Dr Herman Weyl of Zurich devoted a whole book to the "harmony of proportions", as he described symmetry. This was not the "fearful symmetry" framed by William Blake's Tyger, but to geometric forms and transformations. He attempts to define the mathematical philosophy of left and right.

"To the scientific mind there is no inner difference, no polarity between right and left, as there is for instance in the contrast of male and female, or of the anterior and posterior ends of an animal. It requires an arbitrary act of choice to determine what is left and what is right. But after it is made for one body it is made for every body."

According to Leibniz, right and left are indiscernible, until the choice is made. Which way does the earth revolve? Like a right screw, if you face the magnetic pole: like a sinistral screw, if you face south. Right and left are relative concepts. In fact, says Dr Weyl, the whole theory of relativity is an aspect of symmetry, but it is one too abstruse to discuss here. We can, however, recall the famous controversy between Leibniz and Newton concerning the creation of the world. In their simplest forms, the two arguments were (a) from Newton, that motion was a proof of God's arbitrary will in the matter, otherwise there would be reason for matter moving in any particular direction (b) from Leibniz, that it was impossible "to give a reason why God should have put the bodies just at this particular place and not somewhere else; for instance, why He should not have arranged everything in the opposite order by turning East and West about".

Immanuel Kant's opinion is now canvassed, and Weyl sums up his argument: "That if the first creative act of God had been the forming of a left hand, then this hand...had the distinctive character of left, which can only intuitively but never conceptually be apprehended." Leibniz contradicted this, and the argument continued, and gradually ranged itself into the two groups of thinking: scientific, and mythical or religious, which convinced of the rival moral forces of good and evil, began to associate them with right and left respectively.

Weyl ends by quoting Christ's Vision of Judgment in the Gospel of St Matthew. In pictorial form, he includes a close-up of the detail in Michelangelo's "Creation of Adam" from the

Sistine Chapel roof. Adam reclines languidly on the world like someone who has just woken. God from his cloud has just touched his left-hand forefinger with his own right-hand forefinger. Therefore, in Michelangelo's view, creation began (or ended) with the human left hand. Since we know the artist has been credited with being as much left-handed as right, this may be just a personal preference, painted in what we might now call the Sinistrine Chapel!

XXII

PSYCHOLOGY AND THE LEFT

There seems to be disappointingly little material on handedness from the great psychologists, whose findings have affected so many of our traditional beliefs.

Freud is content to quote the views of Stekel, who in his *Die Sprache des Traumes* (1911) stated:

"Right and left in dreams have an ethical sense. The right hand means the path of righteousness and the left hand the path of crime." He then adds an interesting sexual footnote: "Left may represent homosexuality, incest, or perversion; Right, marriage, intercourse with a prostitute and so on, always looked at from the subject's individual standpoint."

Most of the psychologists at least seem to agree that the left does represent the unconscious.

Jung* quotes the Gnostic writings of the 2nd century A.D., in which good and evil are described—following the Vision of Judgment parable, no doubt—as the right and left hand. But they are put in the form of syzygies, that is, pairs of opposites. Good is light and right: evil is dark and left, and also responds to the feminine. "The rightward movement of the Gnostic process," he continues, "is the expression of conscious discrimination. The immediate cause is the rightward movement of our writing. The right is ruled by conscious reason. The left is the side of the heart, the emotions, where one is affected by the unconscious."

So the illusion still persisted that the heart was on the left, and it was to persist for many centuries. The leftward movement of the unconscious is particularly noticeable in the realm of dreams. Here are some of Jung's dream analyses.

* *Aion*: Routledge, Kegan Paul, London, 1959.

Dream 16

"Many people are present. They are all walking to the left around a square. They say that a gibbon is to be reconstructed."

Jung goes into an elaborate and learned analysis over the gibbon or monkey, and explains the movement thus: "Presumably the leftward circumambulation of the square indicates that the squaring of the circle is a stage on the way to the unconscious, a point of transit leading to a goal lying as yet unformulated beyond it. It is one of those paths to the non-ego which were also trodden by the medieval investigators when producing the *lapis* (philosopher's stone)."

Strange are the dreams which Jung considered in his long survey. This one has a Kafka-like quality.

Dream 22

The dreamer is in an American hotel. A dark woman gives him a note about salvation. He takes the lift to the 7th or 8th floor. Then the scene changes. There is said to be a revolution in Switzerland: the military party is making propaganda for "completely throttling the left". The objection that the left is weak enough anyway is met by the answer that this is just why it ought to be throttled completely. . . .

Another dream-interpretation involves the mirror-image of left and right.

Dream 26

It is night, with stars in the sky. A voice says, "Now it will begin". The dreamer asks, "What will begin?" Whereupon the voice answers, "The circling can begin". Then a shooting star falls in a curious leftward curve. The scene changes, and the dreamer is in a rather squalid place of entertainment. The proprietor, who appears to be an unscrupulous crook, is there with some bedraggled-looking girls. A quarrel starts about left and right. . . . The proprietor says, "What they said about left and right did not really satisfy my feelings. Is there really such a thing as a left and right side of society?" The dreamer answers, "The existence of the left does not contradict that of the right. They both exist in everyone. The left is the mirror-image of the right. Whenever I feel it like that, as a mirror-image, I am at one with myself. There is no left side and no right side to human society, but there are symmetrical and lopsided people. The lopsided are those who can only fulfil one side of themselves, either left or right. They are still in the childhood state." The proprietor says, "Now that's much better", and goes about his business.

"The idea of symmetrical proportion," comments Jung, "has been stripped of its cosmic character, and translated into psychological terms. 'Right' and 'left' are used almost like political slogans."

There are several other dreams in this book using the movement towards the unconscious.

Dream 52

A rectangular dancehall. Everybody is going round the periphery to the left. Suddenly the order is heard: "To the kernels!" But the dreamer has first to go into the adjoining room to crack some nuts. Then the people climb down rope ladders to the water. . . .

E. Gostynski studied the stereotyped gestures of a hysterical patient.* He found that the characteristics of the patient's right hand represented "a highly overdetermined condensation of various aspects of her developmental history". Numerous ego defences were analysed through these gestures—reaction formations or denials of infantile wishes, identification with the mother's contempt for the father, regression of the ego to the level of magical omnipotence, defences against an early hand-fetichism, etc. In a consideration of "handedness", Gostynski suggested that cerebral dominance may be the result, and not the forerunner, of an altered mental structure.

"The word symbols 'right' and 'left' cover a physical as well as a mental orientation. The physical orientation towards the right is paralleled by a tendentious shift in the abstract meanings

* *Annual Survey of Psychoanalysis*, Vol. 2: Int. Universities Press, N.Y., 1951.

of 'right' and 'left', characterising a movement away from the left."

The language of psychoanalysis is sometimes difficult for the layman to follow, but here is the brief explanation behind Gostynski's theory:

"The phenomenon of cerebral dominance represents a functional deposit in organic structure. This was acquired during phylogenesis, and was originally the result of one of the steps towards differentiation of mental structure into ego and id, with the deposition of the focus of an archaic superego and a focus of primary repression."

These are bold words, apparently, but they are also rather baffling. If proved, however, they might upset many of the ideas on cerebral dominance.

XXIII

LEFT-HANDED JACK

On August Bank Holiday, 1888, Martha Turner, a prostitute living in George Yard Buildings, Commercial Street, in London's East End, was found on one of the outside landings, stabbed, the postmortem revealed, thirty-nine times with some weapon like a bayonet.

Colin Wilson, in *My Search for Jack the Ripper*,* declares that many criminologists believe this to have been the first murder committed by the man who "exercises a fascination beyond any other mass murderer". The Ripper was never caught, and his identity never established. But the coroner at the inquest on Martha Turner revealed that the wounds had been inflicted by a left-handed man. The woman, says Wilson, had been seen with a guardsman the evening before the murder, and, since the weapon was thought to have been a bayonet, a parade was held of all the guards in the Tower of London, which is not far from the scene of the crime. No arrest was made, for no left-handed guardsman was found. But it was only the first of a series of appalling murders which almost terrorised the city. Jack the Ripper, therefore, may be said to hold a place of honour in any Rogue's Gallery of Sinistrals.

This example raises the question: how far are the police in any country made aware of handedness as a clue to crime, and what instructions, if any, are given by Scotland Yard or the F.B.I. to determine—particularly in the matter, say, of finger-prints on a weapon, or of the kind of butchery practised by the Ripper—whether laterality is a clue? In England, at any rate, it seems impossible to obtain any official information from the

* *Evening Standard*: August 8th, 1960.

authorities. An enquiry on behalf of the present book elicited the following reply from the Criminal Record Office of New Scotland Yard:

"I am directed by the Commissioner to say that Police Records are confidential and for official use only, and it is regretted that he is unable to accede to your request."

It may be thought that such information was if anything, in the public interest, but the official view obviously holds that it is not. Unofficially, information is easier to obtain. It appears that the Criminal Record Office does, in fact, record left-handedness "wherever and whenever it comes to the notice of the enquiring officer concerned". But no question about being left-handed occurs on the questionnaire. Sinistrality is not therefore looked for: as, in the instance of serviceman's questionnaire, a religion has to be quoted, and if non-existent, is cited as "Church of England". This is reasonable, considering that the incidence of sinistrality is probably even smaller than the incidence of church-going, but where a crime has been committed, and evidence is forthcoming, any suggestion of sinistrality would obviously narrow the field considerably.

Investigation among what are known as "underworld" characters, of the Damon Runyon type, but in this case British, have revealed a certain amount of superstition among those who ply their dubious trades. A criminal in London had time to say: "Left-handed screwsmen and petermen* are supposed to be better at their work than the normal right-handed ones. But there's a lot that won't work with left-handed mates—they say they bring bad luck. One left-handed chap I know never went out on a job without being nicked for it."

Moreover, left-handers are conspicuous, particularly if their trade is to do with their hands. One ex-prisoner, who admitted to original sinistrality very reluctantly, claimed that he had once been convicted on evidence that proved left-handedness. He had therefore seen to it that from this time forward, everything he did would be right-handed. There seems, in England, to have been very little research into the

* Underworld slang for a safe-robber.

connection between sinistrality and delinquence, though the Italian Dr Lombroso regarded left-handedness as one of the signs of degeneracy, and frequent among criminal types. The Indian, Dr Das, echoes this:

"The percentage of left-handedness is much higher in an abnormal class of people, e.g. mental defectives, insane, incorrigibles, criminals, etc." The British Home Office Research Unit does not seem to regard the evidence as very important, except where it is a definite factor in a specific case of crime.

One would expect finger-print tests to be important. It is obviously easy to detect whether the hand which held the gun or the knife was a left or right hand—and this, once again, would narrow the field. In a recent English murder case ("The Bodies on the Moor") the male defendant was an ardent pistol enthusiast, and according to the evidence, could shoot equally well with either hand (indicating that he was probably a sinistral who became ambidextral). One police officer in London claimed that he could tell from a man's "dabs" whether he was left or right-handed. Both hands are used for taking finger-prints in England.

Handwriting is another obvious clue. Not all left-handed writing slopes backwards (i.e. from right to left) but a graphological expert could tell handedness by other signs. In the important case of forgery, there is a belief that it is easier to escape detection when forging the signature of a left-handed man. This for two reasons: on a cheque, the bank would be less likely to query the signature because they would be used to variations in the signature; and left-handed writers normally write more slowly which would give the forger more time and care in his work, than if he were copying a signature made instinctively and at speed. There are, however, no known cases of forgers who were left-handed themselves!

Legal procedure, like religious ritual, is based on dextrality, but a curious anomaly exists in the matter of taking the oath. Normally, in every country, the usher tells the witness to take the Bible in his right hand, or to raise the right when swearing under oath. The British Oaths Act of 1888, however, merely states that the witness about to be sworn shall take the Book "in his uplifted hand", but not specifying which one. Presumably, the right hand being by tradition the exalted hand and representative of truth, honour and all the virtues, is the one selected by popular choice, but if there is any assumption that an oath so taken is more binding if one is dextral, then by the same token, a left-handed oath would be more binding if one is sinistral. "I swear by this hand", is a popular phrase in plays. But which hand?

Cases have been known where witnesses were allowed to swear by the left hand if they felt strongly about it: equally, cases have been known where, when the witness instinctively picked up the Bible with the left hand, the usher firmly replaced it in the right hand. Convention is one thing: superstitition is another. An oath taken on the sacred Bible may be merely a convention today, but at one time it would have had all the awesome atmosphere of a religious or superstitious act.

Magistrates' benches are also, apparently, geared to the wants of a right-handed person. This affects, for instance, the position of the register. A London Stipendiary, left-handed, has pointed out that this book, which he has to sign several dozen times daily, measures 30 inches across, with the double page. As his signature has to appear on the extreme right of each page, he is inclined to move the register well to the left of the bench. On his first day this almost resulted in his knocking over the water carafe which is normally placed on the left hand side of the bench. He therefore altered the lay-out by placing the carafe on the right. Such is the "feel" of a traditional court layout, certain visiting counsel remarked that there was "something odd" about the Stipendiary's set-up, but few of them could determine what it was.

XXIV

RULES OF THE ROAD

"The law of the road is a paradox quite,
As you're driving your carriage along:
If you go to the left, you are sure to be right,
If you go to the right, you are wrong"

ENGLISH RHYME, CIRCA 1840

There are few lateral subjects more baffling than the rule of the road, as it is held in various countries. It is difficult to understand why an American drives on the right-hand side while an Englishman keeps to the left, since America was at one time a British colony. It is easier to understand Britain's isolation from the majority of European countries in maintaining her own rule of the road.

The European situation was brought sharply into focus during discussions on that perennial project, the Channel Tunnel between England and France. At one stage the prospect was for a road tunnel, and the delicate question arose—which rule would take precedence, the continental or the English, and at what stage would the change take place? It was with a Gallic gallantry not often displayed by France towards perfidious Albion that M. Guy Mollet, in charge of the French deputation, offered to accept the British left side, throughout the tunnel's length. Now, apparently, the Tunnel is to be an entirely railway affair, so the problem is solved, since French trains run the same way as the British—up on the left side, down on the right. The reason for this came to light during a newspaper correspondence, in which a writer, Mr Hubert C. Studdy of London, gave the following explanation:

"After building their railways, the French, not 'knowing the ropes', found it necessary to ask English signal engineers, who had but recently fixed our own left system, to put up theirs. In pardonable ignorance of the French rule of the road, they naturally arranged the signals for the left-side traffic." This does not apply to trains east of Belgium.

Mr Studdy gave an interesting additional reason for the origin of the left-hand rule of the road.

"An ancient Pope (in the days when the Papacy exercised considerable temporal power) ordained that all road users throughout the Continent should, for their own safety, travel on the left, thus literally and otherwise having the 'whip-hand' for argument with their horses or highwaymen. The hedge on the left was also a protection and shield. At a much later date Robespierre and his fellow-atheists deemed the left rule of the road to be a Christian law, consequently to be abolished."

This is an ingenious theory. It would be remarkable to think that the continental rule was due to the French Revolution, but there is no reason to suppose that this radical upheaval was connected with the innovation. France, at any rate, so often the leader in European affairs, seems to have had a say in many continental conventions.

The second theory, then, concerns Napoleon, and the order of battle. Traditionally, since Richard Cœur de Lion had laid it down, military commanders attacked with the left flank forces first. This meant that, if advancing by road before wheeling into action, they would keep to the left side (few roads being lined by hedges or walls). Napoleon, ever an originator, won many spectacular engagements by reversing this battle order and striking from the right. To facilitate this manœuvre, he ordered his men and vehicles to keep to the right side of the road, and since he was, at one time, master of nearly all Europe, his practice became forcibly adopted. In support of this idea, it can be pointed out that three of the major countries not conquered by Napoleon were Britain, Sweden, and Bohemia (Czechoslovakia) and all three continued to keep to the left side.

Czechoslovakia came into line with the majority some years ago, and Sweden is now following suit. But with the enormous numbers of cars on modern roads, the change-over will be so costly that an additional Swedish motor-tax is being levied to pay for it. It has been said by industrialists that Britain could not, at present, afford to do so, just as, although she invented television, Britain has maintained her original 405 line picture as opposed to the continental 625 line picture. Only recently has one of the three Channels adopted the European system.

The Automobile Association and the Royal Automobile Club of London have received theories like these from many sources. One suggestion is that, with a team of horses, the waggoners, postilions and coachmen always sat on the right, so that they could wield their whips freely—and not necessarily against attackers. When they met another vehicle, it was natural to pull over to the left, so as to be in the best strategic position to ensure clearance. Most roads were so narrow, anyhow, that some sort of manœuvring was necessary.

But what of continental coaches? There is a third theory, in contrast to the French Revolution and Napoleonic theories, and it concerns the postilion. Here the custom was for him to sit astride the left-hand rear horse of the team, so as to be in the best position to control them. This meant that, in passing, the coach or wagon would have to be on the right-hand side for passing safely.

The practice seems to have operated in America, and may account for the dextral way of driving. The Conestogas, boat-like wagons used for hauling wheat from Pennsylvania's Conestoga Valley to the nearby cities, had postilions who also sat on the rear left-side horse, and therefore pulled over to the right when passing another wagon. So, it is said, the right side became adopted in the United States and in Canada. From such small almost random beginnings came the largest car industry in the world, with right-hand drive.

In Britain, however, the "Keep Left" rule had been made

law as long ago as 1835, although it first appeared as an order in the 1772 Traffic Act relating to Scotland. It concerned traffic within six miles of Edinburgh, four miles of Glasgow, and two miles of any other Scottish town. The British Highway Act of 1835 laid down penalties for not keeping to the left side, and to many this would seem to be the logical side, at least for horse traffic. A dextral horseman mounts his steed from the left side, throwing his right leg into the saddle. Posts for mounting horses in Britain are invariably to be found on the left and logical side: and yet, Britain found herself almost in isolation.

No wonder some anonymous wit of the time wrote:

> "The law of the road is a paradox quite,
> As you're driving your carriage along;
> If you go to the left, you are sure to go right,
> If you go to the right you go wrong."

In these days of international acrimony and misunderstanding it is remarkable to find how little ill-feeling these divergent traffic laws have involved. Thousands of British motorists invade the continent each year in their left-hand drive vehicles, and seem to suffer no hardship. British drivers are often winners of continental rallies and races. Yet it is obvious that overtaking, to quote only one instance, is more hazardous for them.

A list of countries still adhering to the left side, or "British" rule provides a strange consortium: the Commonwealth, Bahrein, Burma, Eire, Iceland, Indonesia, Japan, Mozambique, Nepal, Somalia, South Africa, Sudan, Sweden, Thailand and Yemen!

A note on Japanese traffic customs comes from an Italian traveller, Marini Fosco:*

"The road was bad, stony, dusty, full of potholes. We met lorries driven in the most outrageous manner. In Japan, as in England and Sweden, you drive on the left, but Japanese lorry

---

* *Meeting with Japan*: Hutchinson, London, 1957.

drivers drive on the side that suits them; they know that in an accident, the other party will come off worse. This discloses an unpleasant side of the Japanese character, fully conveyed by the Japanese word *ibaru*, which means throwing your weight about."

XXV

CAUSE OR JUST IMPEDIMENT
Stammering and Stuttering

"Demosthenes overcame and rendered more distinct his inarticulate and stammering pronunciation by putting pebbles in his mouth."

PLUTARCH

"Those that stutter and are bald will be soonest melancholy."

BURTON: *Anatomy of Melancholy*

"I knew a L-Lord once, b-but he's d-dead now."

CHARLES LAMB, AT A DINNER

Why do some people stammer and stutter? Is it simply the result of a nervous affliction, or is there a deeper physical and medical reason? How many unfortunate stammerers are, in fact, left-handers who have been shifted, with little sympathy or understanding, and forced to write with the right hand?

This is one of the most fascinating of all the facets on handedness. The author's attention was brought to it in a vivid way by having to edit, for radio programmes, the speeches and other public pronouncements of King George VI. The monarch's speech impediment became more and more acute, until, for the last Christmas Day broadcast which he made to the nation (1951), a practice founded by his father King George V, it was necessary to cut out, on tape, the pauses in his talk, in order to make a coherent message. King George had hitherto refused to make any compromises about these broadcasts, or to have them "doctored". His official biographer, Sir John Wheeler-Bennett, comments:

"The origins and causes of Prince Albert's stammer are

difficult to discover. He was undoubtedly a highly strung, easily excitable and nervous child, and his early nursery experiences were not calculated to have ameliorated his condition."*

Sir John recalls that his first nurse ignored him to a degree which amounted virtually to neglect, and being "sadistic and incompetent", would feed him while driving in a Victoria, a habit which may have laid the foundation for his other complaint, a gastric one.

"But he did not stammer when he first began to talk," the royal biographer continues, "and it appears to have developed during his 7th and 8th years. It has been attributed to his being naturally left-handed, and being compelled to write with his right hand. This would create a condition known in psychology as a 'misplaced sinister' and may well have affected the speech."

Soon after he had been made Duke of York, and taken his seat in the House of Lords, the Prince found himself on a very different field of activity—the tennis-court. Partnered by Dr (later Sir) Louis Greig, he triumphed in the final of the R.A.F. Doubles, after being beaten by Greig in the semi-final of the singles. King George V telegraphed his congratulations. The left-hander had made good this time—with his left hand.

In the All-England Championships of 1924 at Wimbledon, however, he was not so fortunate. This was the first and last appearance of a member of the Royal family in the world's most famous lawn tennis event. Again partnered by Louis Greig, he came up, in the very first round, against that redoubtable pair A. W. Gore and Roper Barrett, and failed to win a set. But it proved to all those who watched that the Duke of York, though he wrote with the right hand, played tennis with his left. The same was true of his golf.

There has always been a strong sinistral or at least ambidextral trait in the Guelph family, which, during the First World War became the House of Windsor. Although writing with his right hand, the present Prince of Wales shows signs of

* *King George VI*: Sir John Wheeler-Bennett, Macmillan, 1958.

sinistrality when kicking a football or digging, but polo he plays dextrally.

The case of King George VI can be chosen in priority because its results involved such an ordeal for a man destined to be constantly in the public eye, and listened to by the public ear. But there are, of course, many other cases of well-known stammerers and stutterers for whom the consequences were not so tragic. Among monarchs, we can include Louis II of France, described by a contemporary chronicler as: "Louis the stuttering, who left two bastard sons." Charlemagne, Charles the Great, has been called left-handed but no evidence seems available about its effect on his speech. Of England's Charles the First, Humphrey Lestrange wrote: "His vocall impediment was to wise men an index of his wisdom . . . since there was never, or rarely, known a fool that stammered."

Looking further back in history, we have Demosthenes, a well-authenticated case, referred to not only by Plutarch but by the Elizabethan dramatist, John Lyly (a sort of court provider of the kind of plays the Queen liked to see). Lyly, in his *Campaspe*, has another theory about the speech of Demosthenes, saying that, "with often breathing up the hill he amended his stammerings".

Cicero, augur as well as author, is said to have been another stammerer—an odd complaint in one who was obviously never at a loss for a word. But both Macaulay and James Anthony Froude, the historian, record the moment when, in an important debate, Cicero "stammered, blundered, and sat down".

Charles Lamb was well known for his hesitancy in speech. He even described it himself when on one occasion, "I stammered a bow and went home". In the *Oxford Dictionary* he is reported to have made, "a witty retort conveyed in his usual roll of stammers, 'I n-nev-never heard you d-do anything else' ". Lamb's remark about knowing a Lord might bring to mind the possible advantage of having a delayed action in speech delivery. Aneurin Bevan, a shifted sinistral from the Welsh mining valley of the Rhondda, eventually found it a useful Parliamentary weapon rather than a handicap, but there is little doubt that, until the time when he was established as a politician, the stammer was a genuine hardship.

Dean Swift has been credited with an impediment in speech. At least he realised the affliction existed. Of one character he wrote:

"And though you can hear him stut-tut-tut-ter,
He barks as fast as he can utter."

Swift had a piercingly honest approach towards all human failings, and it may well be that, in this passage, he was thinking partly about himself.

The case of Lewis Carroll—the Rev. Charles Lutwidge Dodgson—is described in another part of this book, since Dodgson was a mirror-character in his own right as an author, quite apart from the facts of his own life. But his stammer was well known to Alice Liddell and her friends, and is referred to in her memoirs. The question remains: how much is this impediment of speech caused by the changing of handedness under discipline or even duress, and what do the experts recommend as treatment in such cases?

One of the clearest analyses of the problem is made by Sir Cyril Burt in his study of the Backward Child. Why he asks, are there disorders of speech? Is it, as some experts have argued, directly connected with the enforced transfer from left hand to right, or is there another cause?

Stuttering and stammering have been held as human infirmities since the earliest times, but the idea has persisted to our own days, paraphrased to meet a new conception, in warfare. Rudyard Kipling wrote of the Maxim machine gun, "the little demon", which "set up an irritating stammer". An echo of this came from Wilfred Owen's: "What passing bells for those who die as cattle?" which includes the image of the "stuttering rifles' rapid rattle" pattering out their "hasty orisons".

Burt, in his examination of London children found no conclusive evidence of the reason for a stammer in the normally educated, but among those of a lower mental calibre, more than twice the number of stammerers had been switched. He quoted Terman* as claiming that between a third and a half of stammering children in London were shifted sinistrals. The theory of Edward Lee Travis† seemed to support this contention as far as American schools were concerned. "Most stutterers," wrote Travis, "are left-handers who have come to use the right hand instead of the left. Their acquired 'motor facility' is out of harmony with their native psychological lead." In conjunction with Dr Bryng Bryngelson, he made an examination in Iowa, with the following results: out of 200 stammering children, 62 per cent were originally left-handed and had been shifted, and the University of Iowa confirmed that, out of several hundred similar cases checked over three years, 43 per cent were originally left-handed.

This is a powerful argument for assuming that the switching-over can be blamed automatically for almost all stammering. But again, this is doubted, not only by Cyril Burt, but by Dr Margaret Clark, who agrees that prejudice and tradition have played a large part in this, and that much depends on how the switching-over of hands is conducted by the school authorities. In St Louis, for instance, Burt discovered that, of the left-handed children taught to use the right hand, over 90 per cent showed no sign of speech disturbance, and in the schools of New Jersey, where right-hand writing is compulsory, stammering is almost entirely absent.

As the Duchess in *Alice* might have said: "There must be a moral in this somewhere, if only I could find it."

The moral is surely to be found in the methods employed by those parents or teachers who undertake the task of altering a child's natural, preferred habit.

"Stammering," writes Burt, "is one of the most tragic of all the minor disorders of school life. It holds back the child's development in many obvious ways. The stammerer can never enter freely into any interchange of conversation. . . . He is shy

---

* *Hygiene of the School Child*: London, 1914.
† *Speech Pathology*: Travis, Appleton Century, New York, 1931.

of answering in class. . . . Hence, nearly always, the uncured stammerer becomes backward at his lessons. At home his relatives lose patience with his slow and irritating utterance, and seldom fail to criticise his failing upon all public occasions. Everywhere he is likely to be looked upon as foolish or queer; and few of his comrades can resist the temptation to mimic or mock him. . . . He renounces all ambition . . . He becomes diffident, embittered, or morbidly eccentric; and looks forward to nothing but a life of moral suffering. . . ."

Yet, as Burt continues, there are few disabilities which, if recognised and treated in time, can be more readily or more surely cured. It is a matter of changing the hand in such a way as will be acceptable to the child. Obviously there must have been different methods in Iowa and in New Jersey.

More evidence on this subject comes from Samuel Storrey Orton, former professor of Neurology at Columbia University. He states, at the outset, that "there exists no inconsiderable prejudice against left-handedness, which in many instances is so strong as to amount to the belief that the left is abnormal."*

Dr Orton declares: "There is certainly no justification for this belief, and there is reason to believe that a high degree of specialisation in either hemisphere makes for superiority, and that the good left-hander is not only not abnormal, but is apt to be better equipped than the indifferent right-hander."

The idea that all stutterers are originally left-handed he declares as very superficial, but he warns that the ages of 2–3 years and 6–8 years may be the critical ones for the co-ordination of speech, reading and writing. From a wide experience, he divides the stammerers into four probable categories:

The first consists of those whose shifting has been enforced. Then there are those children who are slow to choose a master hand—in other words, to recognise a cerebral dominance— those whose family history has a record of stammering, and a final minority for whom no specific cause can be found. Orton's critical-age period remains as either 2–3 years or 6–8.

* *Reading, Writing and Speech Problems in Children*: Orton; Chapman & Hall, London, 1937.

There may well be a perfectly normal period of speech development until this latter stage is reached. Then comes the hard task of tackling the impediment in a child old enough to realise his sense of inferiority, awkward enough to try and avoid discussing it, yet unable to understand why the stammer has started.

Orton cites a case in which a boy's stammer had been observable for only three weeks. He immediately obtained the parents' support in retraining him to use his left hand for writing, and within another few weeks the impediment had disappeared for good. His method of explaining the disability was to tell the child about cerebral dominance, but he put it in the much more palatable way, describing: "The two halves oi your brain struggling as to which shall be boss." This is, in fact, a very apt description. As to the brain itself, the speech centres must be placed, as one would expect, on the side opposite to the preferred hand, but as Orton has pointed out, it is impossible to *prove* which is the dominant hemisphere of the brain unless a stroke has occurred, or, in technical language "a cerebral lesion with aphasia". It is, of course, possible by surgery to reverse the cerebral dominance (as in experiments on Rats). Lord Brain, an aptly named expert on the cerebral subject, wrote: "The appearance of a 'motor speech' centre in the left hemisphere in man made that the dominant hemisphere and the right hand the dominant hand, in contrast to the ape, in which right and left hand developed with equal frequency."* W. W. Roberts adds: "True human handedness occurs after the beginnings of speech, by which it is directed and to which it is linked. In the great majority of cases such handedness persists through life."†

Whatever the cause, the cure is generally agreed. It is an irony that the malady occurs mainly in countries with a high degree of training in manual acts such as reading and writing. Burt finds the incidence at its highest in Greece, Sweden and Germany (where left-handed writing in schools is forbidden).

* *The Lancet*, Vol. CCXLIX, 1945.
† *Journal of Mental Science*, Vol. XCV, 1949.

In the United States, where such writing is permitted, it is much lower, and there was apparently no evidence of it at all among the Chinese of a quarter of a century ago.

It is this blend of fear, embarrassment and the feeling of making a fool of one's self in public which make the stammerer's position so difficult.

The theory of cerebral dominance is obviously the most important factor in explaining not only speech defects but handedness. In another work,* Lord Brain declares the fact that injuries on one side of the head are apt to paralyse the opposite side of the body was known to the ancients, as long ago as Hippocrates, the Father of Medicine. This became the notorious "falling sickness" or thrombosis. An interesting sidelight of history occurred in the discovery, in 1953, of the death mask of King Edward III in Westminster Abbey. It was noted that the mouth twisted at the left-hand corner, in just such a way as would indicate a stroke on the right side of the brain. It is also known from contemporary records that an illness suffered by the King robbed him of the power of writing: therefore the assumption was made that Edward had been sinistral.

Lord Brain, writing in the light of recent investigations by two psychologists (Humphrey and Sangwill), does, however, admit that the contralateral theory is by no means universal or automatic. Though the left cerebral hemisphere is the major one for speech in right-handed persons, the same is by no means always true with left-handed persons.

M. E. Humphrey, of the Oxford University Institute of Experimental Psychology, noting variable preferences among his left-handed patients, submitted a questionnaire to seventy individuals, half left, half right. He pooled his experiences with a fellow psychologist, Oliver Zangwill, of the National Hospital, London, who had been considering the effects of brain injuries and speech. They examined nearly five hundred cases of unilateral injury at the Oxford Head Injuries Bureau, and continued to make further detailed reports on smaller groups

* *Speech Disorders: Handedness and Cerebral Dominance*: Butterworth, London, 1961.

of sinistral patients. The results, published by Zangwill,* form a strong challenge to the conventional contralateral theory. The first examination's findings were "consistent with the hypothesis that aphasia in sinistrals may result from a lesion of either hemisphere", but "it must be said that the patients in this small group appear to show a distinct tendency towards 'left-brainedness' in all their speech functions. This would seem to entail revision of the old rule. . . . It also raises the possibility that even in those who are fully left-handed the dominant hemisphere may be the left."

There is not space here to set out their subsequent examinations in detail, but of the individual cases, many aspects were considered, including frequency of sinistrality in the family, and the specific educational disability known originally as "word-blindness" and now as "dyslexia". Out of 10 sinistral patients reported in 1956, no less than 7 were considered to have a left hemisphere dominance. Zangwill quotes other authorities, including the German Professor Claus Conrad, and L. Roberts of the Montreal Neurological Unit, in support of his own findings. The "old rule" of the brain controlling the opposite side would only hold for fully right-handed individuals with a dextral history.

"No longer," Zangwill sums up, "can the human race be viewed as divided into two mutually exclusive categories— sinister and "right-brained", dexter and "left-brained"— handedness, in particular, being less clear-cut than right-handedness and less regularly associated with the dominance of either hemisphere. Indeed cerebral dominance is in all probability itself a graded characteristic, varying in scope and conclusion from individual to individual. Its precise relation to handedness and its vicissitudes still remains to be ascertained."

These are important conclusions, and the next few years may well see one of the most frequently accepted theories being discarded, in so far as the left-hander is concerned.

The recent researches of Oliver Zangwill into what used

* *Cerebral Dominance and its Relation to Psychological Function* (The Henderson Trust Lectures, no. 19): Oliver & Boyd, Edinburgh, 1960.

to be called "word-blindness" carry the story a stage further. The new word for this disability, "dyslexia" (a word which is in Webster's *International Dictionary* but has, as far as one can discover, escaped the *New Oxford Dictionary*), was used as long ago as 1950 by the Danish neurologist, B. Hallgren. This not only affects reading, but a more general difficulty in distinguishing right from left. Sangwill's tests in this matter revealed a number of cases with a tendency towards mirror-writing.

There are any number of left-handers who will agree with the sinistral who said: "I'm hopeless at giving street directions —first right, second left and so on, though I can follow out the route on my own, by instinct."

A London school for Dyslexics has been founded at Coram Fields in Bloomsbury.

Note on Spoonerisms

The "Spoonerism" is named after the celebrated Dr Spooner, of Oxford, and became so well known it merited a place in Murray's *Oxford Dictionary*. It would appear that Spooner is only, in fact, known to have uttered one of these phrases, in which syllables or words are transposed. This was his immortal "Kinkering Kongs" for "Conquering Kings". Eventually the Spoonerism became popular in Oxford (about 1880) with such manufactured examples as: "Let us have hags flung from the window in his honour", or "He arrived in the town drain." As recently as 1934 the author heard the late Monsignor Ronald Knox, in a characteristic speech at the Oxford Union, refer to the Spring which "bites the young bloods".

There is some element of satire in all this, even a possible social mocking of the illiterate by the intellectual. But it can also be associated with cerebral mix-ups. Writing in *Brain* in 1880, one Hughlings Jackson suggested that Spoonerisms were the result of "right-brained Hurry". "Such blunders occur, I think, in persons whose speech is only slightly defective. I believe that these troubles of speech are owing to hurry on the right half of the brain, to hurried reproduction of the words of the subject proposition."

XXVI

PEN-PUSHING
Left-Handed Writing

When did handwriting first begin, and in which direction did it go?

There is not much disagreement about this among the experts. The first alphabet, and the first attempts to write or carve letters in a sequence, belongs to the Phoenicians, a Semitic tribe who inhabited a coastline which today would extend northward from Haifa into the Lebanon. Being celebrated seafarers and traffickers, they brought with them more than merchandise to the shores of Egypt and Greece. Their direction of writing, as with Hebrew and Arabic today, was from right to left, and the earliest Greek writings follow this. Variations included vertical writing and inscriptions (found also among the Romans and Egyptians) and a curious alternate right–left and left–right called *boustrophedon* (literally "ox-turn") in imitation of the beast ploughing and turning after every crossing of the field, to procede in the opposite direction. Etruscan writings of 750 B.C. have been found which are straightforward right to left, as in mirror-writing. A hundred years later, boustrophedon writings were being made, such as the celebrated Gartyna inscription. This seems to have been the moment of indecision. In which direction to write—leftwards or rightwards?

"Finally," says Abram Blau, "the Greeks settled upon the rightward direction of writing which became the fixed convention for the western world." This was about the 5th century B.C. The schism between the two ways of writing, though unnoticed by historians, was almost as dramatic as the later division of Christian and Muslims in religion. Arab and Semitic tribes continued to write from right to left, as they still do. Hindus and Ceylonese did likewise.

There have been attempts to prove from this, and from wall-drawings and frescoes, that these were a primarily left-handed people. Hebrew has been called "a left-handed language". But there seems to be no substance for the argument. True, to start writing on the right-hand side is the logical course for the left-hander, and the actual alphabetic signs and curves of Arabic and Hebrew are performed much more easily that way, by the right-handed. Surely one can only take the view that the Greek alphabet, as it emerged, straight and square rather than in curves, was more suited to the right-to-left movement, which also involved the good-luck, sun-wise movement. Moreover, the Greeks were the masters of culture, and capable of change: the Arabs had scarcely reached the writing stage. This still does not explain why the *first* natural instinct had been to form letters from right to left.

A "pen-pusher" or "pen-driver" is defined in Partridge's *Dictionary of Slang* as a clerk. But it would more appropriately apply to any left-handed writer, for the action is literally that of pushing the pen from left to right, while the dextral writer lets the pen follow the movement of the hand, and can immediately see what he has written. The sinistral hand, in some positions, may actually obscure the words.

It has often been believed that left-handers usually make poor writers, partly for this reason. This is not necessarily so, but certainly the effort to write well is a greater strain for the left-handed child. In the days of steel-nibbed pens, moreover, there was a far greater chance of them blotting their work, since the inkwell being invariably on the right, their hand movement, after refilling the pen, covered the whole expanse of paper. Dr Margaret Clark quotes one Miss Cole, an American expert in penmanship for left-handers.*

"If the left-handed child is independent enough to succeed literally single-handed in his contest with his teachers, some at

* *Psychology of the Elementary School Subjects*: Farrar & Rinehart, New York, 1934.

least of whom will try to change him, then his troubles have only just begun. All systems of writing are based on the assumption that the writer will use his right hand. The youthful and determined left-hander is usually forced into a system not in the least adapted to his needs."

Miss Cole added that the number of left-handers entering first grade in U.S. schools in any one year was as high as 150,000.

Sir Cyril Burt agrees with this situation.

"I have seen teachers going round a class, showing other pupils how to place the paper and hold the pen, but leaving the left-hander to discover these things entirely for himself. Actually, he needs more help, not less, if he is to learn how to manage his left hand efficiently. His paradoxical task is to produce with the left hand a style of writing evolved for the right."

In other words, pen-pushing is involved. In Dr Clark's phrase: "Writing with the left hand is not the same as writing with the right, with only a change of hand. . . . In many schools, pupils are not *taught* to write with the left hand, only permitted." She quotes one boy who told her: "When my teacher saw that I was worse with my right hand, I was allowed change back to the left."

Such an experience can bring about a sense of failure in any child, who may be willing to attempt the changeover but, having failed, has to regard his left-hand writing as being under some sort of stigma. It is probably true that young sinistral writers write more slowly and suffer more from hand-fatigue, and that this may not solely be due to the physical act of pen-pushing. There is, as Edward Lee Travis has pointed out* a secret sense of shame at being different in writing, and a social fear. It is the equivalent of William Blake's Little Black Boy:

> "O why was I born with a different face,
> Why was I not born like the rest of my race?"

* *Speech Pathology*: Appleton, New York, 1931.

FOUR LEFT-HANDED CHAMPS

Above, left: "Babe" Ruth, baseball southpaw whose name speaks for itself. *Above, right:* Gary Sobers of the West Indies, said to be the greatest cricketer in the world. *Below, left:* The late King George VI of England playing at Wimbledon. *Below, right:* President Harry S Truman, a left-handed bowler.

MORE FAMOUS LEFT-HANDERS

Above, left: F. Lee Bailey, the famous criminal lawyer who takes on "impossible" cases. *Above, right:* Rock Hudson, popular movie idol. *Below, left:* Paul Wittgenstein; the loss of his right hand did not halt his career. *Below, right:* Huntington Hartford; the A & P heir is also a cultural entrepreneur.

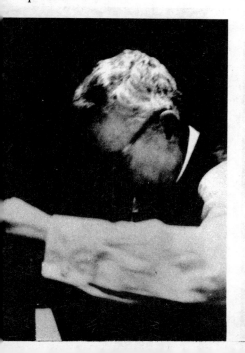 

Substitute "hand" for face, and the thought is the same. A boy will not be conscious of anything wrong if he kicks a football with his left foot, or plays table tennis with his left hand (it is often a great advantage) but writing is another matter. In the early stages, Travis points out, writing is closely allied to speech, and there is the strain of substituting written words for spoken. The speed of thinking is slowed down to the pace of handwriting.

This sense of shame—or embarrassment—and the way it can be removed as the handwriting improves, is vividly shown by two letters of Lord Nelson in the British Museum. One was written not long after he had lost his right arm during the attack on Santa Cruz, in the Canary Islands, in 1797. He was struck by a grape-shot as he was landing, and the arm was amputated without anaesthetics. Later he wrote to his Commander in Chief, in an awkward, childish hand:

"A left-handed Admiral will never again be considered as useful, therefore the sooner I get to a very humble cottage the better." Specimens of his right-handed writing twenty years before show it to be firm and clear, though signatures became increasingly careless. Three years after the loss of his right arm, he was afflicted by partial paralysis after an illness at San Juan. "I have entirely lost the use of my left arm," he wrote, "and very near all my left leg and thigh." To have survived the loss of his right eye also, at the Siege of Calvi in Corsica, argues a great will for survival in England's most famous Admiral. Of his wife it was said: "Fanny was invaluable to a one-armed man who never became dexterous at cutting up what was on his plate."

The British Museum's other letter is the last one Nelson wrote.* It was written aboard *Victory* on October 19th, 1805, and was to Lady Hamilton: the left-handed style is now smooth and flowing.

"My dearest beloved Emma," it began, "the dear friend of my bosom the signal has been made that the enemy's combined fleet are coming out of Port. . . . May the God of Battles crown

* *Egerton Ms.* 1614 F.125.

my endeavours with success at all events. I will take care that my name shall ever be most dear to you and Horatia both of whom I love as much as my own life. . . ."

The slant is to the left, but the actual words in this, one of history's most famous letters, are very clear. Over the page, a postscript dated October 20th, the eve of Trafalgar, concludes: "May God Almighty give us success over these fellows and enable us to get a Peace." Below is a note added in Lady Hamilton's hand: "This letter was found open on his desk and brought to Lady Hamilton by Capn. Hardy. Oh miserable wretched Emma oh glorious and happy Nelson."

What should parents and teachers do about left-handed writing by their children or pupils? The question is obviously one of real importance, and coercion or indifference alike can be dangerous to a child's whole future. Most authorities agree that switching over, if attempted at all at school age, must be done with tact and understanding. To quote Abram Blau, that firm believer in the Master Hand:

"Much as we recommend a parental and pedagogical bias in favour of dextrality during training in infancy, pre-school years, and early elementary grades, *it is extremely unwise to persist in pressing against left-handed tendencies when the child cannot be won over to dextrality.* . . . If the child seems to be very fixed in his sinistral habits . . . it is the better part of wisdom to re-assure him and encourage a more comfortable adjustment to his sinistrality."

Orton, Clark, Burt, Travis, Cole and others agree: which should be a warning to any parent or teacher who enforces a changeover. Often there is a difference of opinion between home and school—or ignorance between them. Attempts were made on the present author, at an early age in school, to insist on the right hand being used, but medical advice given to the parents resulted in his being allowed to follow his preference.

Handwriting is, as Dr Clark has stated, the ultimate preference, just as it is the most important to the left-hander himself. There are cases of sinistrals who have accepted the change-over at school, but have reverted to left-handed writing on leaving.

As for the years of early instruction, the natural sinistral is up against it, as Miss Cole asserts in her views on teaching left-handers:

"Because so few of them are found in any one place, they will be trained in penmanship methods appropriate for right-handed children. Day after day throughout their first six school years, they will be taught by conscientious teachers to write badly."

The result will be, among those 150,000 left-handed school entrants in the United States alone, writing which is barely legible and produced awkwardly. They are "merely the innocent victims of an inappropriate method of instruction".

Much of this can be avoided if the particular needs of the left-handed child be recognised. There are several variations adopted in the holding of the pen. A familiar one is what can be called "the hook", where the hand is actually above the line of writing, and the pen faces inwards towards the body. There are people who can write thus with astonishing speed and facility, in much the same way as the practised mirror-writer, but it looks extremely awkward and usually is. The habit probably arises because the writer placed the paper in the position recommended for right-handers, with the slant towards the left. It is of the utmost importance to *reverse* this position of the paper, slanting it towards the right. Then, with the pen in line with the left shoulder, the operation becomes more natural, and the hand is not entirely obscuring what has been written.

Before the permitted use of the fountain pen in schools, pen-pushing for the left-hander was obviously a laborious and messy business, particularly if the nib was thin and sharp, and liable to dig into the paper. There were also difficulties with fountain-pens, nearly all of which had nibs designed for right-handed writing, with the nib-points slanting down from left to right. One honourable exception is the Waterman Company, which has for long produced a nib slanting in the opposite direction, and specifically described as being for left-handers (with one of these pens this book was written). With the arrival

of the ballpoint pen and later still the felt-tip pen, much character
has gone out of handwriting. Graphologists—among early
amateurs were Goethe, Edgar Allen Poe, Madame de Stael and
Gainsborough—have been baffled in their deductions by the
spidery conformity of a line with no shape in it. But it must be a
consolation to left-handed children. No longer are the inkwell
and the steel nib there to torment them.

Deductions by experts over handwriting can quickly reveal
left-handedness, and it is comparatively easy for the ordinary
person to diagnose it, simply by the slant of the letters. In left-
hand writing, they usually slope "backwards", i.e. from right to
left, or they are upright. The two examples by Lord Nelson
make this clear. Dextral writing follows the movement of the
pen by leaning over with it.

XXVII

ALL DONE BY MIRRORS

"Why, it's a Looking-glass book, of course!
And, if I hold it up to a glass, the words will all go the right
way again."

ALICE, in *Through the Looking Glass*

THE most famous examples of mirror-writing are the Leonardo
Notebooks. But another practised hand was that of Lewis
Carroll, who performed it to amuse his young girl-friends, and
produced the famous page in *Through the Looking Glass*. An
exact definition of this curious form of Calligraphy can be
found in the booklet by Dr Critchley entirely devoted to the
subject.*

"By the term mirror-writing (*ecriture en miroir*: *Spiegelschrift*:
lithographic writing: levography: *abductionschrift*: *scrittura
speculare*) is understood that variety of script which
runs in an opposite direction to the normal, the individual
letters being also reversed. The writing is therefore illegible
until held up before a looking-glass; a familiar example
of mirror-writing is seen in the imprints on a blotting-pad."

Dr Critchley has traced the first reference to it in literature to
1698, by Rosinus Lentilius, reporting the case of a left-handed
epileptic girl who wrote in this fashion, and the additional case
of a soldier who had lost his right arm in battle, and began to
write mirror-wise with his left. Earlier than this, of course,
Vasari had noted Leonardo's writing, but had made no comment on it.

* *Mirror-Writing* by Macdonald Critchley, M.D., M.R.C.P. London, Kegan
Paul, 1928.

In the 19th century, the habit first became associated with hemiplegia, the stroke which affects one side of the brain, and the opposite side of the body. One German doctor quoted 21 cases out of 58 who took up mirror-writing after right-sided paralysis.

There are, apparently, other adult causes, some relating to dissociation of attention, under the influence of drugs or anaesthetics or alcohol—in other words, absent-minded writing in the literal sense. But the main source seems to lie with children, and their earliest efforts to form letters. Sir Cyril Burt declares that, although mirror-writing is found especially among backward left-handed children, it is by no means always a subnormal trait (no one could accuse Leonardo or Lewis Carroll of being lacking in mental calibre!)

Certain letters are often reversed. The "lower-case" b and d and p and q are mirror-images of each other. S and n are also frequently written the wrong way round. If children get accustomed to letters being reversed, why not whole sentences? The most frequent age for mirror-writers, in Burt's opinion, is between 5 and 9, and it is certainly more common among the left-handed (who, as we have seen, are writing in an unnatural movement when pen-pushing from left to right of the paper). Most mirror-writers can read their own writing, a task found impossible by most others. The transcribing of Leonardo's *Notebooks* must have been a thankless task.

Is mirror-writing merely a freak-phenomenon, or has it an important bearing on handedness?

Dr Critchley goes into considerable detail on the various theories as to its origin.

"It is well known that the outer world is impressed upon the human retina and represented cortically in a reversed manner; the normal mind finds no difficulty, however, in correcting this distorted image. Vertical relationships are the easiest to rectify, so that up and down orientation is never in doubt. There appears to be some lingering confusion in right and left lateral relationships so that discrimination is made with less promptness and with a greater margin of error in a horizontal plane. . . ."

The suggestion is, therefore, that the mirror-writer, while having a normal vertical reaction, has a defective horizontal one. Orton adds that he may well also have a lapse in the dominance of the brain-hemisphere which controls his writing with the opposite hand, and this may lead to doubt and confusion as to how words should look and writing should be done. The second part of the theory—that of mental dominance—is the more generally accepted one, and gains strength from the fact that to write from right to left *is* the natural thing for a left-hander to do, just as his natural, instinctive movements are from right to left; he will even stir a cup of tea "widdershins".

An additional attribute to mirror-writing is that the action relieves fatigue. (This has been suggested in the case of Leonardo da Vinci, who seems to have done most of his writing at night, after a hard day's work in the studio.) Critchley quotes the remarkable modern example of an unnamed American author who developed a "bi-manual" mode of living which allowed him to switch between right-handed and left-handed activities, thus using each brain-hemisphere alternately. His claim was that he could, in this fashion, exist on only three hours' sleep!

This would also seem to mark him as a Lewis Carroll character, straight from the pages of the *Looking Glass*, the book full of mirror images such as Tweedledum and Tweedledee. It is surprising that the prospect of using first one side of the brain and then the other does not occur in the White Knight's soliloquy, as an invention of his own.

Mirror-writing, unless it comes naturally, is as unlikely a feat to be able to accomplish, or contemplate, as conjuring, even to left-handed writers. The fact that those capable of carrying it out range from Leonardo da Vinci to mental defectives only makes the subject, as Alice would say, "Curiouser and curiouser".

In addition to mirror-writing as an individual phenomenon, there is the mirror world, which became logical only in Carroll's *Through the Looking Glass*. The American editor of the *Annotated Alice*,* Martin Gardner, is also a mathematician who takes pleasure in introducing, as Dodgson himself did, puzzles for the amateur. In one of these collections,† he approaches the mirror world in an equal spirit of gaiety, quoting from authorities as widely spaced as Kant and the Chinese. The well-known Chinese 'monad' circular symbol is divided equally, though not symmetrically, into the opposing elements of Yin and Yang (resolved into the whole truth of Tao) but, says Gardner, it was two Chinese physicists who received the Nobel prize in 1957, for proving that some elementary particles are not symmetrical at all, and do not mirror each other. Professor Oppenheimer described this as a "gay and wonderful discovery".

Kant is quoted as saying: "What can more resemble my hand, and be in all points more like, than its image in the looking-glass? And yet I cannot put such a hand as I see in the glass in the place of the original."

In music, counterpoint is the equivalent of the mirror. Gardner cites the extreme example of Mozart, who once wrote a canon with a second melody, which was the first one both backward *and upside down*, so that two players could read the same notes from opposite sides of the sheet.

Turning to words, Martin Gardiner became absorbed with opposites, particularly the palindrome. His examples include: "Draw pupil's lip upward", "A man, a plan, a Canal —Panama!" and the famous remark of the First Man on Earth, "Madam, I'm Adam", with her equally famous palindromic reply, "Eve". To these could be added the celebrated, "Stiff, dairyman, in a myriad of fits".

"We are," Gardner asserts, "an asymmetrical mind dwelling in a bilaterally symmetrical body." The German physicist

---

* *The Annotated Alice*: New York, Clarkson N. Potter, 1960: Penguin Books, London, 1965.

† *Mathematical Puzzles and Diversions*: Scientific American, 1956–1958. London, George Bell, 1961.

Ernst Mach put it this way, in 1900: "The very fact that we can distinguish our right from our left implies an asymmetry of the perceiving system."

Gardner concludes: "Physicists will be speculating right and left for a long time to come."

It is not surprising that he found the fantasies of Lewis Carroll a rich field for research, and the activities and character of the fellow-mathematician, C. L. Dodgson, of equal interest. He knew that Dodgson could draw double pictures which made a different image each way up (Rex Whistler has drawn modern examples of this curious art-form) and that he had a musical box which could play tunes backwards—another device to amuse his young friends. From *Sylvia & Bruno* he quotes the significant palindrome in which EVIL is the opposite of LIVE (a useful moral point for the Reverend Dodgson to make). But it is clearly in *Through the Looking Glass* that the mirror images and words reach their height. *Adventures in Wonderland* had hinted at it. "Do cats eat bats, or do bats eat cats?" wondered Alice, and when she came to the mushroom, sidedness played its part. When she nibbled the left side she became larger, and vice versa.

But in *Through the Looking Glass* everything is inversion: Alice walks backwards to meet the Red Queen; she travels the wrong way in the train; the Queen screams before she pricks her finger, and promises jam every other day; the story of Jabberwocky begins with the first verse in mirror-writing; Tweedledum and Tweedledee are mirror images, and so on.

An account of the original idea behind *Through the Looking Glass* was related by a distant cousin of Alice Liddell—another Alice, of the Raikes family—in *The Times*, on January 22nd, 1932. It was apparently Dodgson who discovered that she was "another Alice" and invited her to see something "rather puzzling" in his uncle's house near by in Onslow Square. (Dodgson's little girls were always very trusting, and with justification.) She found herself in a room full of old furniture with a tall mirror standing across one corner.

"Now", Carroll said, giving her an orange, "tell me which hand you have that in." "The right," she said.

He then asked her to go and stand before the mirror and tell him, "which hand the little girl you see there has got it in". After some contemplation, Alice Raikes said, "The left hand", and Dodgson asked her to explain this. Finally she ventured: "If I was on the other side of the glass, wouldn't the orange still be in my right hand?"

"I can still hear his laugh" she recalled. 'Well done, little Alice,' he said, 'The best answer I've had yet'."

Later she heard from him that, through her reply, she had given him the idea for the book; and, of course, she received her presentation copy.

This is very relevant to left-handedness, since there are various indications that Dodgson was originally a Sinistral, but was "switched" in childhood. This would account, not only for his interest in polarity and sidedness (left-handers are always more aware of this than right-handers, because of their own peculiarity and because most of them are partially ambidextral) but for his mirror writing and his stammer. Alice, who later, as Mrs Hargreaves, wrote her own reminiscences about the early days at Oxford, refers to this impediment a number of times. The American authoress, Florence Becker Lennon, in her biography of Carroll* supports the view of original sinistrality, declaring that, "he took his revenge by doing a little reversing himself". But strangely enough, Martin Gardner disagrees, and finds there is little evidence for it.

The truth, as is so many cases of early upbringing, may never be known. Switching a sinistral in those days was taken as such an obvious practice, akin to the rules of hygiene, that nurses and parents scarcely thought about it, and might not even recall that one of their charges or children had, in fact, started life left-handed. It is this lack of information which makes research into the subject a slow and difficult process. So often, the evidence did not seem to be worth noting down. But in Lewis Carroll's case, despite the lack of proof, there

* *Victoria Through the Looking Glass*: London.

exists a very strong supposition that the author of *Alice* was originally a Sinistral. Cyril Burt, noting the mirror-writing plus the stammer, comes to the same conclusion.

It is, perhaps, not surprising that the versatile, enquiring mind of H. G. Wells, master of the semi-scientific thriller, should have given the question of left and right some thought. The result comes up, however, as something of a surprise, in the mysterious story of the schoolmaster, Gottfried Plattner.* He taught at a small private school in the South of England, and dabbled in chemistry. One day a boy brought some greenish powder into the classroom, which he claimed to have found done up in a packet in a disused lime-kiln near the Downs. Plattner tried mixing the powder with various substances—water, hydrochloric acid, nitric acid, and so on. It was only when he applied a match to the mixture that the fantastic thing happened: there was a blinding flash, an explosion, and the unfortunate man literally disappeared. Nine days later, he suddenly reappeared, ragged and bleeding, in the headmaster's garden.

Nobody, it seems, believed his explanation: that he seemed to have been disembodied, in a spirit world, while capable of seeing the real world. His return to reality he put down to a fall, which broke the bottle of the mixture in his pocket, and produced an explosion similar to the one which had removed him. The story of his spirit experiences does not really concern us; they include a vision of the Hand of Death stretching forward to claim a dying man. What is intriguing is the physical state in which Plattner found himself after reassuming the living human state. Everything about him had been changed from right hand to left hand.

"Mathematical theorists," wrote Wells, "tell us that the only way in which the right and left sides of a solid body can be changed is by taking that body clean out of space as we know it—taking it out of ordinary existence, that is, and turning it somewhere outside space. . . . To put the thing in technical language, the curious inversion of Plattner's right and left sides

* *The Plattner Story and Others*: Methuen, London, 1897.

is proof that he has moved out of our space into what is called the Fourth Dimension, and that he has returned again to our world."

The experience, whatever it was, had resulted in a thorough displacement. He could only write, painfully, with his left hand, and in mirror-fashion. He could not throw with his right hand, he was perplexed at mealtimes with knife and fork, his ideas on the rule of the road (he was a keen cyclist) were very confused, and a medical examination showed that the unsymmetrical parts of his body had been misplaced, particularly the liver and lungs. His left eye, which had once been larger than the right, was now smaller, and his heart beat on the right side.

There is no moral in the story, which is in fact an early example of Wells' rather tantalising glimpses into what was to be called Science Fiction. In the unfortunate Plattner's case, it was certainly a drastic way of shifting a dextral.

XXVIII

A GALLERY OF EXPERTS

SIR THOMAS BROWNE

The first gesture in defence of the sinistral was made in 1648 by Sir Thomas Browne of Norwich, a scholarly doctor with an enquiring mind and a prose style unequalled in English for its torrential splendour. In that year, unaffected by the Civil War although supporting the Royalist cause, he published his "*Pseudoxia Epidemica*, or Enquiries into Very Many Received Tenets and Commonly Presum'd TRUTHS, which examined prove but VULGAR ERRORS."

Browne was something of a recluse, but he had studied, not only at Pembroke College, Oxford (later the college of his admirer, Samuel Johnson), but also at the Universities of Montpellier, Padua and Leyden, where he took a doctor's degree. His attitude to life is a curious mixture of the classical and the scientific, the humanist and the Christian, the superstitious and the practical.

In the tradition of the great scientists and artists, he indulged in endless experiments, even testing out the effects on the human digestion of eating spiders and bees. And yet he refused to accept the Copernican system of the universe, and believed in astrology, alchemy, magic and witchcraft. It is known that, as a renowned citizen of Norwich, he attended witch trials, and once his evidence helped to condemn two women to death.*

The scientific worthies of his time evidently did not take kindly to the publication of the *Vulgar Errors*, and Browne's biographer, Edmund Gosse, believes that he was deliberately excluded from membership of the Royal Society, a body more

* See Chapter IX (Widdershins & Witches), p. 71.

august than learned. (In later years, King Charles II delighted in teasing Royal Society meetings with scientific conundrums.) Some of the "errors" Browne exposed were admittedly absurd: that a diamond "is softened or broken by the blood of a goat": that an Elephant "hath no joints": that a Wolf, first seeing a man, "begets a dumbness in him": that the "left eye of a hedgehog fried in oil procures sleep": that "the flesh of peacocks corrupteth not".

But on the subject of handedness—a subject, till that day, of Roman superstition and mythology, and not unconnected with witchcraft—Browne gets, literally, to the heart of the matter. He denied that the heart was necessarily on the left side, which in effect destroyed the reason for the primitive warrior to defend his left, or heart side, with his shield, leaving the right to wield the weapon.

Having established this, Browne proceeds to examine the curious phenomenon of left-handedness. He admits that throughout history, the right hand has been favoured, quoting the Book of Genesis and the mealtime habits of Greeks and Romans, who leaned in their reclining way—the attitude reflected in the paintings of Lord Leighton, Alma-Tadema and Fortunino Matania, as well as in a long heritage of Hollywood films—on the left side, "so that their right hand was free and ready for all service". He mentioned the left-handed Benjamites in the Book of Judges but misquoted them as 7,000 instead of a mere 700. He quotes the experience of Jonah, who met "sixscore thousand, that could not discern between their right hand and their left, or know not good from evil". He notes that the Amazons amputated their right breasts in order to shoot their arrows.

As a practical measure, he recommends the use of one predominant hand, although right-hand preference "hath no regular or certain root in nature". He goes on: "There will otherwise arise anomalous disturbances in manual actions, not only in civil and artificial but also in Military Affairs, and the several actions of war."

Then comes the famous quotation which every left-handed

will remember, and which has been repeated in every book on handedness.

"Many, in their infancy, are sinistrously disposed, and divers continue all their lives left-handed."

In his debunking of popular fallacies, Browne does not join the ranks of those who despise the sinistral.

"Whether Eve was framed out of the left side of Adam, I dispute not: because I stand not yet assured which is the right side of a man, or whether there be such a distinction in nature."

This astonishing country doctor, who has been compared with Montaigne and Pascal, but who, in his restless examination of the physical and metaphysical alike, might more resemble John Donne or Aldous Huxley then asks: "What substance is there in that Auspicial principle, and fundamental doctrine of Ariolation,* that the left hand is ominous, and that good things do pass sinistrously upon us, because the left hand of man respected the right hand of the Gods, which handed their favours unto us?"

Not for another two centuries at least does the question of left-handedness appear again in the books of an established writer. Sir Thomas Browne, in fact, is one of the few established writers, as distinct from the neurologists, educationalists and psychiatrists, who have publicly given the matter a thought. His remarks obviously made little impact at the time, and for those two centuries the "sinistrously disposed" were presumably shifted to dextrality in various ways, and with varying effects on their mentality.

On the more specific anatomical side, Browne brings to bear all his professional knowledge, dealing first with the disposition of the viscera in the human body, a theory revived in the 19th century.

"For the seat of the heart and liver in one side, whereby men become left-handed, it happeneth too rarely to countenance an effect so common; for the seat of the liver on the left side is monstrous, and rarely to be met with in the observations of

* Soothsaying or fortune telling.

physicians. Others, not considering ambidexters and left-handed men, do totally submit unto the efficacy of the liver; which, though seated on the right side, yet by the subclavian division, doth equidistantly communicate its activity unto either arm; nor will it solve the doubts of observation; for many are right-handed whose livers are weakly constituted, and many use the left in whom that part is strongest; and we observe in apes and other animals, whose liver is in the right, no regular prevalence therein."

He prefers the now popular theory of cerebral dominance—and indeed, is about the first man to suggest it in writing.

"Therefore the brain, especially the spinal marrow, which is but the brain prolonged, hath a fairer plea hereto; for these are the principles of motion, wherein dextrality consists, and are divided within and without the crany. By which division, transmitting nerves respectively unto either side, according to the indifferency or original and native prepotency, there ariseth an equality in both, or prevalency in either side . . ."

"First, if there were a determinate prepotency in the right, and such as ariseth from a constant root in nature, we might expect the same in other animals, whose parts are also differenced by dextrality: wherein notwithstanding we cannot discover a distinct and complying account; for we find not that horses, bulls, or mules, are generally stronger on this side. As for animals whose forelegs more sensibly supply the use of arms, they hold, if not an equality in both, a prevalency oft-times in the other, as squirrels, apes and monkeys; the same is also discernible in parrots, who feed themselves more commonly by the left leg. . . ."

This can be confirmed by a visit to the Aviary of any zoo today. Browne also quoted Aristotle's opinion that the right claws of lobsters and crabs were slightly larger, and therefore more often in use.

The Doctor also professionally dismisses a further Vulgar Error, the belief that, in the sexual act, semen from the right testicle will beget a boy, and vice versa.

"The seminal arteries which send forth the active materials, are both derived from the great artery, over which it must have passed to attain unto the testicle. . . . The seminal ejaculation proceeds, not immediately from the testicle, but from the spermatic glandules; and therefore Aristotle confirms (and reason cannot deny) that although there be nothing diffused from the testicles, an horse or bull may generate after castration; that is, from the stock and remainder of seminal matter, already prepared and stored up in the prostates or glandules of generation."

SIR DANIEL WILSON

This distinguished sinistral Scotsman reached the climax of his career in 1881 when he was elected President of Toronto University. Toronto in particular and Canada in general owe a lot to his educational ideas. He came to the new world with the reputation of being one of Scotland's principal archaeologists. He was also an artist, drawing the scene of his native Edinburgh, a poet, and educational reformer, and became interested as a left-hander himself, in the origins of handedness, and its results.

His first investigations were described in a long article for the *Canadian Journal* of 1872, when Wilson was Professor of History and English Literature at Toronto. (The copy in the British Museum in London is marked "with the Author's complimenments", in a handwriting which is clearly dextral, since Sir Daniel eventually taught himself to write with that hand.) His lively mind ranges wide over the whole subject. He first defines the hand:

"The wonderful complexity of its structure, its nice delicacy of touch, and its adaptation in all ways for being the organ of an intelligent volition, fitted for the execution of every requirement of ingenuity and skill, alike its recognition as one special and distinctive feature of man's organisation. Man," he continues, "converts one hand into the special organ servant of his will; while the other is relegated to a subordinate place, as its mere aider and supplementer."

He quotes extensively from many sources and authorities which occur throughout this book. His fellow-Scot, Professor Buchanan of Glasgow, is quoted as saying: "The preferential use of the right hand is not a congenital but an acquired attribute of man. It does not exist in the earliest periods of life. Nevertheless, no training could ever render the left hand of ordinary men equal in strength to the right"—an opinion which seems belied by the performance of "power-service" tennis players and baseball pitchers who are left-handed. If anything, Wilson inclines to the physical theory of greater weight being distributed to the right of the body, a theory now contested. But at least the Toronto professor pursued his enquiries to the extent of examining the dissection of a dead man known to be left-handed, and discovering that in this case, the organs were indeed heavier on the right side.

He also quotes the anatomist Hyrtl, from Vienna, who in his handbook of anatomy of 1860, declared: "The blood is sent into the right subclavian artery under a greater pressure than to the left, on account of the relative position of these vessels, and that in consequence of the greater supply of blood, the muscles are better nourished and stronger, and therefore the right extremity is used."

Delving back into history and pre-history, in both the 1872 and later enlarged edition of his discoveries,* Wilson is aware of the Hebrew language, in which the word for hand (yamin) also means south, and of the important distinction between the position taken up by the classical augurs, the Greeks facing north, the Romans south. He quotes Cicero as saying: "Why should the raven on the right and the crow on the left make a confirmatory augury?" From Egyptian history, he notes that, on the wall of the Abu Simbel group of statues, now saved by a rescue operation, Rameses is seen slaying his enemies with a club held in his left hand, and in the temple at Karnak, Thothmes III holds his offering in a similar way. Wilson is not, however, convinced of that theory of Professor Erlenmayer that the Egyptians were a left-handed people. When looking at early

* _Nature Series: Left-handedness_: Macmillan, New York and London, 1891.

manuscript drawings of English horsewomen in Anglo-Saxon days, he finds two of them sitting side-saddle on the right side, contrary to the later custom of sitting left-sided, with the right hand free for the whip, as in the Great Seals of King Henry VIII's daughters, Mary and Elizabeth.

By contrast, from the New World, he can quote Red Indian language as distinguishing between and comparing right and left. Fu Mohawk, the right hand has the sonorous title of "ji-ke-we-yen-den-dah-kon", which means, "I know how". The left hand—"ske-ne-kwa-dih"—simply means, "The other side".

Whether watching the porters coming off a Mississippi steamer and noting on which shoulder they carried their burdens, or enumerating the difficulties encountered by south-paws in the matter of scissors, rifles, candle-snuffers and the scythe, Sir Daniel Wilson provided one of the first all-round examinations of handedness in its many aspects. It is lively enough to include the story of the ambidextral golfer at the Montreal Club, who took two sets of clubs round with him, to the discomfiture of his opponents. Even in those early days, the suggestion was made that the Club should import some left-handed clubs from Wilson's native Scotland, the home of golf. There is, too, a regional note about polar bears, told to him by one, Dr John Rae.

"A curious story was related by an Eskimo about a bear throwing a large piece of ice at the head of a walrus. The man added that he threw it with his left paw, as if this were some-thing very unusual. This would seem to indicate that left-handedness was not very common among the Eskimos. . . ."

This Daniel comes to judgment with the conclusion that, with the great majority, right-handedness is mainly the result of education. "In every sudden and unpremeditated action, the prompt use of the left hand shows that there remains, after the utmost educational training, some inherent impulse, resulting in a greater aptitude in the one hand than the other. My own experience," he adds, "being left-handed myself, shows the education of a lifetime contending with only partial success to overcome an instinctive natural preference. The result has been, as in all similar cases, to make me ambidextrous, yet not strictly speaking ambidextrous."

The search for a suitable brain of a left-hander to be dissected was conducted by Wilson for years, until he despaired of discovering the solution until after his own death, for, as he publicly remarked: "My own brain has been in use for more than the fully allotted term of threescore years and ten, and the time cannot be far distant when I shall be done with it. When that time comes, I shall be glad if it were turned to account for the little further service of settling this physiologic puzzle."

But the "long-coveted opportunity" did occur during his lifetime. One Thomas Neilly, an Irishman who had served in the army, and had been so inveterately sinistral that he was always placed as "the left-hand man of the line", and was allowed the exceptional usage of firing from the left shoulder, died at the Toronto Provincial Asylum, and Wilson was summoned to the autopsy. The brain was removed, and the two hemispheres weighed. To Wilson's great satisfaction, the right hemisphere was distinctly heavier.

SIR CYRIL BURT

This eminent authority on Psychology, of which he was Emeritus Professor of the University of London, has an international reputation in the study of child development. His most popular work contains a detailed chapter on the whole aspect of left-handedness.* He denies that, in the vast majority of backward children whom he has examined, mainly in London, that general ill health or physical weakness is the main factor.

"Far more important, from the standpoint of classroom instruction, are the more limited and specialised defects of sense and muscular co-ordination—defects of sight, hearing, speech and hand-movement."

Burt's main contribution was to concentrate, not on any one of these defects, singly, but to regard backwardness as the primary factor in itself, and to recognise the individual defect as

* The Backward Child: University of London Press, 1937.

one of many contributory causes. His definition of left-handedness is: "A consistent tendency (whether congenital, or induced post-natally by accident or by some other change in the hand or its neuro-muscular apparatus) to undertake new dexterities with the left hand rather than the right."

The detection of left-handedness, therefore, does not depend entirely on the spontaneous reactions of a child when asked to perform a certain task, or when left to perform it himself. His reaction to an unfamiliar task is even more important. Burt adds the equally important bodily gestures: Which thumb is placed on top, when closing the hands? Which hand is uppermost when folding the arms, as in the case of Mona Lisa and Leonardo da Vinci. In two-handed operations, such as holding a cricket bat or sweeping a lawn, Burt claims that it is not enough to ask which hand is uppermost: it is, which hand executes the more delicate and more active task of guiding and directing the instrument? This may vary between a cricket bat or baseball bat, a broom, and a spade, because the functional movement may be different. From enquiries in America, Burt deduces that, "when a man is seen throwing with the right hand and batting with the left, then it is certain he will sweep and pitch hay with the left hand". He adds that he has never heard of a left-handed scythe.

Burt's percentages of left-handedness, as we have seen, rise sharply when applied to backward and mentally defective children. This he ascribes to their difficulties in muscular co-ordination. He calls many of them ambisinistral: it is not so much that they are dexterous with the left hand as *gauche* with the right. Left-handedness with them is rather a mark of an ill-organised nervous system than of a dull or a deficient mind.

As to the consequences of being sinistral, Burt admits that in school, the left-hander is handicapped, and this applies not only to writing and drawing, but to reading, spelling and even composition. He metaphorically crams a left-hand foot into a right-hand shoe, gets his words mixed up, pens his lines more slowly. The temperamental consequences may even be worse. "Day, after day, at his desk in the schoolroom, at his games in the playground, over the dinner-table at home, the left-hander feels, and is made to feel, that he is peculiar, that he is not as other children are. . . . If harsh methods are publicly used, he may come to hate school and human companionship altogether, and grow egocentric, moody, and full of secret resentment."

The one exception one might make is over games, where he might strike like a budding Babe Ruth, kick like a Ferenc Puskas, play a backhand like a Drobny.

The teacher is recommended to go into each case-history and family-history, to find if the sinistrality is likely to be inborn or hereditary, and whether it affects merely a few activities or the whole being: whether, in fact, it is a habit rather than a physiological necessity. Further, it should be discovered, as soon as possible, what kind of employment the child is likely to take up on leaving school. If it is manual work, then the physical operation of a machine in a factory might be detrimental or even impossible to a left-hander. (The same would be true of any budding sinistral violinist wanting to join the school orchestra.)

"Almost the whole of our civilisation," writes Burt, "from the door-knobs in the house to the steps on the bus, from the lathes in the shop to the handles on egg-beaters, sewing machines, gramophones, and the like—all are designed on the assumption that we are a right-handed population. Hence, anyone who grows up left-handed is bound to be penalized in a hundred directions."

ROBERT HERTZ

The principal of the Sociological school (*Année Sociologique*) in Paris, the celebrated Emile Durkheim, numbered among his pupils a promising young student whose special preference was the study of Maori and Indonesian tribes. Robert Hertz used the immense resources of the British Museum for most of his research, between 1904 and 1906. With the outbreak of World War I, Durkheim's *Année Sociologique* was scattered, and many of the students died. Robert Hertz was killed leading his section in the attack on Marcheville on April 13th, 1915, at the age of 33. It is ironic that his main published work had been on the subject of Death and Funeral Rites among the Maoris, and that he was engaged on a major religious work concerning Sin and Confession.

The other essay published belonged to a very different category: a study of the Right Hand, and the reasons for its superiority. This, originally appearing in the *Revue Philosophique* in 1909, was translated into English and issued as recently as 1960.* The full title is "The Pre-Eminence of the Right Hand: a Study in Religious Polarity". Much of Hertz's thinking has become outdated by later studies, but he must rank as one of those who contributed much material of interest, at a time when handedness was so hotly discussed.

Hertz had found some inspiration for his thesis from his studies of Indonesia and the Maoris. The Maori expression *tama tane*, "male side", meant virility, paternal descent, the east, the right (in the Antipodes, the sun would rise on the right for anyone facing north). "*Tama wahine*", the female or left side, covered everything contrary. "All evils, misery and death", ran a Maori proverb, "come from the female element." Similarly, the priest in the local ritual placed the Wand of Life facing the east, and the Wand of Death facing the west, in the sacred ground. In Indonesia, he was told by a certain Dr Jacobs, who had returned from there, that the native children frequently had the left arm completely bound, and were told not to use it. He also knew the superstition concerning the left thumb—that contact with it might be fatal, for there poison might be concealed: an imaginary *tabu* which has been known in many tribes.

But Hertz's main line of deduction is through his sense of religion; its duality or polarity, matching the functions of the two hands.

"What resemblance more perfect," he begins, "than that between our two hands! And yet what a striking inequality

* *Death and the Right Hand*: translated by Rodney and Claudia Needham: Cohen and West, London, 1960.

there is! To the right hand go honours, flattering designations, prerogatives: it acts, orders and *takes*. The left hand, on the contrary, is despised and reduced to the role of a humble auxiliary: by itself it can do nothing; it helps, it supports, it *holds*."

He echoes Chinese thought in describing the right hand as the symbol of aristocracy, the left hand of the common people. But he also realises that, given the theory of cerebral dominance, the left-hander, being of necessity partly ambidextrous, is capable of considerable skill and resource. But the crux of the matter is in the interplay of both hands. "If organic asymmetry had not existed, it would have had to be invented."

The blend of deep Catholic conviction and an exhaustive study of the habits of primitive tribes no doubt accounts for Hertz's particular theory of religious polarity. Christian and Muslim ritual, as we know, is firmly dextral in its use of hands and movements, but among the tribes there is obviously a much more intense feeling about the difference between the sacred and the profane. "Dualism which is of the essence of primitive thought, dominates primitive social organisation. . . . The two phratries (parts) are reciprocally opposed. . . . Everything that exists within my own part is sacred and forbidden to me: this is why I cannot eat my totem, or spill the blood of a member, or even touch his corpse, or marry in my clan. Contrarily, the opposite part is profane to me: the clans which compose it supply me with provisions, wives, and human sacrificial victims, bury my dead and prepare my sacred ceremonies."

Belief in the supernatural obviously colours Robert Hertz's views. The right hand is not only, by statistics, the dominant hand. It is somehow, also, in a state of grace. God himself has a dualism. He can be beneficent, loving, dependable; or, like the jealous and angry God of the Old Testament, he can "visit the children unto the third and fourth generation, of them that hate me!"

Hertz can believe that the preference for the right hand is somehow a sign of moral pre-eminence. "For centuries the systematic paralysation of the left arm has expressed the will animating man to make the sacred dominate over the profane, to sacrifice the desires and the interests of the individual to the demands felt by the collective consciousness. . . . It is because man is a double being that he possesses a right and left that are profoundly differentiated."

It must be remembered that these words were written when Robert Hertz was a young man in his early twenties. They show a submission where one might expect rebellion. But at least, he had studied the various biological and anatomical theories for handedness in man, and agreed that these probably did account for a much greater proportion of dextrals. Only when the disparity was recognised by the tribe was all honour done for the more popular or "standard" side, and all dishonour awarded to the minority side. The fact of sun-worship would therefore hardly seem to come into it, and Hertz has hope of a better balance between social opinion on left and right:

"If the constraint of a mystical ideal has for centuries been able to make a man a unilateral being, physiologically mutilated, liberated and foresighted community will strive to develop better the energies dormant in our left side and in our right cerebral hemisphere, and to assure by an appropriate training a more harmonious development of the organism."

ABRAM BLAU

This Professor of Psychiatry at the New York University College of Medicine produced, twenty years ago, a Research Monograph which amounts to the most formidable onslaught on left-handedness to be published in modern times.* It is subtitled, "A Study of the Origin and Meaning of Right and Left Sidedness and its Relation to Personality and Language."

Dr Blau first became interested in the subject ten years before he wrote his monograph, through having treated a number of neurological patients with language defects such as stuttering. Study of these cases led him to consider the origin of handedness, and later, the psychological make-up of the sinistral. Blau, who has been quoted on a number of occasions in this present

---

* *The Master Hand*: American Orthopsychiatric Association Inc., New York, 1946.

book, is obviously an expert to be reckoned with, and his assessment of the sinistral character and the desirability of re-training to the Master or dextral hand is worth considering in detail, since his conclusions cut across many of the theories long held by other authorities. On balance, they do not give the left-hander much to be proud of or thankful for, living as he does in a right-handed world—a phrase Blau himself uses.

The Italian psychiatrist Cesare Lombroso regarded left-handedness as a sign of degeneracy, and pointed to the greater proportion of sinistrals among criminals, psychopaths, and mental defectives. (The Italian word for left-handed— *mancini*—means, as has been pointed out, evil or deceitful.) Blau retorts: "Yet, there is equal if not more confirmation that most left-handed individuals appear to be intelligent and not anti-social." This is about his last complimentary reference to the left-hander.

"Sinistrality," he writes, "represents a failure in learning the conventional dextrality. This failure may arise from one of three conditions: an inherent deficiency, faulty education, or emotional negativism." This latter he regards as probably the most common type of sinistrality, a symptom of infantile psychoneurosis.

"My theory of negatavistic sinistrality is that it springs from a contrary emotional attitude to the learning of right-handedness. This is based on the presumption that the environment contains all the necessary, normal social cues and traditional pressures for the acquisition of dextrality and that the child has enough mental and physical capacity to acquire it."

But does the naturally sinistral child accept this? Not on your life. The cues are disregarded, and actually opposed, so that left-handedness is the result.

"Sinistrality is thus nothing more than an expression of infantile negativism and falls into the same category as . . . contrariety in feeding and elimination, retardation in speech, and general perverseness in so far as the infant with meagre outlets can express it."

This might seem to be more the attitude of a conventional

schoolmarm than a qualified psychiatrist. To be left-handed is, in other words, simply to be cussed or naughty. But Dr Blau continues to trace reasons for this refusal to conform, and bases his findings on the emotions. Infantile refusal, or negativism, can easily be traced to lack of love and attention by the mother. His psychiatric studies of many left-handed children, he believes, bear out this theory of maternal rejection in early infancy. He quotes a number of examples which might well make good material for a play by Tennessee Williams. Maternal rejection has been, indeed, a stock dramatic subject back to the days of the Greeks, and it was well known to Shakespeare. Was Hamlet, therefore, left-handed—or any of the disputed children of Lady Macbeth? And what of paternal rejection—could King Lear have begotten a left-handed daughter in the rebellious nega-tavistic Cordelia?

Dr Blau obviously does not claim that all children with this reaction are left-handed, or that this reaction necessarily leads to sinistrality. This would be to revive the scapegoat, and the persecution of the witches who went round widdershins. But he does claim: "It has been my experience from very careful social and psychiatric studies that the abounding majority of left-handed children have this sort of background."

At this point it should be made clear that Dr Blau has rejected any hereditary incidence of left-handedness, and indeed seems to have discarded the explanation of cerebral dominance. It is all a behaviour characteristic.

Well, let us continue. We are next invited to compare the two personality types—the dextral and the sinistral. The dextral, obviously, is compliant where the sinistral is negeta-vistic. Blau realises man's derogatory attitude to the left-hander through the centuries, "that he is gauche, awkward or unusual; at worst, that he is deficient mentally and physic-ally". He then suggests a rule-of-thumb explanation, which expands as his monograph proceeds. His psychiatric treatment of sinistral adults has apparently conclusively confirmed the negatavistic character structure, with histories of early in-fantile emotional troubles. One might ask, which came first, the left-handedness, or the cussedness? Certainly he has no answer as to why some naughty and rebellious children remain right-handed, and show no signs of veering to the left, and puts it all down, once again, to the influence of mother.

But there is more to read about the character of the sinistral type, and it does not make pleasant reading. If a child is negatavistic, this trait may not merely affect refusal to obey, but refusal to defaecate. Blau calls on the testimony of Freud to imply that obstinate characters are probably also constipated characters, in the anal sense.

By the same analysis, the sinistral personality is, according to Blau, close to what has been called a compulsive character. He quotes the American psychoanalyst Hendricks in defining this type:

"He is overmeticulous in dress and social manner, devotes an excessive care to the collection of useless articles, is either brutal or coldly aloof, accepts and enforces a very rigid moral code, is often secretly superstitious and openly very obstinate, is with great difficulty diverted from a rigid course of sternly intellectual thought, constantly experiences the greatest difficulty in making decisions."*

Much of this would, it might be thought, apply to someone like Adolf Hitler. He was determinedly right-handed, swastika and all.

But we find Dr Blau considering this blend of the constipated and the compulsive to be typically sinistral, and he sums up the personality-structure of the left-hander thus:

"Some of the outstanding features of the character type are obstinacy, inordinate orderliness, parsimony, rigidity, a tendency to over-intellectualisation, and self-wilfulness. This character type is not always a liability but may be a real asset if directed along socially acceptable and useful lines. . . ."

For this relief, much thanks, the sinistral might say.

But Dr Blau cannot be accused of merely denigrating the characteristics of the left-hander. His book has added considerably to the general knowledge of the subject, and the theories about handedness.

* *Facts and Theories of Psychoanalysis*: Hendricks, Knopf, New York, 1941.

"Today," he writes, "the question has broken its academic boundaries. The phenomenon of handedness has assumed considerable significance in the minds of scientists, most of whom centre their interest mainly in the effects of left-handedness and its forced alteration."

He admits that "lefties" are at times viewed with admiration and respect, especially if they are southpaw baseball players, tennis players or footballers. But he recognises the disadvantages of being known to be left-handed, the stigma, the derogatory phrases, and so on. "Why a small percentage of the human race persists in using the left or unconventional hand, despite taboos and rigid social barriers imposed by society to prevent such usage, has long been a challenging problem to scholar and scientist."

Blau's own explanation cuts across many earlier ones. He does not concentrate on hand alone, or, as in other cases, on hand and eye alone. "We cannot dissociate the phenomenon of preferred laterality from the whole person or the whole of life." His object is to analyse right and left laterality as if they were two sides of a penny, each complete in itself, but contributing to the coin as a whole.

Preferred laterality, he goes on to say, is not an inherited trait. "There is absolutely no evidence to support the contention that dominance, either in handedness or any other form, is a congenital predetermined human capacity . . . the theory of heredity must be put down as erroneous."

"Preferred laterality is dynamic and has many forms. Complete informity of dextrality or sinistrality in all bilateral functions in one individual is extremely rare. We find a variety of combinations along a scale from complete right to complete left, with the curve of distribution skewing in favour of the right side."

Blau is firmly of the opinion, as we will have gathered, that sinistrality represents, "a mishap to the normal development of dextrality". He finds no factual evidence that it is a Mendelian recessive trait.

XXIX

THE LEFT HAND IN EVERDAY LIFE

Among kitchen and household utensils, the iron and the potato-peeler have for long been a handicap to left-handers. Potato-peelers for sinistrals became available, according to information from department stores, some years ago, and there are models available which are for both left- and right-handed use—allowing, therefore, no excuse for avoiding the traditionally irksome duty.

With irons, the difficulty experienced by left-handers is that the flex is usually attached to the right hand side of the iron. When used dextrally, it is free of the ironing-board. When used sinistrally, it hangs towards the body, and therefore gets in the way of a free motion. Since the pad for the iron is normally on the right-hand side and the sheet rail pointing from right to left, the sinistral has had to reverse the whole procedure. Today, however, there are both boards and irons available for left-handers, in some cases at no extra cost. One large London store, Harrods, reported a considerable demand for these, and since newlyweds do not always think of asking for them, they are thoughtfully included in the "Bride's List" available for those choosing wedding presents.

Handedness is obviously of importance in the kitchen. Sink-units would normally be placed, for right-handers, so that the draining-board was on the left, since in washing up, the dominant hand is the active one, and the lesser hand places the crockery or cutlery on the board. Much will, however, depend on what position the sink-unit occupies in the kitchen itself. Handles are also an interesting example of handedness. The standard position for the handle on an oven door is on the right: for the handle of a refrigerator, on the *left*. Why is this? Whether the difference was consciously planned at any stage is difficult to say: one can only hazard that, with a hot oven, the more practised hand, i.e. the right, should reach in to take out the dish, whereas with a refrigerator, not so much care is necessary.

Scissors, right-handed, present a problem to any sinistral, because the cutting edge is on the wrong side for them. Left-handed scissors are therefore available, but in most places cost more. Left-handed tailors and dressmakers will find it very difficult to obtain a pair of sinistral pinking shears for cutting cloth. One method adopted is to buy two pairs, and have the blades joined together in the opposite way—but this is an expensive method.

The same is true of garden secateurs, and as far back as Roman times, it was known that no 'scaevola" or left-hander could wield a scythe properly. This handicap was also noted by Thomas Carlyle. It does not seem that sinistral agricultural labourers in England are likely to enjoy many privileges.

Barbers and hairdressers are nearly always dextral. This, again, is the result of the design of the average pair of scissors. Moreover, in automatic hair-clippers, the instrument has a starting switch which can only be operated with the right thumb.

An amusing and rather pathetic account of a quest for left-handed nutcrackers appeared in the London *Times* in October, 1965. The seeker, who lived in Kensington and was left-handed herself, saw a pair advertised in the Christmas brochure of a well-known London store, with a lion head or an eagle head, for seven guineas—a high price for such a humble item. The lion's head above the jaw formed the equivalent of one blade in a pair of scissors, the jaw itself the other. The handle of the top "blade" was on the left, and vice versa. The brochure, however, did not state that the nutcrackers were sinistral, and when *The Times*' anonymous correspondent confronted them in the shop, she found to her sorrow that the mechanism did not, in fact, correspond to that of a left-handed pair of scissors, as she had hoped: the lion's head and jaw were not attached to each other by a screw.

"Feeling somewhat crushed, I was reluctant to leave without some further effort in the cause of the left-handed. So had they, I enquired, any left-handed scissors? "No", came the reply, "but we can always make a pair for you." The reply was given so disdainfully that I felt more than ever like an awkward intruder in the shop."

In knitting, though there is no difference to the appearance of the stitch, left-handers knit with the wool and the working needle in the left hand. It presents no greater problems, though left-handed knitters tend to be slower than right-handed, and it is important, if they are working on four needles, and put the knitting down, to remember, on return, which way round the needles were arranged.

There is a continental method of knitting which is like crocheting: in this way, the knitter holds the wool and the needle from which she is working in the left hand, hooking the wool through the right hand needle. Threading a needle, and sewing comes as easily to the left-hander as the right. Some of the most delicate and exacting work (such as in Madeira) is done expertly by left-handed women.

Among the other domestic habits, left-handers, particularly children, tend to lay the table the opposite way from the normal. This can often be a cause for embarrassment. It is natural for a left-hander to expect to have his glass on the left side, but if the guests are in a row, this could lead to as much confusion as would a sinistral fiddler in an orchestra, or a sinistral soldier who had not been placed as the traditional "left soldier of the line". Wine, moreover, back to the days of the Ancient Greeks, must always be served from left to right. The reverse has always been regarded as a sign of bad luck or in-hospitality. "Passing the port" is a traditional circumambulation which must always follow the sunward path. In the Senior Common Room of Brasenose College, Oxford, the port, suitably decanted, is still sent round the table on a small

THREE LEFT-HANDED THOROUGHBREDS

Left: Charles Chaplin (*left*, and also playing left-handedly) in the film *Limelight*.

Below, left: Harpo Marx, zaniest of the great Marx Brothers.

Below, right: Danny Kaye.

PAUL MCCARTNEY
A sinistral Beatle, with spaghetti instead of guitar.

RINGO STARR
The left-handed Beatle drummer listens to another beat.

KIM NOVAK (*left*). As "Moll Flanders", she even fenced left-handed.

railway track, but it is a one-way track, and any reversing would be forbidden by the ancient custom.

Among sinistrals who are partly ambidextral—and this applies to the majority—when both hands are used in eating, the knife is usually held in the right hand, but a spoon would be in the left. When a single knife is used, for cheese, or cutting bread, the left hand is almost invariably used. The hostess's chief guest, be he sinistral or dextral, will be placed at her right hand. Eating habits in more primitive countries, without implements, come into the category of the Clean and the Unclean Hand, and here the strictest observance must be followed.

Many designers seem to be left-handed, which bears out the contention that a blend of the artistic and the individualistic often arises from sinistrality. In one of London's well-known furniture stores, Heal's, the designing staff at one time had almost a majority of left-handers. One of the practical problems is, of course, the T-square, which is normally made for right-handed people. Left-handed T-squares are not easy to come by, and many sinistral designers are content to try and adapt themselves to the awkward alternative.

A point made by a senior designer at this store, himself left-handed, married to a left-hander and with two left-handed children, is that the layout of a shop usually goes on the assumption that the shopper, on entering, instinctively turns to the right. A study has been made of this in the U.S., which has resulted in the almost universal placing of the most desirable line of goods to the right of the door, so as to attract the eye immediately. Sinistral shoppers would tend to go in the other direction.

In pottery, the potter's wheel can usually revolve in either direction, as operated by the feet, and asymmetry in pottery would only arise when, say, handles were placed on cups which had an asymmetrical design. The legend of the left-handed tea-cup, suggested by the actor Spike Milligan, has long been a music-hall joke, together with the left-handed "flannel" hammer. But if there is a design on one side of the cup only, then the handle should be placed on a given side, in relation to the design.

Turkish coffee jugs in the familiar copper designs have the long handle and the lip on the side (nearer the body) arranged so that they can only effectively be poured by the right hand—not surprising, in view of Middle Eastern attitudes.

Filling in official forms is also geared as a general practice to the movement from left to right, and stamps are placed on the right side of the envelope. It would clearly be more convenient for the sinistral to place his stamps on the left side, particularly if he was attaching a large number of stamps in an office, or for Christmas cards. But since franking of stamps is nearly always automatic, the presence of "cack-handed" envelopes might cause serious dislocation.

Public telephone instruments (and most telephones on office desks) are on the left in the box. Whether people can be said to be left-eared or not is difficult to determine, but although in old superstitions the left ear was the unlucky one, the telephone has made it the common one, and probably the more sensitive one. Moreover, it leaves the right hand free for dialling and inserting money. These simple actions the left-hander learns to do, but when it comes to writing down numbers or notes while on the telephone, he is handicapped, and must hold his right hand across his body, interfering with the free play of the left hand for writing. It was Peter Scott, naturalist and artist, who revealed to the author one advantage he enjoyed—in gliding. Mr Scott, son of the hero of the Arctic, Captain Scott, is himself left-handed, and in recent years became the Gliding Champion of Great Britain. "The instruments in a glider", he explained, "are on the right. I learned how to operate these dextrally, and then was able to use my left hand for making navigational notes on to a pad on my knee." So, it's an ill wind . . . which wafts a glider on to success.

Left-handed writing problems are dealt with elsewhere in this book. Whatever the technique involved, there seems no reason why the sinistral should regard himself or herself as handicapped, despite the unnatural direction of the writing.

Many girls become expert secretaries, whose shorthand is no less good than their dextral equivalents. Much of a modern secretary's time is spent today in transcribing tape-recordings on a stenorette rather than sitting by the boss's desk with notebook at the ready (this may be something of a loss for the boss). Most secretarial bureaus admit that many of their clients are left-handed, and this does not count against them.

In August, 1965, a panel of City men from the London Chamber of Commerce adjudicated in a diploma examination of 150 entrants, to choose Britain's Top Secretary. She was Mrs Nancy Hall, 33, daughter of a railway engine driver, and working for the country's National Coal Board, her boss being director in charge of the Mining Research Establishment. In addition to answering a number of searching questions about sales methods, and immigrants in British society, she had to prove her technical worth with typing at 80 words per minute, and shorthand at 130 words per minute. This she does with her left hand.

Nothing more need really be said about left-handed secretaries. They can obviously make the grade.

Cheque books have the stubs on the left side, so that the dextral can steady the book with his left hand, and keep the whole space clear for filling in first the stub, then the cheque. In 1955, an enterprising New York firm, the Trade Bank and Trust Co., of 7th Avenue and 38th St., advertised a special service of cheque books "for Southpaws". One of the *New Yorker's* equally enterprising reporters went to investigate.* From the director of business development, Mr Robert A. Halpern, "a husky, tanned, right-handed man with greying hair", he learned that the firm had been providing the books since 1945, and that the kindly action was to prevent southpaws from having to cross their hands over while making out the cheque, "like a pianist playing a difficult arpeggio". Mr Halpern added that his own daughter was left-handed, as were two of his secretaries. This American bank practice does not seem to be known at all in Europe.

* *New Yorker*, July 30th, 1955.

In industry, the problems of left-handed workers using tools or machines constructed for right-handed operators do not seem to have received much study in any country except France. In October, 1962, an official study group was set up in Paris to consider methods of re-adaptation for "*gauchers*" or left-handed people in such jobs. Doctors were to study the effects of left-handedness on efficiency in individual cases. The Chairman, Professor Henri Desoille, said that one obvious remedy was to train them to use their right hand as well, "so that they are more balanced". But he realised the additional problem that, if done at school, it could lead to stammering or lack of interest in school lessons. An enterprising small firm in Manchester announced, in 1965, that it would cater primarily for left-handed implements of all types. But these, apart from minor instances, are the only cases we have found of helping left-handed workmen in a right-handed working world.

In dancing, one would expect the use of left or right foot to be important, but there is no general rule in favour of the right, except for ballroom dancing, where the reverse turn is towards the left. Most ballet dancers learn to use both feet with equal skill, but one can detect a left-handed dancer at the practice rail. When relaxing, she will usually put the left foot forward, and will tend to pirouette and turn more easily to the left. Such, however, is the rule of the stage, that the foot commencing the dance may well be dictated by the side at which the dancer enters. By tradition, the first step should be with the "upstage" leg.

Group dancing in circular movements, such as the Jewish "hora" dance, is invariably clockwise, but there are variants. Some interesting discoveries have been made by Curt Sachs.*

"The preference for one side of the body as a problem of culture history was first observed and discussed by Bachofen: the left side of the body is given preference over the right in the cultures in which women occupy an important position—in

* *World History of the Dance*: New York, 1937.

matriarchies, earth and moon religions, and agricultural societies. The right side is favoured over the left in the cultures in which males have the more important place—in patriarchies, sky and sun religions, and among hunters and nobles. We can add a Chinese counterpart: in old China the peasants give preference to the left hand, the nobles to the right.

"This fact seems also to have a certain importance for the history of the dance. In it, perhaps, we may find an explanation for the strange phenomenon—which cannot be ascribed to pure physiological reaction—that in many dances, according to rule, the left foot begins the dance, in others, the right. Thus the *bacubert*, the sword round of Southern France, calls for the left foot, but the *basse dance* of the 15th century for the right. The former is a vegetation charm and therefore rustic; the latter is a dance of the nobility."

According to an old account, when the Highlanders were first persuaded to come down from the hills and fight as regular soldiers for the Scots, many of them could not distinguish between their left and right foot quickly enough to obey commands. So, as an experiment, wisps of hay were tied to one foot, and wisps of straw to the other. The commands "Hay foot!" and "Straw foot!" were then substituted, and the Highlanders responded.

But assuming a quicker degree of co-operation among ordinary soldiers, the command "By the left . . ." is given because the left side bears the weapon and perhaps also the shield, the weapon to be ready for action as the body moves forward. The traditional position of "stand at ease" meant that the left leg was loose, and ready for the first step, while the body, with its viscera heavier on the right, could rest its main weight on the right leg. Burt states that, in right-handed persons, the right leg is said, as a rule, to be a little shorter. He adds that "in most armies the place of seniority and honour is on the right, so that the right-hand man has his right arm free, and the next has his right hand ready to support him. When stationary, armies dress by the right, i.e. the senior; when marching, by the left, i.e. by the weakest."

There could be a slight objection here, in that two-legged animals and birds also advance with the left foot or claw first, and there seems to be no proof that the right leg, say, of a penguin is stronger than the left, nor the right claw of a parrot.

Burt adds: "Incorrigibly left-handed, the author's own experience in drilling as a volunteer was that, after a little practice, he had no difficulty in firing from the right shoulder; but he never could acquire an equal facility with his companions in unfixing a bayonet and returning it to its sheath."

"'Urry up wi' that floor, lass, the blood's rushin' to me 'ead!"

XXX

THE SOUTH SIDE STORY

1. SOUTHPAW 1: LEFT-HANDER: *Specif:* a left-handed base-ball pitcher 2: a boxer who leads with the right hand and foot forward while guarding with the left hand.
2. SOUTHPAW adj. 1: habitually using the left hand: LEFT-HANDED 2: done with the left hand (a laboriously printed southpaw note—John Mason Brown)

.WEBSTER: *New International Dictionary*

SOUTHPAW; a left-handed boxer: pugilistic: U.S., anglicised in 1934, *The Daily Telegraph*, Sept. 21, concerning Freddie Miller, "He is, in boxing parlance, a 'Southpaw'". Ex U.S. baseball slang (1918).

PARTRIDGE: *Dictionary of Slang*

In the old ball park of Chicago West Side, the pitcher faced west: therefore a left-handed pitching arm was south, and from this emerged the name "Southpaw". Its origin is therefore in baseball and only later was it applied to the left-handed boxer, with whom it is now firmly associated. The sinistral phenomenon has, of course, been noted down the ages in sport of many kinds, even dating back to instructions given to Roman gladiators on how to tackle a left-handed opponent. The element of surprise is the strongest weapon in the sinistral armoury, when left meets right.

One of the greatest players in the history of baseball, which dates back for centuries, was George Herman "Babe" Ruth (1895–1948) from Baltimore. He was signed on in the local side as a pitcher in 1913, graduating to the Red Sox and finally the Yankees, with whom he achieved his greatest fame and fortune. In 1927 he set up a record with 60 home runs. In his

lifetime, he earned more than a million dollars playing baseball
—and playing it left-handedly. His various books, however,
make little mention of this remarkable fact, and he did not, to
the present author's knowledge, give any written advice for his
fellow sinistrals in the game. Two other famous players of the
past were Lehmann and Webb.

For expert information on southpaw boxing, the author is
indebted to the well-known British sports writer, Tony van den
Bergh. He confirms the gladiatorial story:

"If instead of looking back a mere two or three centuries,
we turn to the days when Rome bestrode the world, we can see
from illustrations of the time that many boxing gladiators were
southpaws. They were 'gloved'—but 'gloved' with the *Caestus*,
the leather thongs, studded with metal, binding the knuckles
and forearms of the boxers, which enabled the victor not only
to put his man down for the count, but to ferry him across the
Styx at the same time."

Let us accept that only 10 per cent of boxers are left-handed;
a generous figure perhaps. Only five of these ten will box as
southpaws, the others being taught from an early age to adapt
the orthodox stance, even though this will mean that their
strongest punch—the left—will of necessity be shortened, and so
lose authority. Therefore, simple arithmetic will show that an
orthodox boxer will only meet a southpaw opponent on an
average once in twenty outings, and the southpaw will only
meet an opponent of similar stance in the same ratio. Thus,
however skilful an orthodox boxer may be, he is bound to be
inexperienced when faced with a member of the right-foot-
foremost brigade. If he is to win, he must tackle the problem
with imagination, guts, and—most probably—with considerable pain.

On the other hand, the southpaw, rarely meeting one of his
own kind, is used to facing the orthodox; and so is posed with
no new problem. It would appear logical, therefore, that the
southpaw should have vast advantage over his opponents.
Yet the number of southpaws to win world championships are
remarkably few. Only ten southpaws have worn the world

crown; and two of these had somewhat dubious claims.*

No southpaw has held the world heavyweight championship, the highest honour of all. Undoubtedly the greatest of
those who reached the top was Freddie Miller, the Cincinnatti
featherweight, who had no less than 237 contests, of which he
only lost 24; being k.o'd only once in his entire career.
Freddie Miller will be remembered in Britain for campaigns
in 1934 and 1935, when, fighting almost weekly, he handed
boxing lessons to all our leading featherweights and light-
weights, including such ring giants—in skill not size—as the
long-bodied pride of Liverpool, Nel Tarleton, Dave Crowley,
who now owns a bar in Rome, Jimmy Walsh and Seaman
Tommy Watson. Miller, the World Champion, was as fast a
moving boxer as has ever graced the featherweight class; but
despite his speed he still had the ability to set himself for a
punch, as is proved by his forty-three knock-out victories.

The only British southpaw to win a world title was the Scot
from Ayrshire, Jackie Patterson, who held the flyweight crown
from 1946 to 1948. Jackie was essentially a puncher and, indeed, 14 of his total of 91 opponents, failed to pull themselves
off the canvas before the count of ten. From the Empire, came
Jimmy Carruthers, of Australia, a bantamweight who had a
meteoric career, winning the world title and retiring un-
defeated after only nineteen contests. In the past decade
Britain has produced only two really first-class southpaws, in
Dave Charnley—a manager who actually boxes with his
charges—and Brian Curvis of the famous Welsh fighting
family.

Turning over the pages of *Pugilistica*—the boxing "Bible"
which tells the story of bare-knuckle fighting from 1719 to
1863—one finds hardly any mention of wrong-way-round
fighters. Certainly none of the engravings or etchings show

---

* These include: Melio Bettina, Italian-American light-heavyweight (1939);
Lou Brouillard, French-Canadian middle and welterweight; Corbett III (young
Corbett) welterweight, 1933; Tiger Flowers, middleweight; Al McCoy, German-
American, middleweight; George Nichols, Italian-American, light-heavyweight;
John Wilson, middleweight, 1920; Jackie Patterson, Scottish, flyweight, 1946;
Freddie Miller from Cincinnatti, featherweight.

any fighter of the Corinthian period with his right foot in front. Indeed, to a man, the bare-knuckle brigade are shown with their left hands and left feet leading; the hands high and the knees bent, in a stance more reminiscent of fencers than modern day boxers.

Every expert has his own especial answer to the problem of how to encounter a southpaw, the most popular theory being that the orthodox fighter should pour in a stream of right hooks to the jaw and body, on the principle that this is the southpaw's most vulnerable area and the most difficult for him to defend. On the other hand, the southpaw seldom spends a fight throwing lefts at his opponent and one might imagine that the same theory applied to him.

Eddie Pierce, the former light-heavyweight champion of South Africa, was adamant that the best way to deal with a southpaw was to hook him with a left over his leading glove—the right. Booked to fight a Belgian named Deschiemakker, Pierce argued his theory the whole way to Oxford against the opinion of the Inspector of the British Board of Boxing Control who was travelling with him. At the bell, Pierce crossed the ring, touched gloves, stepped back and then threw a smashing left hook to the Belgian southpaw's jaw, sending him crashing to the canvas. Pierce without a glance at his fallen opponent, turned and leant on the ropes looking down at the Inspector. "There you are," he said. "What did I tell you! They get so used to men trying to hit them up the belly with the right, they never expect a left hook. They're suckers for it." He then turned his attention back to the ring in time to see the referee spread his hands wide to denote that the contest was over.

Outside Britain and the Commonwealth, the game of cricket may be looked upon as more of a ritual than a game. Despite the speed of pace bowling and the wide variety of strokes allowed to the batsman, it is the leisurely stroll of fieldsmen to their appointed places between overs, the informal appearance but Olympian authority of umpires, the sacrosanct breaks for lunch and tea, which give cricket its reputation.

Since the earliest days, when top-hatted gentlemen played

on the Downs in Sussex, the left-hander has won an enviable reputation. As long ago as 1892, the staid *Pall Mall Gazette* was asking why left-handed bowlers always became right-handed batsmen. This is certainly not always the case, but many varying examples could be quoted, from the time of the mighty Wilfred Rhodes of England and Warren Bardsley of Australia to the recent spectacular careers of Dennis Compton and Richie Benaud, also of these two countries. There was one Test Match series with England in which the West Indies XI contained more left-handers than right. Gary Sobers is their most striking example, and probably the greatest all-rounder in the world, batting and bowling left-handed.

There is absolutely no prejudice, in cricketing circles, against the sinistral—rather a respect. He starts with the advantage, as a bowler, of being able to deliver the ball "round" the wicket (that is, approaching from right to left) from an angle which a right-hand bowler cannot achieve. As in so many cases in other sports, it is the unusual and unexpected which may claim the victim. As far as batting is concerned, cricketers well know that, when a left-hander faces the bowling, the fieldsmen have to be re-positioned to counter his sinistral strokes. Since this is done at the usual dignified pace, it is possible for a partnership of right-handed and left-handed batsmen to prove a nuisance, or a spinner-out of time, by scoring single runs, and forcing the repeated changing of the field on each occasion.

A very early cricketing memory by a famous sinistral comes in Sir Compton Mackenzie's current series of autobiography:*

"Then there was the cricket match between the small boys of Broadway and a visiting team of small boys in which I took five wickets. This was a complete fluke. Much embarrassed when I was put on to bowl, I concentrated on bowling straight and in order to do this I thought the surest way was to swing my arm directly over my left shoulder. The result was a series of half-volleys which an experienced batsman would have hit over the boundary by stepping out and treating the delivery

* *My Life and Times*: Octave Two, 1891–1900.

as a full pitch. As it was, the inexperienced batsmen I bowled against stepped back and their stumps were spreadeagled. I was entirely at a loss to understand my success as a bowler and not in the least elated by it. Elation came when I held a tough catch at cover-point at the very end of the innings, which left the boys of Broadway victors. The echo of that 'well caught' from the spectators still rings in my mind's eye from seventy years ago.

"Do not let me suggest that I was ever a good cricketer. I suffered from the handicap of being a left-handed bowler and a right-handed batsman. I could bowl without disgracing myself, but as a batsman I was always hopeless. I might not have been such a hopeless golfer as I was if I had started to play with left-handed clubs. I was quite a good shot but I never shot from my right shoulder, and I will back myself to fill a pipe against anybody, for I have always filled a pipe with my left hand."

Hockey is a game played in many countries by both sexes, but it cannot under any circumstances be played left-handedly, owing to the construction of the hockey-stick and the nature of play. The flat striking surface is on the left side: the right side is rounded. According to the All England Women's Hockey Association: "Any player using a left-handed stick would find it almost impossible to keep to the rules. They would find it difficult to receive the ball, or to get the ball away from other players. A 'bully' would also be impossible with a left-handed stick, and so would the avoidance of obstructing. . . ."

In polo, where the relationship between horse and rider is of paramount importance, difficulties can arise for the sinistral. M. G. White has summed up the present position.

"Because collisions in polo are not only very dangerous but can also result in the loss of valuable horses, there are strict rules controlling a player's right of way, i.e. the circumstances in which he can make for the ball with other players having to give way. When the player in possession of the ball is not being challenged by another player he may take the ball on either side of his pony, but hitting the ball forward when on the near side requires a difficult back-hand stroke taken by leaning over the horse's body. When challenged, however, a player has no right of way at all when taking the ball on the near side. He must move over to the off side or clear off altogether. Otherwise, for example, opposing players making for the ball from opposite directions would meet with their ponies head on, whereas by each keeping the ball on the off side of his pony they can meet stick to stick.

"A left-handed player naturally elects whenever possible to take the ball on the near side of his pony, where his stroke is strongest. This means that he has frequently to change smartly over to the off side thus having to make the difficult back-hand motion. In the event of his being 'caught out' on the wrong side of the ball a serious penalty is incurred. Despite the provision for extremely serious penalties in polo, the Hurlingham Club, which controls polo in Britain and many parts of the Commonwealth, now prohibits left-handed play. In earlier years left-handed players had to be specially registered as an indication of their competence and to prevent ambidextrous play in order to confuse the opponent. The American Polo Association, however, still permits left-handed play, though with the higher speeds of modern polo there is a growing feeling that the greater number of occasions in which left-handers could commit dangerous fouls makes their presence undesirable.

"A left-hander in polo is, in balance, at a considerable disadvantage. He is seldom free to use his strongest stroke and being the odd man out is always the first to be blamed in any accident."

Left-handers in lawn-tennis are almost too numerous to mention. But from the days of Jaroslav Drobny to Rod Laver, to name merely the modern examples, the champions have often been sinistrals. As Drobny explained to the author, the initial advantage is in first meeting a right-handed opponent. His forehand is against yours—but you expect that. Your forehand is against his—and that may be something of a surprise for him. The Australian left-handers have, anyhow, established their place in any international championship.

INDEX

A PERSONAL WORD FROM MELVIN POWERS
PUBLISHER, WILSHIRE BOOK COMPANY

Dear Friend:

My goal is to publish interesting, informative, and inspirational books. You can help me accomplish this by answering the following questions, either by phone or by mail. Or, if convenient for you, I would welcome the opportunity to visit with you in my office and hear your comments in person.

Did you enjoy reading this book? Why?

Would you enjoy reading another similar book?

What idea in the book impressed you the most?

If applicable to your situation, have you incorporated this idea in your daily life?

Is there a chapter that could serve as a theme for an entire book? Please explain.

If you have an idea for a book, I would welcome discussing it with you. If you already have one in progress, write or call me concerning possible publication. I can be reached at (213) 875-1711 or (213) 983-1105.

Sincerely yours,

MELVIN POWERS

12015 Sherman Road
North Hollywood, California 91605

MELVIN POWERS SELF-IMPROVEMENT LIBRARY

ASTROLOGY
____ASTROLOGY: HOW TO CHART YOUR HOROSCOPE *Max Heindel*   3.00
____ASTROLOGY: YOUR PERSONAL SUN-SIGN GUIDE *Beatrice Ryder*   3.00
____ASTROLOGY FOR EVERYDAY LIVING *Janet Harris*   2.00
____ASTROLOGY MADE EASY *Astarte*   3.00
____ASTROLOGY MADE PRACTICAL *Alexandra Kayhle*   3.00
____ASTROLOGY, ROMANCE, YOU AND THE STARS *Anthony Norvell*   4.00
____MY WORLD OF ASTROLOGY *Sydney Omarr*   5.00
____THOUGHT DIAL *Sydney Omarr*   3.00
____WHAT THE STARS REVEAL ABOUT THE MEN IN YOUR LIFE *Thelma White*   3.00

BRIDGE
____BRIDGE BIDDING MADE EASY *Edwin B. Kantar*   5.00
____BRIDGE CONVENTIONS *Edwin B. Kantar*   5.00
____BRIDGE HUMOR *Edwin B. Kantar*   3.00
____COMPETITIVE BIDDING IN MODERN BRIDGE *Edgar Kaplan*   4.00
____DEFENSIVE BRIDGE PLAY COMPLETE *Edwin B. Kantar*   10.00
____HOW TO IMPROVE YOUR BRIDGE *Alfred Sheinwold*   2.00
____IMPROVING YOUR BIDDING SKILLS *Edwin B. Kantar*   4.00
____INTRODUCTION TO DEFENDER'S PLAY *Edwin B. Kantar*   3.00
____SHORT CUT TO WINNING BRIDGE *Alfred Sheinwold*   3.00
____TEST YOUR BRIDGE PLAY *Edwin B. Kantar*   3.00
____WINNING DECLARER PLAY *Dorothy Hayden Truscott*   4.00

BUSINESS, STUDY & REFERENCE
____CONVERSATION MADE EASY *Elliot Russell*   2.00
____EXAM SECRET *Dennis B. Jackson*   2.00
____FIX-IT BOOK *Arthur Symons*   2.00
____HOW TO DEVELOP A BETTER SPEAKING VOICE *M. Hellier*   2.00
____HOW TO MAKE A FORTUNE IN REAL ESTATE *Albert Winnikoff*   4.00
____INCREASE YOUR LEARNING POWER *Geoffrey A. Dudley*   2.00
____MAGIC OF NUMBERS *Robert Tocquet*   2.00
____PRACTICAL GUIDE TO BETTER CONCENTRATION *Melvin Powers*   2.00
____PRACTICAL GUIDE TO PUBLIC SPEAKING *Maurice Forley*   3.00
____7 DAYS TO FASTER READING *William S. Schaill*   3.00
____SONGWRITERS RHYMING DICTIONARY *Jane Shaw Whitfield*   5.00
____SPELLING MADE EASY *Lester D. Basch & Dr. Milton Finkelstein*   2.00
____STUDENT'S GUIDE TO BETTER GRADES *J. A. Rickard*   2.00
____TEST YOURSELF—Find Your Hidden Talent *Jack Shafer*   2.00
____YOUR WILL & WHAT TO DO ABOUT IT *Attorney Samuel G. Kling*   3.00

CALLIGRAPHY
____ADVANCED CALLIGRAPHY *Katherine Jeffares*   6.00
____CALLIGRAPHY—The Art of Beautiful Writing *Katherine Jeffares*   5.00

CHESS & CHECKERS
____BEGINNER'S GUIDE TO WINNING CHESS *Fred Reinfeld*   3.00
____BETTER CHESS—How to Play *Fred Reinfeld*   2.00
____CHECKERS MADE EASY *Tom Wiswell*   2.00
____CHESS IN TEN EASY LESSONS *Larry Evans*   3.00
____CHESS MADE EASY *Milton L. Hanauer*   3.00
____CHESS MASTERY—A New Approach *Fred Reinfeld*   2.00
____CHESS PROBLEMS FOR BEGINNERS *edited by Fred Reinfeld*   2.00
____CHESS SECRETS REVEALED *Fred Reinfeld*   2.00
____CHESS STRATEGY—An Expert's Guide *Fred Reinfeld*   2.00
____CHESS TACTICS FOR BEGINNERS *edited by Fred Reinfeld*   3.00
____CHESS THEORY & PRACTICE *Morry & Mitchell*   2.00
____HOW TO WIN AT CHECKERS *Fred Reinfeld*   2.00
____1001 BRILLIANT WAYS TO CHECKMATE *Fred Reinfeld*   3.00
____1001 WINNING CHESS SACRIFICES & COMBINATIONS *Fred Reinfeld*   3.00
____SOVIET CHESS *Edited by R. G. Wade*   3.00

COOKERY & HERBS
____CULPEPER'S HERBAL REMEDIES *Dr. Nicholas Culpeper*   2.00

_____FAST GOURMET COOKBOOK *Poppy Cannon* — 2.50
_____GINSENG The Myth & The Truth *Joseph P. Hou* — 3.00
_____HEALING POWER OF HERBS *May Bethel* — 3.00
_____HEALING POWER OF NATURAL FOODS *May Bethel* — 3.00
_____HERB HANDBOOK *Dawn MacLeod* — 3.00
_____HERBS FOR COOKING AND HEALING *Dr. Donald Law* — 2.00
_____HERBS FOR HEALTH—How to Grow & Use Them *Louise Evans Doole* — 3.00
_____HOME GARDEN COOKBOOK—Delicious Natural Food Recipes *Ken Kraft* — 3.00
_____MEDICAL HERBALIST *edited by Dr. J. R. Yemm* — 3.00
_____NATURAL FOOD COOKBOOK *Dr. Harry C. Bond* — 3.00
_____NATURE'S MEDICINES *Richard Lucas* — 3.00
_____VEGETABLE GARDENING FOR BEGINNERS *Hugh Wiberg* — 2.00
_____VEGETABLES FOR TODAY'S GARDENS *R. Milton Carleton* — 2.00
_____VEGETARIAN COOKERY *Janet Walker* — 3.00
_____VEGETARIAN COOKING MADE EASY & DELECTABLE *Veronica Vezza* — 2.00
_____VEGETARIAN DELIGHTS—A Happy Cookbook for Health *K. R. Mehta* — 2.00
_____VEGETARIAN GOURMET COOKBOOK *Joyce McKinnel* — 3.00

GAMBLING & POKER

_____ADVANCED POKER STRATEGY & WINNING PLAY *A. D. Livingston* — 3.00
_____HOW NOT TO LOSE AT POKER *Jeffrey Lloyd Castle* — 3.00
_____HOW TO WIN AT DICE GAMES *Skip Frey* — 3.00
_____HOW TO WIN AT POKER *Terence Reese & Anthony T. Watkins* — 2.00
_____SECRETS OF WINNING POKER *George S. Coffin* — 3.00
_____WINNING AT CRAPS *Dr. Lloyd T. Commins* — 3.00
_____WINNING AT GIN *Chester Wander & Cy Rice* — 3.00
_____WINNING AT POKER—An Expert's Guide *John Archer* — 3.00
_____WINNING AT 21—An Expert's Guide *John Archer* — 3.00
_____WINNING POKER SYSTEMS *Norman Zadeh* — 3.00

HEALTH

_____BEE POLLEN *Lynda Lyngheim & Jack Scagnetti* — 3.00
_____DR. LINDNER'S SPECIAL WEIGHT CONTROL METHOD *P. G. Lindner, M.D.* — 1.50
_____HELP YOURSELF TO BETTER SIGHT *Margaret Darst Corbett* — 3.00
_____HOW TO IMPROVE YOUR VISION *Dr. Robert A. Kraskin* — 3.00
_____HOW YOU CAN STOP SMOKING PERMANENTLY *Ernest Caldwell* — 3.00
_____MIND OVER PLATTER *Peter G. Lindner, M.D.* — 3.00
_____NATURE'S WAY TO NUTRITION & VIBRANT HEALTH *Robert J. Scrutton* — 3.00
_____NEW CARBOHYDRATE DIET COUNTER *Patti Lopez-Pereira* — 1.50
_____PSYCHEDELIC ECSTASY *William Marshall & Gilbert W. Taylor* — 2.00
_____QUICK & EASY EXERCISES FOR FACIAL BEAUTY *Judy Smith-deal* — 2.00
_____QUICK & EASY EXERCISES FOR FIGURE BEAUTY *Judy Smith-deal* — 2.00
_____REFLEXOLOGY *Dr. Maybelle Segal* — 2.00
_____YOU CAN LEARN TO RELAX *Dr. Samuel Gutwirth* — 2.00
_____YOUR ALLERGY—What To Do About It *Allan Knight, M.D.* — 3.00

HOBBIES

_____BEACHCOMBING FOR BEGINNERS *Norman Hickin* — 2.00
_____BLACKSTONE'S MODERN CARD TRICKS *Harry Blackstone* — 3.00
_____BLACKSTONE'S SECRETS OF MAGIC *Harry Blackstone* — 2.00
_____COIN COLLECTING FOR BEGINNERS *Burton Hobson & Fred Reinfeld* — 2.00
_____ENTERTAINING WITH ESP *Tony 'Doc' Shiels* — 2.00
_____400 FASCINATING MAGIC TRICKS YOU CAN DO *Howard Thurston* — 3.00
_____HOW I TURN JUNK INTO FUN AND PROFIT *Sari* — 3.00
_____HOW TO WRITE A HIT SONG & SELL IT *Tommy Boyce* — 7.00
_____JUGGLING MADE EASY *Rudolf Dittrich* — 2.00
_____MAGIC MADE EASY *Byron Wels* — 2.00
_____STAMP COLLECTING FOR BEGINNERS *Burton Hobson* — 2.00
_____STAMP COLLECTING FOR FUN & PROFIT *Frank Cetin* — 2.00

HORSE PLAYERS' WINNING GUIDES

_____BETTING HORSES TO WIN *Les Conklin* — 3.00
_____ELIMINATE THE LOSERS *Bob McKnight* — 3.00
_____HOW TO PICK WINNING HORSES *Bob McKnight* — 3.00
_____HOW TO WIN AT THE RACES *Sam (The Genius) Lewin* — 3.00
_____HOW YOU CAN BEAT THE RACES *Jack Kavanagh* — 3.00
_____MAKING MONEY AT THE RACES *David Barr* — 3.00

_____PAYDAY AT THE RACES *Les Conklin*	3.00
_____SMART HANDICAPPING MADE EASY *William Bauman*	3.00
_____SUCCESS AT THE HARNESS RACES *Barry Meadow*	3.00
_____WINNING AT THE HARNESS RACES—An Expert's Guide *Nick Cammarano*	3.00

HUMOR

_____HOW TO BE A COMEDIAN FOR FUN & PROFIT *King & Laufer*	2.00
_____HOW TO FLATTEN YOUR TUSH *Coach Marge Reardon*	2.00
_____JOKE TELLER'S HANDBOOK *Bob Orben*	3.00
_____JOKES FOR ALL OCCASIONS *Al Schock*	3.00
_____2000 NEW LAUGHS FOR SPEAKERS *Bob Orben*	3.00

HYPNOTISM

_____ADVANCED TECHNIQUES OF HYPNOSIS *Melvin Powers*	2.00
_____BRAINWASHING AND THE CULTS *Paul A. Verdier, Ph.D.*	3.00
_____CHILDBIRTH WITH HYPNOSIS *William S. Kroger, M.D.*	3.00
_____HOW TO SOLVE Your Sex Problems with Self-Hypnosis *Frank S. Caprio, M.D.*	3.00
_____HOW TO STOP SMOKING THRU SELF-HYPNOSIS *Leslie M. LeCron*	3.00
_____HOW TO USE AUTO-SUGGESTION EFFECTIVELY *John Duckworth*	3.00
_____HOW YOU CAN BOWL BETTER USING SELF-HYPNOSIS *Jack Heise*	3.00
_____HOW YOU CAN PLAY BETTER GOLF USING SELF-HYPNOSIS *Jack Heise*	2.00
_____HYPNOSIS AND SELF-HYPNOSIS *Bernard Hollander, M.D.*	3.00
_____HYPNOTISM *(Originally published in 1893) Carl Sextus*	3.00
_____HYPNOTISM & PSYCHIC PHENOMENA *Simeon Edmunds*	3.00
_____HYPNOTISM MADE EASY *Dr. Ralph Winn*	3.00
_____HYPNOTISM MADE PRACTICAL *Louis Orton*	3.00
_____HYPNOTISM REVEALED *Melvin Powers*	2.00
_____HYPNOTISM TODAY *Leslie LeCron and Jean Bordeaux, Ph.D.*	4.00
_____MODERN HYPNOSIS *Lesley Kuhn & Salvatore Russo, Ph.D.*	5.00
_____NEW CONCEPTS OF HYPNOSIS *Bernard C. Gindes, M.D.*	4.00
_____NEW SELF-HYPNOSIS *Paul Adams*	3.00
_____POST-HYPNOTIC INSTRUCTIONS—Suggestions for Therapy *Arnold Furst*	3.00
_____PRACTICAL GUIDE TO SELF-HYPNOSIS *Melvin Powers*	3.00
_____PRACTICAL HYPNOTISM *Philip Magonet, M.D.*	2.00
_____SECRETS OF HYPNOTISM *S. J. Van Pelt, M.D.*	3.00
_____SELF-HYPNOSIS A Conditioned-Response Technique *Laurance Sparks*	4.00
_____SELF-HYPNOSIS Its Theory, Technique & Application *Melvin Powers*	3.00
_____THERAPY THROUGH HYPNOSIS *edited by Raphael H. Rhodes*	4.00

JUDAICA

_____HOW TO LIVE A RICHER & FULLER LIFE *Rabbi Edgar F. Magnin*	2.00
_____MODERN ISRAEL *Lily Edelman*	2.00
_____ROMANCE OF HASSIDISM *Jacob S. Minkin*	2.50
_____SERVICE OF THE HEART *Evelyn Garfiel, Ph.D.*	3.00
_____STORY OF ISRAEL IN COINS *Jean & Maurice Gould*	2.00
_____STORY OF ISRAEL IN STAMPS *Maxim & Gabriel Shamir*	1.00
_____TONGUE OF THE PROPHETS *Robert St. John*	3.00
_____TREASURY OF COMFORT *edited by Rabbi Sidney Greenberg*	4.00

JUST FOR WOMEN

_____COSMOPOLITAN'S GUIDE TO MARVELOUS MEN Fwd. by *Helen Gurley Brown*	3.00
_____COSMOPOLITAN'S HANG-UP HANDBOOK Foreword by *Helen Gurley Brown*	4.00
_____COSMOPOLITAN'S LOVE BOOK—A Guide to Ecstasy in Bed	3.00
_____COSMOPOLITAN'S NEW ETIQUETTE GUIDE Fwd. by *Helen Gurley Brown*	4.00
_____I AM A COMPLEAT WOMAN *Doris Hagopian & Karen O'Connor Sweeney*	3.00
_____JUST FOR WOMEN—A Guide to the Female Body *Richard E. Sand, M.D.*	4.00
_____NEW APPROACHES TO SEX IN MARRIAGE *John E. Eichenlaub, M.D.*	3.00
_____SEXUALLY ADEQUATE FEMALE *Frank S. Caprio, M.D.*	3.00
_____YOUR FIRST YEAR OF MARRIAGE *Dr. Tom McGinnis*	3.00

MARRIAGE, SEX & PARENTHOOD

_____ABILITY TO LOVE *Dr. Allan Fromme*	5.00
_____ENCYCLOPEDIA OF MODERN SEX & LOVE TECHNIQUES *Macandrew*	4.00
_____GUIDE TO SUCCESSFUL MARRIAGE *Drs. Albert Ellis & Robert Harper*	4.00
_____HOW TO RAISE AN EMOTIONALLY HEALTHY, HAPPY CHILD *A. Ellis*	3.00
_____IMPOTENCE & FRIGIDITY *Edwin W. Hirsch, M.D.*	3.00
_____SEX WITHOUT GUILT *Albert Ellis, Ph.D.*	3.00
_____SEXUALLY ADEQUATE MALE *Frank S. Caprio, M.D.*	3.00

MELVIN POWERS' MAIL ORDER LIBRARY

The books listed above can be obtained from your book dealer or directly from
Melvin Powers. When ordering, please remit 50¢ per book postage & handling.
Send for our free illustrated catalog of self-improvement books.

Melvin Powers

12015 Sherman Road, No. Hollywood, California 91605

WILSHIRE HORSE LOVERS' LIBRARY

Notes